ISBN 978-0-282-84162-1
PIBN 10868632

English
Français
Deutsche
Italiano
Español
Português

www.forgottenbooks.com

Mythology Photography **Fiction**
Fishing Christianity **Art** Cooking
Essays Buddhism Freemasonry
Medicine **Biology** Music **Ancient**
Egypt Evolution Carpentry Physics
Dance Geology **Mathematics** Fitness
Shakespeare **Folklore** Yoga Marketing
Confidence Immortality Biographies
Poetry **Psychology** Witchcraft
Electronics Chemistry History **Law**
Accounting **Philosophy** Anthropology
Alchemy Drama Quantum Mechanics
Atheism Sexual Health **Ancient History**
Entrepreneurship Languages Sport
Paleontology Needlework Islam
Metaphysics Investment Archaeology
Parenting Statistics Criminology
Motivational

HANDWRITING

AND

EXPRESSION

TRANSLATED AND EDITED

BY

JOHN HOLT SCHOOLING

FELLOW OF THE ROYAL STATISTICAL SOCIETY, ASSOCIATE OF THE INSTITUTE OF ACTUARIES

FROM THE THIRD FRENCH EDITION

OF

L'ÉCRITURE ET LE CARACTÈRE

PAR

J. CRÉPIEUX-JAMIN

WITH SOME 150 FACSIMILE REPRODUCTIONS OF THE HANDWRITINGS OF
MEN AND WOMEN OF VARIOUS NATIONALITIES

LONDON
KEGAN PAUL, TRENCH, TRÜBNER & CO., LTD.
PATERNOSTER HOUSE, CHARING CROSS ROAD
1892

TABLE OF CONTENTS.

INTRODUCTION.

THIS translation of M. Crépieux-Jamin's work, *l'Ecriture et le Caractère*,[1] supplies to English readers a method of practically studying character by means of a form of personal expression hitherto but little so regarded in England, viz. by the handwriting, which, as M. Crépieux-Jamin shows, may be viewed as a series of gestures expressive of personality.

The movements which the hand makes in the act of writing, form a tracing upon paper, which observation and comparison of data have shown to be a graphic representation, within certain limits, of the individuality of the writer. This tracing of his nature which a man unconsciously makes when he writes, has the advantage of permanency, which allows an amount of detailed study to be given to facts of this kind, that it is not practicable to apply so readily to many other forms of gesture, which, although equally expressive, are fleeting in their manner of outward manifestation, such, for example, as facial or other bodily gestures and movements.

An interesting little volume by R. Baughan,[2] and one

---

[1] *l'Ecriture et le Caractère.* By J. Crépieux-Jamin. Paris. Felix Alcan. 1888.

[2] *Character Indicated by Handwriting.* By Rosa Baughan. Published by L. Upcott Gill.

by Henry Frith,[1] are the only works of any importance
hitherto published in England upon handwriting as a
form of expression, and so far as can be judged from
various newspaper advertisements and from drawing-
room small talk, the subject of this book is not usually
considered as a serious study.   Moreover, persons who
have had practical proof of the truth of this branch of
anthropologic knowledge, sometimes appear to think
that there is something mysterious about it, and are
inclined perhaps to class this with various so-called
occult arts.   Nevertheless, there are some men whose
mental bent, and habit of observation, cause them to
recognize that no class of phenomena is without significance, and these at least may be glad to see an English
version of M. Crépieux-Jam'n's able work.   Mr. Thomas
Faed, R.A., says in reply to a letter of mine upon the
subject, relating more particularly to indications of the
artistic faculty in handwriting, " I have long been think-
ing of the subject of your letter, and thought often that
I had made out my case—every now and then cases
stepped in that did not fit."   The experienced graphologist also finds cases stepping in that do not fit, and this
serves to remind him of what he is already aware, viz.
the necessity for continuing the careful investigation of
new facts, in order to make good the existing deficiencies
in his study.

Now graphology is simply based upon observation of
certain phenomena, which are as legitimately within the
field of rational inquiry, as are those upon which Darwin
founded his *Expression of the Emotions*, and more

[1] *How to Read Character in Handwriting.*   By Henry Frith.
Ward, Lock and Co.   1890.

recently, Mantegazza, his *Physiognomy and Expression*.[1]
This art, like that of medicine, is open to abuse and
quackery, but that is no reason why it should not be
rationally pursued, and if stripped of guess-work, and
confined to its legitimate field as a branch of practical
psychology, it will well repay the attention of such
readers of this book as may possess a natural or acquired
faculty of observation. The merely curious, who may
not be disposed to give time and trouble to this study,
will not derive much benefit from it, but, on the other
hand, a moderate amount of application on the part of
an observant man will enable him, by the method herein
set out, to gauge truly the general traits of character by
means of handwriting. This is a practical advantage
that is worth having in every-day life, for by it we can
not only perceive, and perhaps thereby be led to appreciate, the good qualities of persons we may have mis-
judged, but we can also use the study as a means of self-
protection ; for an instance, it is no small thing to be
able to know even without seeing a man if he be worthy
of trust. I may here mention on this score one among
several incidents that have occurred to myself. I was
one day in the office of a business man and was shown
a letter where the indications of untrustworthiness were
so pronounced that I told my friend the writer was not
to be trusted. Curiously enough, this was the very
point in question with Mr. ——, who, as he had already
had proof of the reliability of graphology, decided not
to send a consignment of goods upon credit to his corre-
spondent, who not long after became a bankrupt under
somewhat discreditable circumstances. Incidents such

---

[1] See note on page 36.

as this do not, of course, singly afford a logical proof of the truth of graphology, as they might be accounted for by coincidence, but such coincidence many times occurring does afford proof, and the best test of the reliability of opinions thus obtained, is the facility in forming accurate judgment that will be acquired by students who are either already observant, or whose latent faculty for viewing facts accurately may be developed by study of the special data afforded by handwriting, provided that they intelligently use only the positive knowledge already acquired, eschew conjecture, and do not attempt at first anything more detailed than a general outline of character.

M. Crépieux-Jamin's work is by far the best that has yet been written, but it does not profess to be complete, for the reason that graphology has only within comparatively recent years been raised from the level of more or less intuitive guess-work and conjecture, to the basis of rational knowledge, obtained by much careful study and by comparisons many times repeated. M. Crépieux-Jamin has an undoubted right to the first place among graphologists, and his works have attained considerable circulation abroad ; his first book, *Traite pratique de graphologie*,[1] published in 1885, is now in the second edition, and has been translated into German and Danish, a second edition of the former translation being now in the press. The present translation is based upon the third edition of his more recent work, which is also being produced in German and Italian, and the chapter on *The practice of graphology* has been

---

[1] *Traité pratique de graphologie.* By J. Crépieux-Jamin. Paris. Marpon et Flammarion.

specially written for this English version, the Preface in
the original by Dr. Paul Helot has been omitted,
the first chapter has been reduced from some thirty
pages to the nine herein printed, and the preponderance in the original of French illustrations over
the specimens written by Englishmen, Americans,
Germans, Italians, Swiss, and Belgians, has been altered
in favour of a larger number of English handwritings,
as being more interesting to English readers. As
regards the work generally, instead of giving foot-notes,
I have as a rule embodied in the text any fresh matter
that seemed to emphasize or to elucidate the meaning
of the French original, being assisted throughout by
whatever knowledge I may have gained upon the
subject of this book, by some fifteen years' acquaintance
with graphology. All these modifications have been
made with the acquiescence of M. Crépieux-Jamin, some
of them with his assistance.

One main feature of M. Crépieux-Jamin's mode of
treating the subject, is the stress he lays upon the
relative value of graphologic signs as contrasted with
the *absolute* significance which used to be given to
them. This principle of judging the value of any
specified sign according to its surroundings is thoroughly
sound, and is fully explained later on. The conditions essential to successful graphologic analysis, the
cases of conventional, non-spontaneous handwriting,
such as that of copyists, etc., and the various objections
usually raised, are all dealt with in due course ; but it
is desirable here to refer to the most general objection
frequently considered fatal to graphology, viz. that
handwriting of the same person varies. This to some

extent is a fact, and were it not so, this translation would not have been written, for non-variation in the same person's handwriting would imply a lack of change in this outward expression, corresponding to the variation of mood and feeling that all men undergo to a greater or less degree, and such lack of change in the handwriting would deprive graphology of its very foundation as a rational study, and it is under a strictly rational aspect that this book is offered to English readers. Thus, this usual so-called objection is in fact a most valuable witness in favour of the validity of graphology, and persons ignorant of the study may test for themselves, in a crude way, the alteration in handwriting under varying circumstances. Write a letter under the influence of hopefulness and elation, and you will notice the words or lines of your writing tending up-wards ; write in a condition of dejection, and you will see the downward direction of the words or lines. Write under the impulse of strong affection for the person addressed, and you will see your words incline more to the right hand, more away from a vertical position, than when you tax merely your intellect in writing (say) an explanation of a mathematical point, or when writing a letter upon business matters to a person to whom you are indifferent. If you be a calm man, notice how a state of mental excitation will alter the usual calmness and regularity of your words and letters, to a condition of more or less agitation.

Now we recognize handwriting which is familiar to us as readily as we recognize its writer in the street, although we not infrequently remark variation in the writing of the same person at different times, as well as variation in the man himself. The main character is there, the variation is due to numerous causes of fluctuation in mood or feeling ; and as regards handwriting, an experienced graphologist sees what is the outline of the permanent character, as well as the merely temporary changes passing over it. The more numerous the specimens of handwriting of a variable man that are submitted for analysis, the more detailed would be the traits extracted with reference to the mood influencing the writer at the various dates of the specimens ; and referring now to men not easily subjected to temporary variation, and extending the period for the operation of possible change of character, so as to let it range from the time when mechanical difficulty in acquiring the art of writing has been overcome, to the time when old age begins to also cause effort in writing, and obtaining thus a series of spontaneous expressions of the writer's nature, we should then possess a reliable index of the various changes occurring in a man's character during this long period, however little subjected to temporary variation he might be, during those shorter intervals that would affect more variable and impressionable persons. The nearest approach that I possess to a series extending over many years, is a collection of the signatures of the first Napoleon, dating from 1785, when he was a second lieutenant, to the 11th December, 1816, when he wrote a letter to the Comte de Las Cases, his companion in captivity at St. Helena, who was ordered to leave the island, a circumstance which Napoleon much regretted. This is his signature (see next page) written immediately after the battle of Austerlitz, which is so ascendant that it forms (approximately) an angle of 45 degrees with the horizontal line of the page from

Written immediately after the battle of Austerlitz.

which the N starts. Notice now the signature to a letter dated the 14th July, 1815, from the Isle of Aix, when

Written at the Isle of Aix after Napoleon's second fall.

this strong man knew he was mastered ; there is here no ascendant angle of nearly 45 degrees, but we see a droop in the signature below the level it starts from.   And this droop characterizes all the signatures that I possess which Napoleon wrote in captivity, just as when formerly his reckless ambition was leading him on to victory after victory the marked ascendant movement is a very notice-able trait in his signatures written at Milan, Cairo, Auster-litz, Berlin, Vienna, and at Moscow when he *entered* that city as a conqueror on the 12th September, 1812.

It should be stated, however, that variation is most frequently met with in the handwriting of persons who are readily susceptible of impressions from outside phenomena of various kinds, and who are also more or less easily influenced by their receptivity of external impressions.   A man who is governed mainly or entirely by his reason, and whose course of action is but little influenced by susceptibility to impressions derived from other persons or things, will exhibit a great degree of constancy and non-variability not only in his demeanour, but also in his various modes of expression, handwriting among the number. Painters, for instance, on the other hand, require to be readily open to receive impressions, whether from persons, from the varied phenomena of landscape, or from any other source, which impressions, aided by the imagination and individuality of the artist, are by means of his special technical skill finally shown to us in the form of a picture. Now this sensibility to impressions is plainly indicated in handwriting, and is readily perceived by the graphologist, who is therefore at once made acquainted with a most important characteristic of his subject. But this is not the place to go more fully into the general question of objections; I merely deal here with the most usual one, being desirous of not in any way denying variation in the same person's handwriting, but on the other hand, wishing rather to lay stress upon this fact, as helping to establish the basis upon which rational graphology is founded.

A serious warning must be addressed to possible students. Assuming that this book be substantially true concerning the inferences as to character set out in it—and there is a considerable degree of probability that such is the case—a method is given by which the real nature of men and women can be gauged.

Now in fairness to others, students should abstain from ventilating any opinions they may form about character. Let this method be used for self-protection, by all means, but do not let us give a fresh impetus to the discussion of other people's failings. Let us rather use this study as an additional index to our own weak points, and thus employ it as a personal corrective.

A hint may also be given to those readers who may think that, without previous study of handwriting, they have merely to turn to the *table of graphologic signs* in order at once to diagnose character. This cannot be done, for faulty observation alone would lead them astray, as it would indeed upon any other subject where the power of accurate observation and appreciation of facts has to be acquired by practice and study. To quote from page 145 of this book : "The possession of an English dictionary does not enable a Frenchman to speak English, nor is a man a chemist because he possesses works upon that science."

In expressing my appreciation of M. Crépieux-Jamin's amiable and courteous participation in our correspondence, extending over some eighteen months, I may state, that, although *Handwriting and Expression* is not a close translation of his book, any worth it may have as a treatise upon graphology is due to the excellence of the French original.

This introduction is not addressed to irrational enthusiasts, who are likely to do more harm than good to graphology, nor to those who have always a negation ready for subjects upon which they may be ignorant : I speak to such as may already be rationally and cautiously pursuing this study, and to others who regard statements or facts they have not examined, with the philosophic doubt that stands as a sentinel before the gate of their reason.

J. H. S.

19, Abingdon Street,
Westminster, 1892.

NOTE.

MANY of the illustrations now given are taken from the hand-writings of prominent men and women. With a few exceptions their signatures are not printed, for whatever satisfaction may thus be lost by the more curious readers of this book, the study itself is not affected by this omission, and, moreover, the risk is not incurred of exposing those who have kindly increased my stock of data for a specific purpose, to the attacks of the hunter of autographs.

I shall at all times be glad to receive autograph letters, etc., especially those of persons having a marked individuality, and to give a graphologic opinion upon any that may be sent for this purpose.

J. H. S.

APPENDIX TO THE INTRODUCTION.

THE illustration on the next page is reproduced by permission of Mr. Samuel Davey from page 158 of a valuable and most interesting work upon historical documents, etc.,[1] by the Rev. Dr. Scott and Mr. Samuel Davey. Mr. Davey, who is also the editor of the " Archivist," and a well-known collector of, and dealer in, autograph letters, etc., has kindly lent the electro block of these fac-similes for the purposes of this book.

These signatures of Napoleon, which date from 1795 to 1808, not only afford a sufficient illustration of variation in the same person's handwriting—see preceding *Introduction*—but they also possess significance for the student of graphology who has some knowledge of Napoleon's character, and of his career during that period.

[1] *A Guide to the Collector of Historical Documents, Literary Manuscripts, and Autograph Letters, etc. By the Rev. Dr. Scott and Samuel Davey, F.R.S.L. London. S. J. Davey, the " Archivist" Office, 47, Great Russell Street.* 1891.

1795.

1795.

1795.

1796.

1796.   1806.

1796.

1796.

1798.   1807.

HANDWRITING AND EXPRESSION.

THE EARLY DAYS OF GRAPHOLOGY.

Twenty-five years ago—we are writing in 1892—the term graphology was quite unknown; this name was given by the Abbé Michon to the study of character by means of handwriting. It would be premature to write a history of so recent a science, but it may be interesting to give a brief sketch of its development.

Antiquity has bequeathed to us only a single observation concerning handwriting. Suetonius wrote of the Emperor Augustus :—" I have noticed chiefly this in his handwriting : he does not separate the words, and he does not carry to another line those letters which are too many for one, but he places them underneath, and surrounds them with a line." [1] This observation is not followed by any comment.

Until the seventeenth century there is no document which leads us to suppose that graphology had been thought of. In 1622 an Italian named Baldo wrote a

[1] Suetonius, *Octavius Augustus*, lxxxxvii.

B

book called : *A method of ascertaining the habits and the qualities of a Writer by means of his written Letters.*[2] This work was translated into Latin and printed in Bologna forty years later by one Petrus Vellius. Thus Baldo, who was a savant, professor, and philosopher of his time, appears to have been the first to occupy himself with the connection existing between character and handwriting. Certain ideas are developed in this little book with an ease that shows Baldo to have been a close observer, as for instance when he says that a familiar letter to a friend is the best autograph to use for graphologic analysis.

Baldo's essays are interesting, but they do not appear to have been much known. They would have been unknown to-day but for the Abbé Michon, who came across the translation by Petrus Vellius in the library of the medical school at Montpellier in 1875.

The idea of Baldo is sound, for he thought that handwriting being a manifestation of our personality, it should faithfully reproduce some of the traits of character. It appears somewhat strange that this fairly obvious idea did not occur to any of the great writers of antiquity or of the middle ages, but this may perhaps be explained as follows. In those days people wrote but little, even kings and emperors did not all know how to write, and there were public writers, men of that calling, who, usually expressing only the thoughts of others, made use of a special handwriting of a conventional kind. Thus a large variety of the elements of comparison, and the spontaneity of handwriting, were

[2] *Trattato come de una lettera missiva si cognoscano la natura qualita della scrittore.* Carpi. 1622.

absent, and these are the two most favourable conditions for the development of graphology. But at the time of Louis XIV. things were different. People wrote much, and handwriting of a merely official kind became rarer in proportion. As knowledge became more diffused and as people wrote more frequently, graphology began to extend itself in many directions up to the time of the Abbé Michon, who, collecting the scattered works of those who had preceded him, gave a name to the study and caused it to make a decided advance. Graphologic knowledge, like everything else, has had to wait until the conditions essential to its evolution are realized.

A Neapolitan professor of anatomy and surgery, Marcus Aurelius Severinus, also wrote upon the subject contemporaneously with Baldo. Of his work, which was not published, we know little, and he died in 1656.

Leibnitz [3] appears to have perceived the connection between character and handwriting, for *apropos* of a study of human morals (*doctrina de moribus*) which related to character, he said :—" The handwriting also nearly always expresses in one way or another the natural temperament, unless it be that of a writing master, whose writing lacks spontaneity."

In 1792 a German, J. Chr. Grohmann, endeavoured to give a physiological explanation of the fact that a man's character is reproduced in his handwriting. His so-called scientific proofs were very ingenuous, and more-over, he carried graphologic study quite outside its legitimate place, by asserting his power to determine

---

[3] *Opera Leibnizii* : ed. Dutens, vol. vi., *Leibniziana*.

from handwriting various details of the writer's physique, such as the voice, the colour of the hair and eyes, &c. We fear that Grohmann drew upon his imagination in symbolizing the characteristic signs of handwriting, and he must have deceived himself as much as he did others.

Goethe was probably aware of this production of Grohmann's, for in a letter he wrote to Lavater he speaks of the study of handwriting as a known fact. He thus expresses himself :—" There does not exist the shadow of a doubt that handwriting has its analogies with the character and with the human mind, and that it can afford at least a presentiment of the kind of feeling or of the mode of action, inasmuch as we must also admit a certain harmony with the personality, not only in the features and in the general conformation of a man, but also in the facial expression, the voice, and in the movements of the body." Goethe goes on to point out the difficulty of systematizing the facts, assures Lavater of his interest in such researches, and advises him to continue the collection of data upon the subject.

This letter was the cause of Lavater's observations upon handwriting. He was then engaged on his great work upon physiognomy, and all that touched upon the external manifestation of a man's personality interested him. Following the advice of his friend, he collected autographs, and he devoted several pages of his book to the study of handwriting.

Lavater refers to the variation often seen in the same person's handwriting, and says, truly enough, that so far from being an argument against the truth of graphology, it is a proof in its favour, as showing the effect of this or that mood upon our handwriting. He refers also to the difference in handwriting according to nationality, just as there are national traits of physiognomy ; and we may here point out that this variation is to be expected, for if one nation is character- ized by, say, more thrift than another, or by greater excitability, a graphologist would find the signs of thrift or of excitability more frequently shown in the hand- writing of that nation than in the handwriting of a nation not having these characteristic traits so generally diffused among its units.

Lavater finishes with these words :—"Another idea which I leave for the consideration of those who may be, as I am, impressed with it : I notice in the majority of cases an admirable analogy between the manner of speech, the gait, and the handwriting."

In our opinion these last lines of the chapter very appositely sum up Lavater's work ; he had a distinct perception of the affinity existing between handwriting and character, but he contented himself with indicating the importance of the subject and the nature of the methods for studying it thoroughly. Elsewhere he says, " I limit my ambition to preparing materials for my successors."

M. Moreau, a professor at the Paris medical school, edited Lavater in 1806 and enlarged the article dealing with handwriting. In doing so he made considerable advance upon Baldo's work, showing more knowledge and greater precision. Several of his statements have been substantiated by careful investigation and more recent experience, and he deals more fully than did Lavater with the influence of varying circumstances and states of feeling upon the handwriting. His remarks upon this point are sound, and confirm Lavater's opinion that such variation is a valuable proof of the connection between character and handwriting. We can gather from M. Moreau's observations that graphology was seriously practised by a few men, starting from the year 1806.

In 1823 an Englishman named Stephen Collet (Thomas Byerley) wrote some interesting pages upon *characteristic signatures*, and Edgar Allan Poe engaged in a sort of intuitive graphology. He possessed a collection of autographs and gave a rough sketch of some of the characteristics they appeared to posséss, but he seems to have had no definite method.

In 1830 a graphologic school existed in France which was acquainted with graphologic signs of character. To this school belonged M. Boudinet, Bishop of Amiens, Cardinal Regnier, Archbishop of Cambray, and the Abbé Flandrin. Doctor Descuret in his work, *Médicine des Passions*, gave a graphologic portrait of Silvio Pellico, made by M. Flandrin, and the increased knowledge then existing enabled him to attain considerable precision.

From that time the study spread widely, and we find graphologists giving their opinions upon handwriting at Liége, Lyons, and Paris.

A Belgian savant, M. de Robiano,[1] speaking cf a letter in 1854, said to the writer of it: "This is the writing of a caviller, a vain man, of a fussy person"; and this opinion was true. A Jesuit, Pére Martin, worked at graphology, but, as with M. de Robiano, he left no published work.

[1] *Histoire de l'Ecriture*, p. 48.

In 1863 there appeared in Germany a book called by the appalling title of *Chirogrammatomancy*. The author, M. Henze, had for some time previously published his opinions upon the character of those who consulted him, and this work was a summary of these opinions. We can scarcely say that M. Henze had a method to work by, although he may sometimes have arrived at fairly accurate results by intuitive judgment of the handwriting.

An artist, M. J. B. Delestre, published in 1866 an important work upon physiognomy.[5] He devoted a long chapter to handwriting, and progressed much farther than the jottings of M. Moreau and the hints of Lavater upon the subject. M. Delestre also refers to the frequent variation in individual handwriting, and makes the sound statement that, while the variations conform to the emotions of the moment, the fundamental qualities of the writing remain the same, and serve as a basis for judging accidental modifications. The author's description of the connection between many of his graphologic signs and traits of character is in accordance with present knowledge, and M. Delestre has certainly a right to an honourable place among the founders of this study.

In 1872 there appeared a work called *The Mysteries of Handwriting*.[6] Desbarrolles wrote the preface to it, and the Abbé Michon did all the rest. This book was a revelation, and it contained a systematic method and an organized theory.

[5] *De la Physiognomie*, by J. B. Delestre. Paris : Jules Renouard. 1866.
[6] *Les Mystères de l'Ecriture*. Paris : Garnier frères. 1872.

M. Michon starts very fairly by telling his readers that he is a pupil of M. Flandrin, but, while giving publicity to the teachings of his master, he thinks it right to state that he is not merely a compiler, but that he presents a personal work.   This is true.

Soon' after this book was published an interminable quarrel arose between M. Desbarrolles and M. Michon upon the question as to which of them was the inventor of graphology ; as a matter of fact, neither of them was the inventor.

This dispute excited the *amour propre* of M. Michon, and he wrote his *System of Graphology* so as to detach himself from his former collaborator ; this work, however, made no further advance in graphology.   Afterwards M. Michon brought out in succession : *The History of Napoleon the First determined from his Handwriting ;* the journal *Graphology* from 1873 to 1881 ; a *Memoir upon the Faulty Method used by Experts in Handwriting ; A Method of Graphologic Study ; The History of Handwriting ;* and a *Dictionary of the Notabilities of France judged from the Handwriting.*

These last two works have not been completed, but a few numbers of the *Dictionary* have appeared, preceded by a very remarkable study upon *The Handwriting of the French People since the Merovingian Epoch.*

The works of M. Michon, who died in 1881, are of great importance ; he has either discovered or classified numerous signs of the expression of character in handwriting, and the development which he has given to the study is ten times greater than all that appeared before his time.   He once said that the Abbé Flandrin was the first to raise graphology from the level of intuitive guess work and foolish divination to a rational basis of careful examination and comparison of actual data, just as in botany Jussieu was the father of the natural-affinity method of classifying plants in families. But this statement is not correct. Camille Baldo was, perhaps, the actual father of graphology; Lavater, Moreau, Flandrin, Henze, and Delestre its first promoters; but M. Michon himself was the founder in chief of the study as it exists at the present time.

As this chapter deals only with the early days of graphology we must here end it; in a subsequent chapter the names will be mentioned of those who have successfully continued the work of M. Michon.

THE BASIS OF GRAPHOLOGY.

PSYCHOLOGICAL study is certainly gaining ground at the present day, owing to the insatiable curiosity which urges us to investigate our own nature and that of others. Thus graphology, although of such recent growth, ought quickly to make its way even before the eyes of those who doubt its validity, and become through observation and comparison a study capable of much development —exact, certain and unquestionable. In truth, it does not meet with opposition properly so-called, for those who oppose it do not usually gainsay the fact that handwriting contains indications of character, but rather they are sceptical as to the possibility of deducing individuality from this source. If these are to be called adversaries, we ought to add that they afford but relatively slight opposition, and that the number of those who are sceptical or indifferent is continually decreasing owing to the increase of believers or of adepts in graphology. It commences to attract attention, and we can already detect graphologic study in the writings of several contemporaneous authors. This spread of the art is doubtless partly due to the inherent curiosity of man, but it is also due to the confidence graphology inspires, especially amongst close observers. Most of us are to some extent natural graphologists before even knowing of the existence of the art, for we involuntarily form opinions upon the letters we receive and pronounce a judgment which, however scanty or erroneous it may be, is none the less a proof of a certain amount of knowledge, and of some ideas and reasoning upon the subject.

We recognize a feminine hand (though not always necessarily a woman's hand) in writing which is slender and much inclined, we read pretension in written characters adorned with pen-scrolls and excessive flourishes, and letters which are agitated and unequal tell us of the nervous and unsettled temperament of the person who traces them. Graphology has had but to regulate and develop this intuitive perception which most people possess ; this has now been done to a considerable extent by experience and observation, although the limits of graphologic study have by no means been reached. The essentially human instinct which urges us to investigate personality may now be profitably employed in the study of handwriting. And this *coming* of graphology will have the effect of drawing attention to another branch of expression, perhaps a little overlooked now-a-days, that of physiognomy.

At the outset M. Michon [1] was met with general incredulity. All the critics, Francisque Sarcey at the head of them, wrote very amusing journalistic articles upon the new discovery, and it seemed to be taken for granted that an intelligent man could not study the subject without compromising himself in the opinions of others. M. Michon replied to this attack by organizing numerous meetings open to the public; he widely diffused his journal and succeeded in popularizing his book in spite of all the opposition he met with. His chief method of proof consisted in offering a practical

[1] See p. 3 of the first chapter.

demonstration to sceptics ; he said, " Give me the hand-writing of a man whom you know intimately but of whom I know nothing, and I will tell you his aptitudes, passions, and tastes." This is more a process of popularizing graphology than a scientific demonstration of its truth. Moreover, in some cases this course is imprudent, for we must remember that in order not to compromise graphology in such a test, it is necessary that he to whom it is offered has a correct judgment, and that he really knows in detail the nature and character of the man whose handwriting may be submitted for analysis. Now, those who study character know that it is often very difficult to obtain these two conditions, especially the latter. People suppose that they know a man because they have observed two or three traits of his character, and it may happen that these are merely intentional manifestations on his part, a sort of conventional bearing assumed in order to conceal his true personality.

Graphologic study is in three sections ; that of *general signs*, that of *particular signs*, and that of *resultants*. General signs are gathered from the handwriting as a whole by considering the height, the width, the inclination or slope, the regularity, &c. They require less observation than particular signs ; habit teaches us without much difficulty to assign regular handwriting to calm and reflective minds, eccentric handwriting to eccentric persons, and confused handwriting to those who lack clearness in thought and expression. Investigation of particular signs requires more detailed work ; these signs are given by the words, the letters, the finals, by the punctuation, &c. It must be evident that only patient analyses and frequent comparisons have enabled us to state that the small *n* shaped like the small *u* denotes kindness of disposition, that capital letters unduly large denote imagination, and being very low in height show hypocrisy. It is necessary to possess a certain amount of judgment in order to apply in special cases the rules which form the basis of this study, and which, in analogy with bodily gesture and movement, give, in general, the signification of gentleness to the curve, and to the angle that of firmness or obstinacy. Concerning resultants, their acquisition depends upon the acumen of the graphologist, and they form a distinct class of observation of a higher order than the analysis of handwriting. Farther on we will study in detail each of these three sections of graphology.

The objections that we meet with emanate only from those who are quite unacquainted with this study. As soon as people obtain some idea of it, and when they have even slightly looked into graphology, they recognize the absence of validity in their objections. One objection raised is that a man can vary his handwriting *ad infinitum*. This is an error; if we examine several specimens by the same writer we see that the changes affect only certain details ; the basis, the foundation of the handwriting does not vary. These variations in detail display the fluctuations caused by enforced or voluntary personal impressions, as a cloud in the sky passes away without modifying it. Another objection, that graphologists can alter their handwriting at will, is easily met. If the graphologist shuns the exposure of a significant trait in his handwriting, he must employ a process of elimination or of the introduction of non-natural signs, and this is very difficult in handwriting which has to keep up a natural appearance ; and, if non-natural in appearance, a graphologist would soon detect its sophistication.   Still another objection : each country has its type of handwriting ; this is a fact of no value as an objection, but which at once draws attention to the truth that different nationalities show their difference of character by a special type of handwriting, which is, in fact, one of the most valid arguments for graphology. Just as each nation has special external characteristics, so it is only natural to find this variation in national handwriting ; it is the contrary proposition which would go against the validity of graphology.

But it is scarcely necessary for us to lay stress upon these objections ; to-day many men of intelligence and education find graphology worthy of their consideration from the mere examination of its results, despite its lack of a scientific theory.[2]   But apart from its results, which furnish practical evidence of its truth, we shall now endeavour to give *a priori* and theoretical proof of its validity, starting from physiological movement, which is the real basis of graphology, and meeting at the end psychology,[3] upon which our study is equally dependent.

Our nervous system, which conveys sensorial impressions to the brain, can also, in accordance with our will, excite the muscles and compel them to contract and produce movement.   The muscles are always ready to act ; they are perpetually in a state of readiness, waiting

---

[2] Graphology is extensively studied in Paris and in other parts of France, also in Germany, Austria, Italy, and Denmark.   The Société de Graphologie at Paris carries on graphologic research in a systematic way, and has a Journal and a large number of members.

[3] See the chapter upon *Resultants*.

for the stimulus of the motor nerves. But this condition is not yet one of expression; it is a state of
muscular tonicity. But when, responding to nerve
action, the muscles are in contraction, they at the same
time produce movement and physiognomical expression, gesture.

The different parts of the body possess a nervous and
muscular system which is the more complex as the
diversity of their respective functions is greater. The
face, which contains important organs, possesses very
numerous and delicate muscles, serving to protect these
organs and to admit of the fulfilment of their functions.
The hand is also furnished with a large number of
muscles which bear witness to the importance and
diversity of the movements it is required to make.
The arms of a man are almost constantly in action, and
they make such a number of movements and gestures
in proportion to the other parts of the body that, when
we speak of gesture, it seems almost that a movement
of the arms is implied.

Amongst all the uses for which our hand serves us
there are none which require more delicate and complex
movements than painting, drawing, and handwriting.
In fact, while we are acquiring the art, writing is nothing
more than a drawing more or less rough and crude.
Little by little we gain facility and a muscular suppleness which finally enable us to write very rapidly, and
thus we get rid of the mechanical difficulty at first
experienced, and which is an obstacle to ready transmission of the results of brain movement through the
motor nerves and muscles to the paper on which
we write. This action of writing is carried into effect

by a voluntary process resulting from co-ordination of ideas. We are conscious of perception, and there results an idea, a thought, more or less distinct which leads to some act. Whether this act be carried out by movement of the face or of the hand, whether these gestures be guided into a certain channel of ex-pression, as in the act of writing, or whether they have more freedom as to the mode of their manifesta-tion, as in general personal gesture, they always express themselves in close connection with the feeling or thought which produces them, and in more qualified affinity with the personal character.

We can already deduce two important graphologic signs from the preceding observations. Handwriting being one of the indispensable means used in developing our intellect, we may infer that handwriting which is defective and very slow or laboured, comes from a mind delayed in its development, that is, from a condition of intellectual inferiority. Rapidity and ease in hand-writing, necessitating at least some amount of mental training, is therefore an indication of relative superiority in this respect to the former example.

However, whether writing be more or less rapid, when it is free from obvious effort in production, and in accordance with the normal activity of the writer, and traced without other purpose than that of noting down the thoughts, it has a particular physiognomy that observation shows us to be in accordance with the character. The careful and precise man reveals himself by his arrangement of the headings, the margins, by accurate punctuation, while the sight of a letter without punctuation, and whose lines are straggling and confused, tells us of want of care, of mental confusion ; and the personality of the writer usually confirms this opinion. Ascending handwriting belongs to sanguine, ambitious men, while that which sinks down and descends across the page appertains to a state more or less unhappy and of discouragement. Avaricious men have their words and letters crowded close together ; such waste no space upon the paper. Lavish or wasteful persons, on the contrary, write but a few words in one line, and their long final strokes are fitly connected with this trait of their character. The gentleness of disposition which shows itself in personal gesture by soft and rounded movements, is revealed in handwriting by curves, by non-angular finals, while hardness corresponds with angular finals and pen-strokes. Handwriting sloping forward shows sensitive-ness; if vertical, force of character is the indication given. Rapid, nervous handwriting expresses activity, agitation ; that which is very calm and rounded tells us of indolence, of inactivity. Simplicity of character is recognized by simplicity of form in the words and letters ; and oddness, eccentricity, are shown by notice-able singularity in the formation of the handwriting.

The affinity between character and handwriting is sometimes so pronounced, that the physiognomy of a letter will at once bring the character of its writer before us, even if he or she be a stranger. This is the case with handwriting which is very impulsive, bristling with notes of exclamation, with words unnecessarily repeated or with syllables omitted ; such relates to animated, enthusiastic and heedless natures.

It follows from these facts that, in recording a thought

on paper, the pen registers the normal or the immediate impressions of the writer. These written signs may be viewed similarly to other gestures used by persons in speaking. But handwriting has this advantage over other modes of expression, that the tracing of all the little gestures made when writing, is permanent and not fleeting. Hence the facility for study and comparison of the data afforded by this mode of expression.

There is practically no limit of condensation for gesture in handwriting. The tracing caused by hesitation, for instance, is sometimes shown by strokes so slight that only the microscope enables us to discern them. We find also in handwriting little hooks, in size $\frac{1}{500}$th of an inch, which abruptly terminate the words, similar to the slight actions, brief and brusque, with which certain speakers end their sentences.

Having identified handwriting with personal gesture, it is permissible to investigate in the former all phenomena which are included by the latter; these embrace indications:

   1. Of personal superiority and inferiority.
   2. Of the intellect.
   3. Of the moral character.
   4. Of the will.
   5. Of the æsthetic sense.
   6. Of age.
   7. Of sex.
   8. Of a state of health or of illness.

The investigation of age by means of handwriting is necessarily limited to merely broad distinctions; sex cannot be invariably determined, and a state of health or of illness is only generally indicated by this mode of personal expression.

We shall show later that two or more graphologic signs may be combined in order to discover a less obvious condition of personality than is indicated by a single sign. This study of *resultants* admits of much development. We have pointed out as far back as 1885, in our *Practical Treatise on Graphology*,[1] the advantage this study affords to our science.

It is essentially a psychological study, the development of which is independent of graphologic analysis of handwriting. Resultants constitute a means of ascertaining traits of character that handwriting cannot directly afford. Personal gesture by itself does not enable us to discern injustice, mental penetration, devotedness to a cause, etc. This is also impossible in the case of handwriting, since it is merely a series of gestures ; but, nevertheless, it is possible to ascertain such qualities as those just named by means of the method of resultants, which relates to the accurate combination of two or more traits directly obtained from handwriting, in order to get one which is not thereby immediately indicated. As time goes on we may hope, by this method, to discover more of these indirect characteristics than are now known, but undue haste will only mislead us, and moreover, we cannot too strongly protest against those graphologists who expect to find resultants, or even special signs, as some do, indicating anything outside of the eight kinds of personal traits which we have mentioned as being within the possible scope of rational

[1] *Traité pratique de Graphologie*, par J. Crépieux-Jamin. Marpon et Flammarion, éditeurs, à Paris.

graphologic study. There are some who investigate handwriting for the profession of its writer, others for the temperament (*i.e.*, whether bilious, lymphatic, etc.), the colour of the hair, the shape of the hands, the entire physique. M. Michon himself believed that he could see in words whose letters were separated a sign of sterility.[5]

An eager experimenter in this direction has com municated to us the signs which he uses for ascertaining the avocation of a writer. All his indications are not equally far-fetched, but none of them merit more than cursory attention.

Several graphologists have fallen into this error of analogy of forms, and have made it the basis of their study. We have seen, however, in the preceding pages of this chapter that the connection of handwriting with character can only be established by analogy with *gesture*. Any indication that handwriting may perhaps afford concerning the profession of individuals is, we think, due to the fact that the constant sight and use of certain objects tend to their reproduction in handwriting more or less consciously, sometimes deliberately. For instance, musicians will interpolate musical signs in their handwriting ; poets will sometimes write prose in a similar fashion to verse, with large margins on each side ; mathematicians will occasionally use the symbols so familiar to them, even in writing a letter ; while writing-masters will produce calligraphy rather than a more natural style of handwriting, etc. But all musicians, all poets, all mathematicians, and all

[5] It is but fair to M. Michon to state that this error is almost lost among his truths.

writing-masters do not act thus, and signs of this species may apply to other professions; it is wiser for the graphologist not to use them, since they are in no way connected with the true basis of our study. For example, the cross which some priests make at the head of their letters or by their signature does not by its presence indicate the smallest trait of character. It is a mark which is but very slightly influenced by variations of personality, and it does not even tell us for certain that the writer is a priest; many laymen and religious persons make this cross, and thus it is no more a graphologic sign than is a printed heading of a page.

Regarding the investigation of facial traits by means of handwriting, followed with so much rabidness by several graphologists, this error is, we think, to be explained by their confusing anatomical form with expression, with gesture. There is no connection between a *retroussé* nose or brown hair with any special graphologic sign, nor could there be such, because we can only establish an entire congruity between phenomena of the same order and of the same nature.

Dealing now with the investigation of temperament by these means, it would appear, if this contention be sound, that it would be possible, proceeding from the known to the unknown, to determine the character of a man from his temperament, and *vice versa.*

Dr. J. R. wrote to us : " I have tried to ascertain the temperament from handwriting. People of *sanguine* temperament have handwriting which is regular, clear, eager, free. With *lymphatics* the writing is nerveless, feeble, lazy. With *nervous* people it is small, sharp, lively, capricious. With *bilious* men it is concentrated, free from any expansive movement, and without flourishes."

Now this is not a matter of special graphologic signs, but of opinions formed by Dr. J. R. by the aid of a few signs under his notice. These particular opinions appear to us to be fairly near the mark, but the development of a study of character upon such a basis would be rather a matter of conjecture, because we can, and do to a large extent, escape from the influence of our temperament.

We have now to clearly determine the question: Is graphology, separated from any idea of the marvellous, and from the errors we have just pointed out, a science? From the preceding pages we see that graphology is a science as regards the observation of its data, and an art in experimentation. Other sciences, except mathematics, are on the same footing; we know very well that professors of physics do not succeed in all their experiments, there is not only a science of physics, but there is also a way of realizing conditions favourable to successful experimentation. We call chemistry a science and music an art, although chemical experiments form an art, and musical harmony is a science. How ought we to regard graphology? We venture to say as a science, since Darwin and Mantegazza consider that personal expression is amenable to science.

Graphology is in process of development, and it already affords serious results—in fact, no other method is better adapted for acquiring knowledge of men—but its progress is inseparable from that of physiology and psychology, and, notwithstanding the number of works that have been written upon these subjects during the last few years, it must be admitted that the bond existing between mind and matter is not yet stated in a definitive manner. Graphology would derive much advantage from such a work, but we cannot ask for this. Owing to this lack of knowledge it is not possible to draw up a thorough psycho-graphologic classification, for in order that a classification of any knowledge may be definitive, it is necessary that the matter to which it relates be completely elucidated, that it be a science, exact, certain, and complete to such a degree that all progress concerning its basis becomes impossible.

It is needless to say that graphology is far from realizing these conditions, and any classification presented as definitive is condemned at once. We will endeavour to formulate a table of signs as rational as possible, but, at a time when graphology and psychology are in full process of evolution, we will thoroughly guard ourselves from attempting a classification which the least fresh discovery would at once render incomplete or faulty.

Touching, now, the means of ascertaining, with the greatest degree of accuracy, a man's character from his handwriting ; to thus diagnose his natural character it is primarily indispensable to use only a natural manifestation of his character. This elementary remark is not so needless as might be thought, since the most common objection made to graphology is that a man can change his handwriting at will. We can also change at will the nature of our other personal gestures and expression, but this does not invalidate the truth that gesture expresses the feelings. A man who gives for analysis a purposely distorted specimen of handwriting cannot reasonably complain of graphology, any more than he who makes a grimace when being photographed, can accuse the photographer of not giving him his natural expression.

In order to avoid chance of error from this source, it is not sufficient for the graphologist to ask for a natural specimen, he must also make sure that what is sent to him fulfils this condition. Deception of this kind may be discovered, for then the handwriting is generally more or less vertical, unequal in size and shape, and constrained, *and the writer may deceive himself.* But, in fact, most people understand by a free and natural handwriting that which is usual to the writer.

Now, the requirements of certain avocations cause many people to adopt a certain *official* style of handwriting. It is of a rather insignificant, very legible type, which is to be met with among copiers of manuscripts, clerks of the lower grades, and others. When we see a really intelligent man using this kind of handwriting, we can be nearly sure that he has another which is more akin to his own individuality; and if he looks through his papers, he can usually find a few lines relating to non-official affairs which would confirm the truth of this statement. As regards people who are actually of quite mediocre ability, it is probable that this insignificant kind of handwriting is, or has become, natural to them and is in fact the expression of their own lack of individuality. This might certainly be affirmed of those unhappy copiers of legal documents, whose daily work, long continued, has rendered them almost incapable of doing anything else.

Speaking generally, official handwriting as compared with that which is free and spontaneous, is analogous to measured movements as contrasted with free gesture. Graphologically it cannot be entirely rejected as an index of character. Just as a man of measured bearing sometimes betrays himself in various external physiological ways, such as a tremor of his voice, a perturbed glance of the eye, involuntary muscular contractions, pallor, and especially by intermission in keeping up his conventional or official bearing, so also does a writer frequently disclose after another fashion those sides of his character which he wishes to conceal.

The use of erroneous graphologic signs is another source of error in the analysis of handwriting. Moreover, the value or significance of graphologic signs is not the same in all cases. In a later portion of this work we have endeavoured to diminish the chance of error from these sources as much as possible, by pointing out signs which are of doubtful value, and by showing the *relativity* of the value of ascertained signs according to the stamp of handwriting which contains them. There are, however, so many signs that have already been thoroughly tested and ascertained to be true, that we can state with confidence that there is no other art or science of observation kindred to graphology, which admits of so thorough an insight as to character.

Another cause of inaccuracy lies in the fact that handwriting is not, as gesture is, a direct expression of individuality. In transferring the latter to the paper on which we write, we employ three intermediate agents—pen, ink, and paper. Any one of these may be defective in such a way as to make it impossible to analyze certain signs, or to cause us to think wrongly that others are absent. But admitting that pen, ink, and paper be free from any material defects, and now-a-days this is usually the case, handwriting is still only a representation of our character effected by three different intermediaries which play the part of witnesses, and the evidence of others, however reliable it may be considered, never inspires us with so much confidence as does the direct observation of facts.

Moreover, it is necessary to know if the writer be ill or well. The handwriting of a man who is feeling the first attacks of a serious illness will hardly contain the sign indicative of gaiety, however much he may be naturally inclined towards joyousness. Also, the handwriting of convalescents undergoes considerable alteration as they regain health.

To sum up, we may say that notwithstanding the sources of possible error which we have just named, and which perhaps we may have somewhat unduly emphasized, experimental graphology gives us a high degree of certainty under the following conditions:—

I. That the specimen submitted for analysis be genuine and spontaneous.

II. That the signs used by the graphologist be only those which have been well established by experience, and not those whose accuracy may be in course of proof.

III. That the pen, ink, and paper used by the writer be of ordinary conditions, i.e., free from any material defect.

IV. That the specimen be written by a man in
     ordinary health, or if not, that his pathological
     condition be stated.

But the novice in graphology will still have his
ability well tried. When a man knows how to observe
he sees many things which others do not see. In
sciences based upon observation it is not only necessary
to reason accurately, but we must also observe and be
sure that we observe truly. The observation of specially
indicated signs is fairly easy, it is the A B C of graphology ; but the just appreciation of their value, relatively
to the whole specimen as concerns the character under
analysis, is a matter that we cannot guarantee to teach
to everybody. We will give directions, but we cannot
supply absolute means for accurate analysis under all
circumstances. The basis and general method of
graphology should appeal to any sound intellect, but its
thorough and accurate practice as an art requires the
mind of an observer.

We have still to speak of the way by which new signs
may be discovered and tested. At first, empirical
knowledge was the only method of constituting graphology. It could not be otherwise, for only by much
seeking about and by many tentative conjectures can
sciences of observation be even partially formulated.
We have, say, a number of specimens of handwritings
in which we notice the same peculiarity, whatever it
may be ; we then endeavour to trace in the writers one
identical trait of character, which may be allied to the
sign we have observed. Or again, given ten persons
whom we know to possess an identical characteristic,
we should obtain specimens of their handwriting and

see if we could find in each of them the same graphologic sign. At other times, by a kind of intuition, a
graphologist suspects that this good quality, or that
defect in a character, is likely to be represented in handwriting by a certain sign, and *vice-versa*. But it is only
actual experience many times repeated that should be
decisive in each of the foregoing methods of procedure.
But this may not always be satisfactory as regards the
accuracy of the results obtained. For some people know
very little of their real personality, and others are not
sufficiently exact in defining different gradations of the
same class of personal characteristics. Now, the confirma-
tion by such people of the opinion formed by the graphologist is likely to lead him into error, if he be not very
careful, especially if this should cause him to be too readily
satisfied with his discernment in any particular instance.

A totally different and most interesting test has been
made of the truth of graphology. MM. H. Ferrari,
J. Héricourt, and Charles Richet thought of applying
hypnotism as a proof of its validity.[6] It has been
proved by actual experiment that the personality of
a man may be temporarily changed when in the
hypnotic state. If it be true that the form of handwriting is really dependent upon various conditions of
personality, it must then follow that each change of
personality causes a corresponding variation in the
handwriting. The results of the experiment have confirmed this. A young man, totally ignorant of graphology, was put into the hypnotic state. " It was by turns
suggested to him [7] that he was a cunning and artful

----

[6] *Revue philosophique*, directed by Th. Ribot, professeur au
Collège de France. April, 1886.
[7] *Revue philosophique.*

French peasant, then that he was Harpagon,[8] and finally that he was a very old man, and a pen was given to him. At the same time when it was noticed that the traits of the physiognomy and the general bearing of the subject underwent changes, and became harmonious with the idea of the person suggested to him as being himself for the time being, it was also observed that his handwriting showed similar variations not less marked, and to an equal extent assumed a special, individual character quite in accordance with each of his new conditions of personality. In fact, the *written gesture* was changed just as the general bearing and gestures were changed. By that fact only, the principle of the possible truth of graphology is established; but this hypnotic experiment also proves its effective reality, forasmuch as that the variations in handwriting which were observed side by side with those of the personality of the subject hypnotized, reproduced, at least as regards general traits, those very characteristics which are attributed by graphologists as being kindred to the characters of the various persons hypnotically suggested to the subject of the experiment."

We cannot be accused of having exaggerated the importance of graphology in stating that it is a science of observation. Based upon physiological movement, demonstrated by the comparative method, it will be of the greatest importance when all its various parts have been well studied, and when it is possible to formulate all the laws which regulate the various movements of handwriting.

---

[8] The miser in Molière's comedy, *L'Avare.*

THE SIGNS.

I.

WE have pointed out the reasons for the existence of graphology as a serious study; they may be summed up in the following proposition. *Handwriting may be considered as a combination of gestures expressive of personality, and thus a relation exists between character and handwriting of the same order as between character and gesture.*

We now proceed to give instructions for practising graphology as an art by analysis of its signs.

A special feature in handwriting is called a *graphologic sign*. For instance, a clear handwriting is one where the lines are distinctly separated, and the words of which are tolerably wide apart. Now, clearness of hand-writing is a graphologic sign.

There are *general signs*, such as the handwriting ascending or descending upon the page, being written in straight or serpentine lines across the page, being large or small, etc. There are also *particular signs*, which relate to the letters, the finals, the margins, etc.

At present we know about 170 distinct signs; but in order that our readers may not be dismayed, it is well to state that at least half of these may be considered as multiplex, or as duplicate manifestations of the same physiological movement.   Thus the study of signature flourishes, of finals, of different ways of crossing the small *t*, may all be respectively included in the study of the curve, the angle, and the line.

When we come across signs in a specimen which are not given in our nomenclature, it is usually practicable to compare them with already-established signs, and thereby to arrive at their value.   Would-be graphologists who follow only the letter, and not the spirit and method of the art, can never hope to pass mediocrity.

Investigation of signs and their adaptation to personal traits form the technical portion of graphologic study. This is of the utmost importance, for it is the basis of deductions as to personality, whose sum forms a graphologic portrait.   Notwithstanding the important results which have been attained, and which are set out in this chapter, the latter must certainly not be considered complete.

We are of opinion that this study contains the key to character, and also that practical psychology as illustrated by graphology, admits of being defined in the form of principles, much in the same way as mathematies are definitely formulated.   Long psychological analyses, which we have met with, appear to us to be a sign of incapacity and of subjectivity on the part of the writers ; we shall therefore endeavour to strike out a fresh line.

For the sake of clearness we shall express ourselves in the form of propositions, which will then be amplified.

II.

The meaning of a trait in handwriting is investigated by considering it as a physiological movement, and by bringing it into general connection with the corresponding psychological state, taking into account also the constancy and the emphasis of the trait observed.

Take, for example, rapid handwriting. It is irrational to think that a series of rapidly-written characters is the normal and ordinary production of a feeble and phlegmatic nature. Our movements are responsive to cerebral excitation; if they be vigorous, the motive power is then vigorous; if they be quick, we infer that rapid movement animates their motor. Rapid handwriting[1] responds to quick, nervous excitation; it ought also to be allied to a psychological state which admits of this excitation, and which gives a quick conception, animation, and precipitance.

Clear handwriting[2] indicates order, a clear and bright intelligence. We can hardly attribute clear, orderly, and precise external action in handwriting to a blundering, disorderly, and confused mind. Clear handwriting is allied to distinct and definite nervous action; it shows a clear mind.

Let us take another example. The bar across the small *t* is a sign which necessitates a certain definite action of the will of the writer in order to put it in its place. For this reason this small sign is of great im-

[1] See p. 24 for remarks concerning the handwriting of copyists, etc., which must not be confused with the kind of rapid writing now alluded to.
[2] See definition on p. 30.

portance in graphology. We are able, for instance, to determine the animation of the writer by noticing the animation with which the *t* is crossed. In movements which are quick and animated we often employ an excess of energy, so as not to fail in our intention, preferring rather to exaggerate than to act more cautiously, and therefore more slowly. Thence it results that a long bar to the *t* indicates animation. It is easy to understand similar physiological analogies to the will that are shown by handwriting. We can readily conceive that delicacy of personality shows itself by slender lines, and that energy is portrayed by vigorous strokes of the pen. A bar of the *t* which is very heavy and short shows pretty clearly the violent, perhaps brutal nature of the writer ; and finally, we see consisteney and stability of mind in the regularity and uniformity with which these apparently trivial, but really significant, signs of the will are made.

It must not be supposed, however, from the preceding remarks that, because a long bar to the *t* shows animation, and a strong bar energy, it must therefore necessarily follow that a bar both long and strong indicates a large degree of activity. Dr. Paul Helot was the first to point out that such exaggerated bars to the *t* are frequently found in the handwriting of persons who are but quite moderately endowed with will power, and who, after having left some of the *t*'s without any bar, will all at once put undue force into the bars of others, quite out of proportion to the end to be attained. Something like a man who would shoot sky-larks with a field-piece. Thus *t*'s crossed in this way indicate weakness rather than strength of will, being the action of people who proceed less by consistent reason than by spasmodic and unsuitable efforts : and we see these large bars of the *t* followed by others which are very small and weakly traced.   It has also been noticed that when people are writing to dictation, they usually make longer and stronger bars to the *t* than is their habit. This fact agrees with every-day observance, for a passive, non-responsible act generally lacks reserve and firmness.

An angle, from its very nature, shows a certain decision in handwriting which we do not see in the curve.   It is a kind of voluntary, definite, and hard act, which is quite in accordance with the bearing of a man who would show firmness in opposition.   This is a sign of will power, of resistance, and, in some cases, of obstinacy.

The curve, on the contrary, shows us rather a mark of gentleness and absence of harshness ; it seems natural to resort to gentle, undulating movements as distinct from harsh and abrupt ones, when we wish to attract, and to retain what we have attracted.

In all the signs and numerous illustrations which follow, physiological movement is considered as analogous to the corresponding mental condition.   A characteristic trait in handwriting is viewed as a material expression of cerebral action.   A constant movement, a pervading characteristic of handwriting, corresponds with some one constant and general trait of personality ; a more detailed trait, an intermittent sign, is allied to some minor and intermittent feature of the individuality.

The intensity of signs may be accurately gauged

by comparing their extensiveness, frequency, and emphasis, with the intermediate values which lie between the slightest and the most pronounced manifestations of the same sign.

An instance of the varying degrees of intensity of a sign which may be verified by most of us, is that the handwriting inclines more in a letter which is written under the impulse of considerable affection for the person addressed, than in one which relates merely to some affair of business.

III.

Our organism sometimes reacts with similar external results under psychological conditions which are different; thus a graphologic sign does not necessarily represent only a single trait of character.

There is a kind of low-toned, convulsive laughter, the external expression of which is very similar to one form of weeping. We may sometimes hear one or the other of these emotions expressed, without being able to say from which condition it proceeds, notwithstanding that such laughing and weeping denote opposite senti-ments. Moreover, the two emotions may be expressed at the same time. A child of mine being inconsolable because an unripe apple had been taken from him, I began to tickle him, and he then shouted with laughter *without ceasing his sobbing*. Afterwards, in moving away from him I stumbled, and assumed a rather ridiculous position, and the child began again to laugh and cry at the same time. Thus there seems to be an affinity of expression between sobbing and laughing, despite the apparent contradiction of the two.

There are also instances where external expression is connected with different, or even contrary, passions or conditions from those which it is ordinarily reputed to express. The calm of sleep is not unlike, sometimes it is very like, the calm of death; the sigh of joy resembles the sigh of sorrow. Joy sometimes causes weeping, and violent grief in some cases brings out a convulsive laugh. The keenest affright we have ourselves experienced was caused by a mirthful cry from a child, who was playing about. This shrill cry reminded us exactly of one which had come from a little girl whom we had seen run over by a carriage.

We learn from anatomy that a large number of muscles respond to very different, and even contrary, functions. For example, one of the muscles of the neck serves to express anger, fright, dread, and suffering. M. Mantegazza has pointed out several other cases of synonymous external expression.[3] There is conformity of gesture between panic and madness, and between admiration and affright.

The pleasure of feeling thoroughly well, and the complacence of a person quite satisfied with himself, are shown by a similar external expression. There are analogies of still more weight, because they include a large number of facts at one time. Pleasures and pains experienced by aid of the sense of hearing are expressed by us much in the same way as pleasures and pains that touch our affections. Also, those of sight are expressed similarly to intellectual joys and griefs.

---

[3] *La Physiognomie et l'Expression des Sentiments.* By P. Mantegazza. Now translated into English, and published by Walter Scott, London. (*Physiognomy and Expression.*)

Modesty and shame, extreme physical cold and fear, extreme heat and anger, have respectively an outward expression closely allied.

So in graphology, many signs have different acceptations. We have just shown that this is to be expected. We now proceed to show that it is really the case.

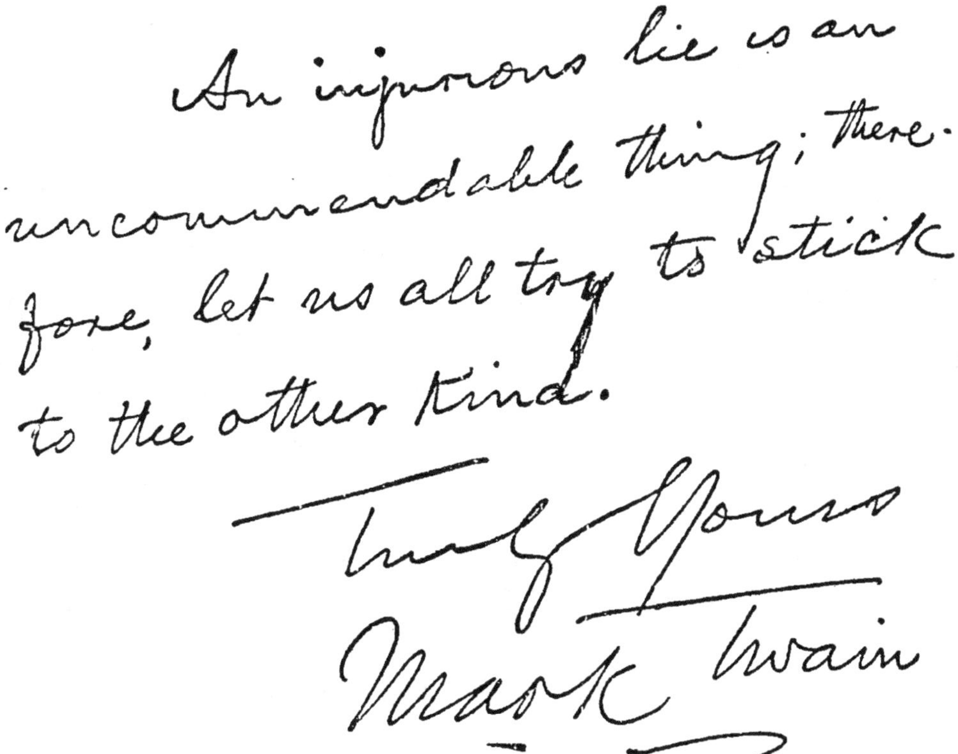

An injurious lie is an uncommendable thing; there-fore, let us all try to stick to the other kind.

Truly Yours

Mark Twain

Fig. 1.—Ascending handwriting: ardour, ambition.

Ascending handwriting (*fig.* 1) shows ardour. In fact, men whose movements are ascendant and expansive, and who find a certain pleasure in the muscular effort which is thereby necessitated, are ardent men. But this expression equally belongs to ambitious men. By analogy with their ascending handwriting, the writers are active, for ardour and ambition can scarcely exist without activity. It is also probable that they are of cheerful temperament, for nothing is more opposed to sadness than ardour and activity. We may also regard hopefulness, joyousness, and chance mirth as possible additional meanings of ascending handwriting, for these call into existence a certain ardour and mental animation.

However, the quality which is ambition in the case

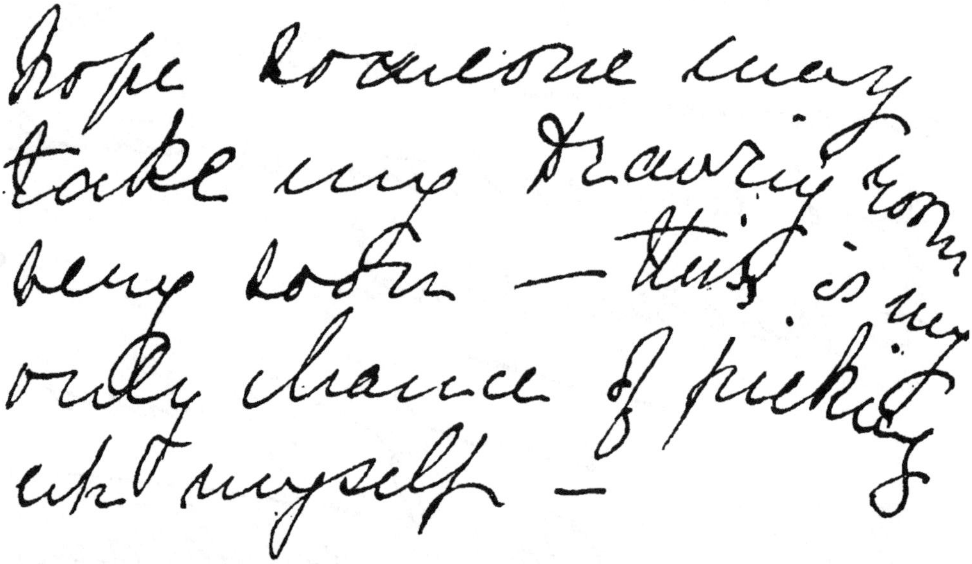
hope someone may
take my drawing from
being sold — this is my
only chance of picking
up myself —

Fig. 2.—Descending handwriting: sadness, discouragement.

of a man of superior type, amounts only to ridiculous vanity when allied to a man of an altogether inferior type.[4]

Thus we see that ascending handwriting has two principal meanings, two which are likely to exist with it, and two or three corollary traits.[5]

Descending handwriting (*fig.* 2) tells us of sadness.

[4] See the chapter, *Resultant Characteristics.*

[5] The determination of the various significations of the same sign necessitates study that is both important and delicate, and

When sad we avoid action and expans i v e, centrifugal movements ; w e hang the head, and the body tends rather to sink down than to expand. Such depression is certainly contrary to gaiety, and thus melancholy, which is one form of sadness, is shown by descending handwriting.

Bodily fatigue, mental uneasiness, fear, and want of self - confiden c e, which paralyse ardour and ambition, as does discouragement also, are all frequentaccompani-

which admits of almost indefinite extension. Thus we do not present the table which follows this chapter as an absolute code, but as a guide to enable the student to grasp the spirit of the main indication of graphologic signs.

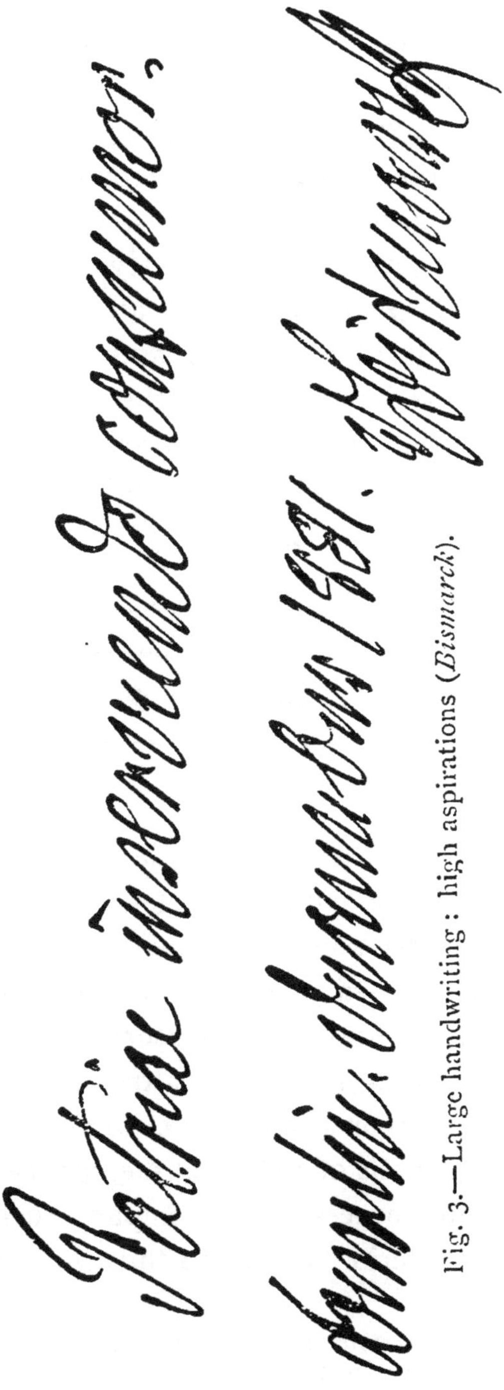

Fig. 3.—Large handwriting : high aspirations (*Bismarck*).

ments of this graphologic sign. In fact, descending handwriting is a pathologic indication of no small importance to an observant physician.

Large handwriting (*fig.* 3) signifies pride. It may denote generosity, greatness of soul, high aspirations, for largeness and fulness of bodily movements and actions, as opposed to petty doings, give the idea of power and greatness, and of an elevation above trifles. But uneducated persons and children write large. With these it results from the mere mechanical difficulty in writing, which is laboured, and which shows an inferior state of cultivation and a slow intelligence. Pres-

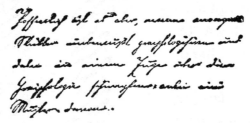

Fig. 4.—Small and slender handwriting: minuteness, delicacy.

byopes[6] also make large letters when they try to dispense with spectacles.

Very small handwriting (*fig.* 4) shows pettiness, an unnecessary attention to small matters. People of this stamp find their pleasures in little things, trifling ideas, finicking manners, paltry actions. With such, life is always on a small scale. This personal condition is characteristic of a state of mediocrity. Now, a narrow mind must necessarily accompany such a condition in a man of inferior[7] type, and thus this narrow mind is a trait of

[6] *Presbyopia* is far-sightedness accompanied by indistinct vision of near objects.
[7] See the chapter, *Resultant Characteristics*.

character which is evinced by very small handwriting emanating from an inferior man. But, in the case of a distinctly superior s man, this graphologic sign would express acuteness rather than pettiness—an intelligence which would inquire into every detail.

Intelligence is a trait which follows of necessity from this minute investigation of details. But in all cases, very small handwriting shows a love of detail and minutiæ.

In some cases short-sightedness may cause this style

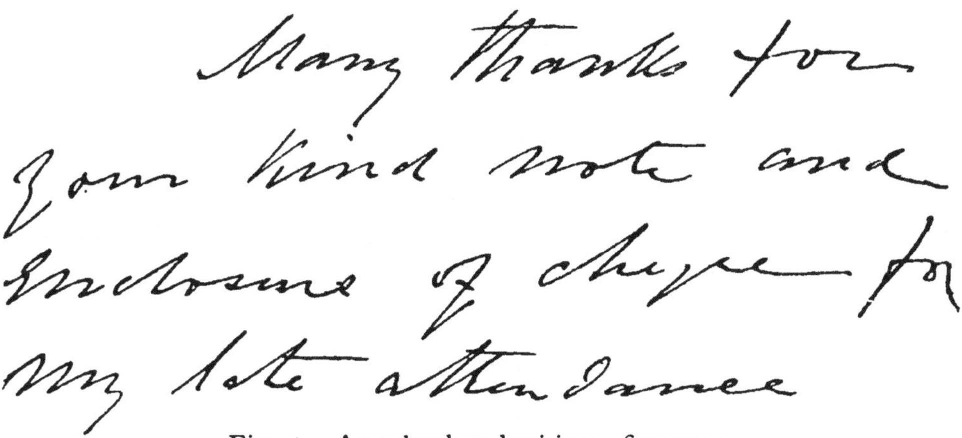

Fig. 5.—Angular handwriting: firmness.

of writing. But we have dealt quite sufficiently with this sign, and we pass to,

Angular handwriting (*fig.* 5), which indicates firmness; this form of will-expression may easily run into obstinacy, especially with quite commonplace people. Hardness is the necessary consequence of external expression which is angular to excess. In angular handwriting the absence of grace and charm is compensated by the clearness, the positivism,[9] and the sincerity of the

[8] See the chapter, *Resultant Characteristics*.
[9] This word is used in its philosophic sense.

angle. But egoism and selfishness follow from this sign when it is too much accentuated.

Rounded hand-writing (*fig.* 6) shows gentleness. This is a pleasing grace with superior men, but it is a weakness in men of inferior type. The curve is of much importance from the artistic standpoint; it is one of the conditions of what is beautiful. Rounded handwriting is thus a sign of the æsthetic sense. If unduly exaggerated, this shows weakness and want of vigour; and finally, imagination, being allied to grace, may be shown in handwriting by the curve.

Temperate hand-writing (*fig.* 7),

Fig. 6.—Rounded handwriting: graciousness, gentleness.

where the strokes of the pen, especially as regards the finals of letters and words, are kept in check and restrained, is indicative of discretion and reserve. In our opinion this is the most important graphologic sign of a superior individuality, because it shows voluntary attention and care to the definite arrangement and control of instinctive impulses and suggestions. Like all graphologic signs, it has an inferior significance if found in the handwriting of inferior persons. Thus, a common man would by this same sign show his distrust of others, while in a

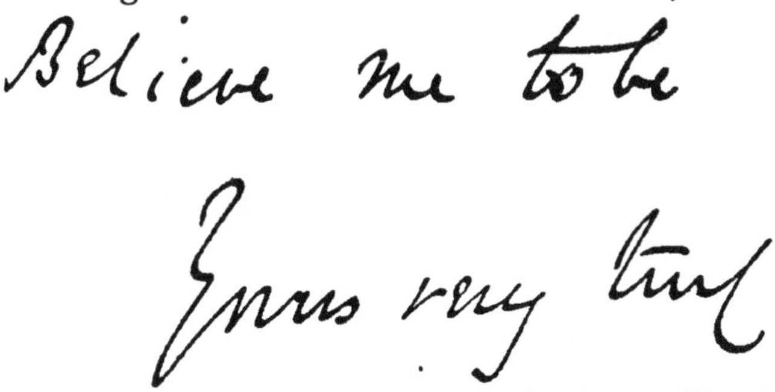

Fig. 7. — Temperate handwriting: reflection. Cleanly-traced handwriting: precision of thought.

cultivated mind the sign would indicate merely prudence, and, in the case of a distinctly high order of man, it would denote good judgment. Economy, positivism, the desire of others' approval, dignity, haughtiness, a good education, modesty, and dissimulation, are also shown by a certain reserve and discretion in personal action.   An economical man does not waste his ink and paper by making long finals to his words ; a positivist naturally eschews those large movements which accompany imagination ; he who seeks the approval of others will often assume a reserved expression of face, which

¹ See note on p. 41.

serves him as a shield for faults which he desires to conceal; and this reserve of expression is characteristic of a proud or dignified man, who is careful not to commit

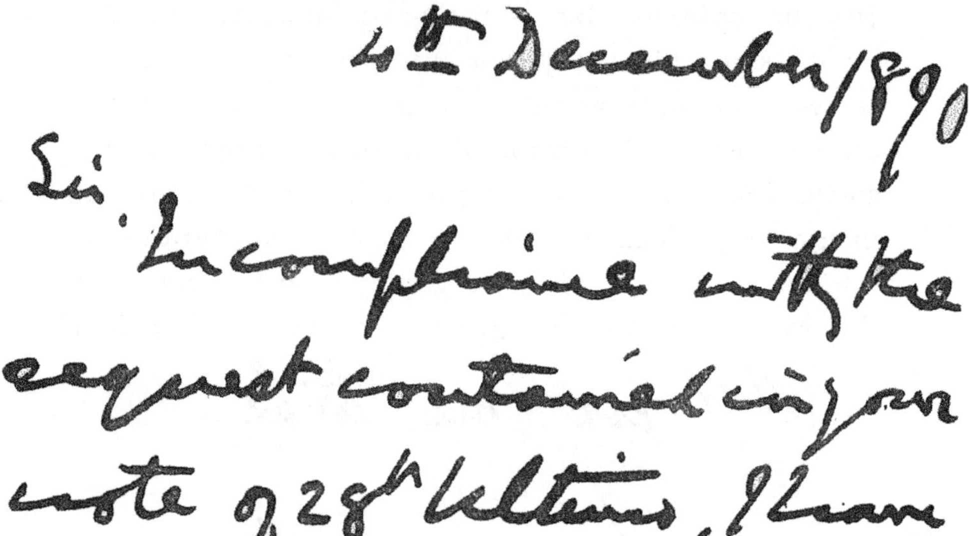

Fig. 8.—Handwriting containing pronounced pen-movement: imagination, impressionability.

himself by any external manifestation of his nature; the bearing of eminent men also shows this reserve and discretion. Of necessity a hypocrite must keep himself in check ; while modest people restrain their actions out of modesty, and timid persons from an instinctive dislike of attracting notice.

Handwriting containing pronounced movement (fig. 8) is of no less importance than the preceding type, of which it is the direct opposite.   Various meanings attach to these pronounced strokes of the pen, some of which rove far away from the other strokes, perhaps on account of the special incidence of these signs, or due, it may be, to a change in the mental condition with which such movements are associated.   They show imagination and

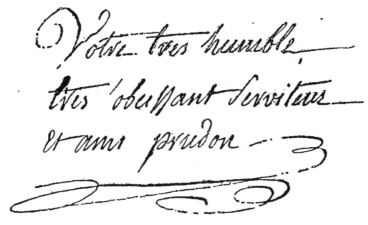

Fig. 9.—Hesitating handwriting: indecision.

exaltation, and even madness if the handwriting be wanting in co-ordination and harmony.

Moderate movement of this kind is one of the signs of gracefulness, which requires movement for its expression.   It is also one of the chief indications of vivacity and impressionability, and of lively and communicative persons, who employ numerous gestures. Thoughtlessness and loquacity are frequent accompaniments of this sign, and boastful pride is shown by the exaggeration of such movements.   From the nature of the preceding traits we may infer that an inferior judgment is the necessary consequence of excessive movement of this kind in the handwriting, and, although we have pointed out eleven possible meanings of this graphologic sign, we do not pretend to say that it may have no others.

Hesitating handwriting (*fig.* 9) shows indecision. This is a very obvious connection between handwriting

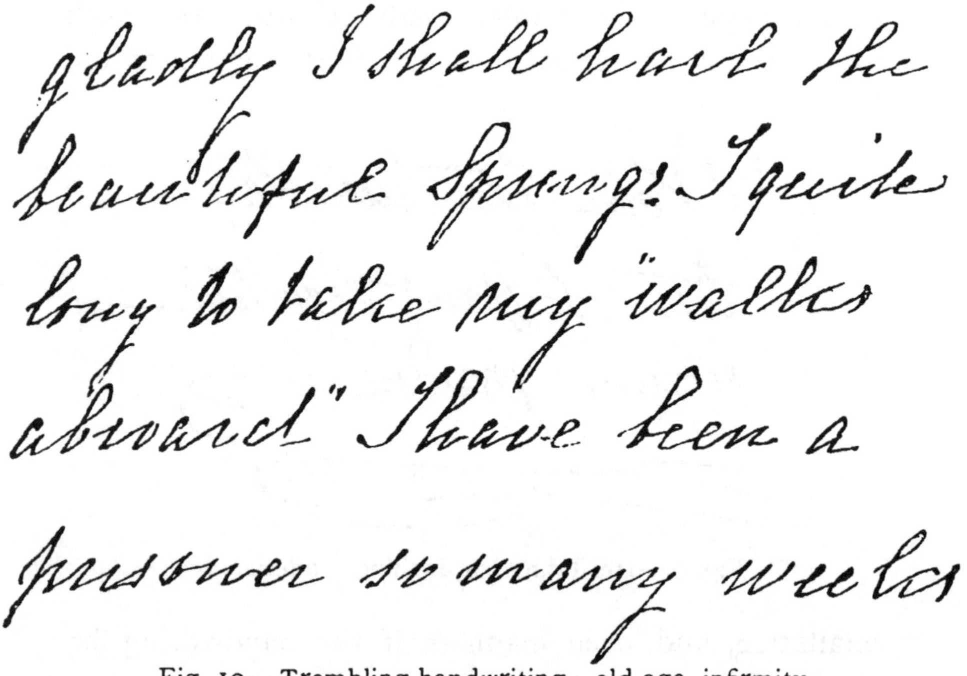

Fig. 10.—Trembling handwriting : old age, infirmity.

and character, for if an idea presents itself to us under two aspects we hesitate in its expression, and the vacillation of our mind is carried into the action of the pen upon paper. But let us remember that other causes may produce a hesitating appearance in writing, such, for example, as fear, apprehension, and timidity. These last motives quickly give rise to a *trembling handwriting*, (*fig.* 10), which is also caused by anger, indignation, old age, personal excesses, various nervous diseases, by cold or by fatigue.

Flourishing, ornate, affected handwriting (fig. 11) is a sign of pretension, for an unaffected man speaks, walks, and writes simply. We come across writing-masters and schoolmasters of an inferior type, but more specially schoolmistresses, who form their capital letters with the flourishing scrolls which they teach to their pupils. Such persons have not sufficient individuality to possess an individual handwriting, and they employ

Fig. 11.—Flourishing, ornate handwriting : pretension, studied effect.

their calligraphic flourishes even in their friendly corres-pondence. And their ornate handwriting is a witness to their own insignificance. With young people this is often a sign of coquetry, vanity, or conceit, or it may be that their individuality has not yet had time to unconsciously throw off the merely conventional style that may have been taught to them. But be it well understood that a true æsthetic sense may aecom-pany curves akin to flourishes, if they be truly graceful and found in a handwriting which is harmonious.

Inclined handwriting[2] (*fig.* 12) shows sensibility.
That which arouses our kindly feeling, our tenderness, our love, induces a bending, inclined movement,
a tendency to sympathy. Hence the inclined attitudes
of feeling people. There is no other graphologic
sign which has so many possible significations and
which lends itself more readily to combinations of signs.
We shall see later on, when we deal with resultants,

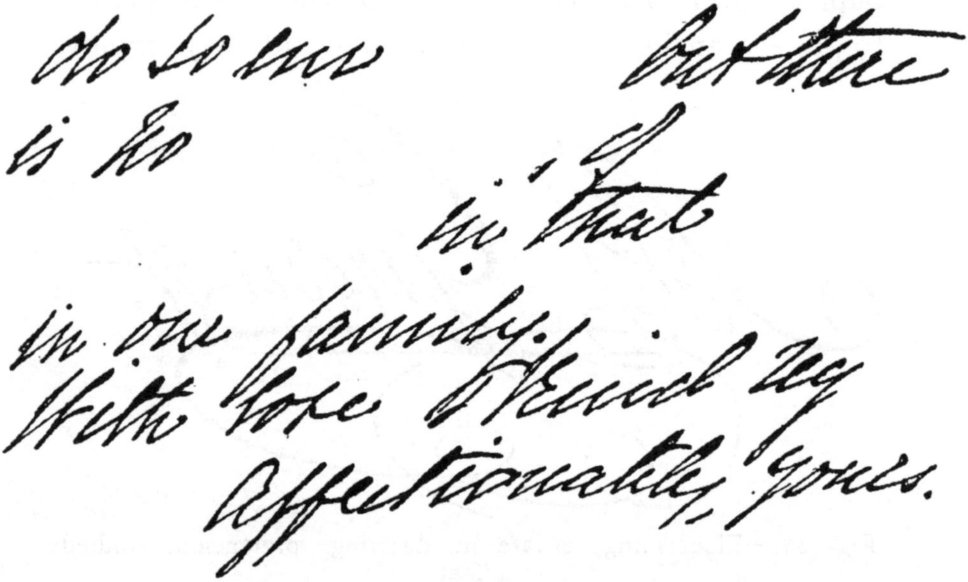

Fig 12.—Inclined handwriting : sensibility.

that this is a concomitant sign with excitability,
passion, irritability, love of admiration, affection, com-
passion, hatred, love, admiration, fear. Extreme sensitiveness may bring about a morbid condition and lead
to unhealthy enthusiasm and madness. This quality is
the prime factor in the play of the passions.

So far, we have discussed only the general characteristics of handwriting. Its particular and more de-

[2] *I.e*, sloping from left to right.

tailed signs do not lend themselves to accessory meanings as do the general traits we have been illustrating ;
their graphologic speciality appears to involve a speciality of character, as distinct from a general type ; but
they are not, however, quite exempt from accessory traits.

For instance, *filiformed words*,[3] viz., those whose final
letters are scarcely formed, denote impenetrability ;
we know that men possessed of this quality are rather
given to avoid clearness and precision in their statements. They avoid a too definite expression which
may reveal themselves. Acuteness and a certain distrust of others always accompany this impenetrability,
and hypocrisy is also frequently to be found there. But
precipitation may in some cases be the cause of the
filiformed words ; a man in a hurry contents himself
with expressing his meaning, he does not stop to complete all his words.

Even one of the first signs that we have discovered, the
bar of the small *t* becoming thinner and ending in a point
(*fig.* 69), may show a critical mind, sarcasm, aggressiveness, irritability, hasty temper, or nervousness, and occasionally it may even denote all these traits at the same
time.

A simple horizontal stroke of the pen indicates positivism, reason, probity, justice, love of clearness in
expression, order or suspicion. Moreover, this same
line can tell us if the writer be quick, energetic, brutal,
etc. These remarkable significations were known to M.
Michon, and this being so, it is the more incomprehen-

---

[3] *I.e.*, having the form of a thread.
[4] *I.e.*, not of necessity denseness to impressions, but the faculty
of not being easily read by other men.

sible that he based his theory upon the *absolute* value of graphologic signs, instead of upon their *relative* value according to the environment in which we find them.

But it is not so difficult as might appear to ascertain the true meaning of a graphologic sign in handwriting, in spite of the facts apparently to the contrary which we have just pointed out. How shall we distinguish, without knowledge of the productive causes, whether a specific sign indicates fear or madness, whether another sign shows a voluptuary, or a state of great suffering? This we can do by observation of the other external expressions in handwriting which will accompany one or other of these conditions. For handwriting being but a series of various manifestations of personality, it enables us, by viewing and comparing several traits, to judge as to whether a specific quality *may exist* in a man, or whether it *must result* from this more general weighing of the facts.

When we commence the study of handwriting, we ought to take special note of the probable interpretations of signs, and to set apart those which are doubtful; and then, by a process of elimination, a careful observer should arrive at satisfactory results.

The intensity and the frequency of a sign are evidences in favour of the validity of the accompanying traits which it may indicate; its faintness and its intermission have the contrary effect. Moreover, the general effect of the specimen will always serve as a guide to a just appreciation of details, for the facts themselves will never be contradictory—the onus of a faulty interpretation of them rests with ourselves—they are complete as to a man's character, in framing upon paper the contrasts and shades of his nature.

IV.

*The same personal charactistics may be expressed by
different signs, or by combinations of signs (RESULTANTS),
and we cannot infer from the absence of a certain sign the
existence of the quality opposite to that which such sign
indicates.*

There are characteristic traits which may be shown
by several different graphologic signs. Animation is
usually expressed in handwriting by long bars to the
t, but it is also shown by this bar being short and ending in a point. Rapid handwriting, ascending handwriting, and in some cases filiformed words, are moreover signs of animation.

Firmness, again, is indicated by handwriting which is
rigid, or vertical, or angular, by emphasized strokes of
the pen, by a certain bar of the *t* which is free of the
letter, or by another which is hooked round the base of
the *t* like that in *fig.* 75. If none of these signs be
found in a specimen, it is certainly probable that the
writer is not of firm character. This is, however, only a
presumptive deduction based upon the absence of certain positive signs, and not arrived at by the existence
of the sign which is the opposite to firmness. It could
only be more than presumptive, if we knew for certain that
firmness is shown in handwriting by no other sign than
those just named, and by no combination of other signs.

We lack this certainty as to all the different signs
which may express the same quality, and we shall continue to do so as long as new signs, and new meanings
of signs, are in process of discovery. Moreover, there is
no limit to the number of resultant signs, and every
trait of character may perhaps be expressed by such

combinations, even when those special signs are absent which we believe to indicate this or that personal trait. For example, more or less entire want of judgment, which is to be deduced from the sign of eccentricity (fantastic shape of the letters), or of a too lively imagination (large movements of the pen), of vulgarity (a vulgar type of handwriting), or of mental confusion (the lines confused, and disorder in the writing), may very likely be shown quite independently of these four signs, by a series of resultants whose chief factors are : great sensibility, nervousness, want of energy, naïveté, pretension, etc. We are forced to recognize this possibility of a characteristic being shown either by one special sign, or by a combination of signs, when we reflect upon the multitudes of different handwritings, and, to take a special instance, upon the small proportion of their writers whose judgment is sound.

The most experienced graphologists are often unable to detect the sign in a handwriting, which corresponds to a quality known to be certainly possessed by the writer. We need give only a single illustration of this. Signs characteristic of the æsthetic sense are letters of typographic form, and graceful curves. We have observed a third sign of this, viz., handwriting the letters of which are separated. Now, according to a theory of negative signs which says : " The absence of a positive sign is a sure indication of the quality directly opposite to its meaning,"[5] we ought to discredit the existence of taste for the beautiful, and love of art, in many eminent artists who write without letters typo-graphically shaped, without graceful curves, and without

[5] Michon, *Méthode de Graphologie*, p. 40.

the separation of letters just referred to.   This would be irrational, and in all probability there is a special sign, at present unknown, or an unknown combination of the signs of various aptitudes and faculties, which expresses in handwriting such recognized artistic ability.   But however that may be, we ought to consider a case of this kind as an existing graphologic *defect of omission*, and not transform a gap in our knowledge into an error, by the application of this theory of negative signs.   We ought rather to make careful experiments so as to fill up this hiatus, having all due care not to compromise the knowledge of positive signs which we already possess.

V.

Recently Discovered Signs.

IN the table of signs which this book contains, we have indicated those whose significance is well authenti-cated, by placing a (?) only after some few interpretations about which we are at present not quite sure.

We should have liked to give the name of the dis-coverer of each sign, but in many cases it is very diffi-cult to say who is, or was, the actual finder.

For instance, while nearly all the general signs can be traced back to M. Michon or to his predecessors, we ourselves have materially affected their meaning by applying to them a relative principle, and to the hard and fast interpretation once given to them, we have added others which sometimes possess an equal, if not a superior importance.   Thus we shall not go into much detail as concerns this matter, but it is only right to mention M. Barbier de Montault, M. Adr. Varinard, Dr. Eugéne Schwiedland, and Dr. Paul Helot as being discoverers of entirely new signs since the death of M. Michon.

To M. Barbier de Montault belong one sign of pride (*fig.* 44), the sign of religious sensibility (*fig.* 140), and that of self-complacence (*fig.* 6).

M. Adr. Varinard has pointed out hypocrisy (the small letters *o* and *a* being open at the base), the quality of extending protection to others and pride in so doing (the final stroke of the first letter of a word covering that word).

Dr. Eugéne Schwiedland has made known the signs of gaiety (*figs.* 34, 74 and 85), the spirit of contradiction (*fig.* 35), a taste for bodily exercises (*figs.* 36 and 37), and has also pointed out the signature flourish of intriguers (formed by lines which are entwined).

Dr. Paul Helot has found the signs indicative of shortness of breath (*fig.* 126), of the desire for improvement (*fig.* 28), of complication (*fig.* 25), of simplification (*fig.* 88), of ill-considered effort (*fig.* 60), and of distrust (*fig.* 86).

We ourselves publish the signs of mental culture (*figs.* 98 to 103), those of superiority and inferiority (*figs.* 87 to 97), and some new indications of art, a disagreeable character (*fig.* 33), of a person easy of access (*fig.* 32), of effeminacy (*fig.* 108), of mental flexibility, versatility (handwriting which varies in size according to the size of paper), of irrational enthusiasm (*fig.* 31), of a critical mind (*fig.* 69), of badness of nature (*fig.* 70), of acquired kindliness (*fig.* 29), of enterprise (*fig.* 65), of tardy resolution (*fig.* 66), of unceremoniousness (*fig.* 72), of the constraint of quick people (*fig.* 73), of the want of originality (*fig.* 49), of mental clearness (*fig.* 108), of coquetry (*fig.* 56), of envious pride (*fig.* 42), of presumption (*fig.* 45), of vulgar vanity (*fig.* 47), of dissimulation (low capital letters), of pride of domination (*fig.* 48), of party-spirit (*fig.* 38), the defensive signature-flourish (*fig.* 77*a*), the aggressive signature-flourish (*fig.* 78), and that of rational egoism (*fig.* 83). Also the sign of indecision (letters of unequal height), of mental activity (letters varying in slope), of quick sensibility (various inequalities in the handwriting), of moderation (lines tending towards a horizontal direction after previous lines have been markedly ascendant).

The preceding "recently discovered signs" are here merely enumerated, only a few of them being accompanied by a description of their respective characteristics in handwriting. This latter explanation will be 'found in the subsequent table of graphologic signs.

VI.

Verbal description of the Signs.

As a rule, graphologic signs are easy to recognize. We can distinguish without difficulty a clearly arranged handwriting and one which is confused, words whose letters are of equal height, long or short bars to the *t*, thick or slender strokes of the pen, etc. Still, in taking up the study of graphology and in gauging the intensity of the signs, it will be of use to the student to have the verbal description as well as the actual facsimile of the various signs, the latter illustration being specially useful for purposes of comparison. We shall give both, and

⁶ Illustrations which are given in other parts of the book are not repeated here. The reference-table at the end shows at a glance upon what page any illustration is printed.

the table which follows will also give, in the same order as this definition of the signs, the different meanings which may attach to each of them.

GENERAL SIGNS.

Ascending handwriting (*fig.* 1) is that whose lines ascend from left to right.

Descending handwriting (*fig.* 2) is that whose lines descend from left to right.

Large handwriting (*fig.* 3) is that whose letters are tall.

Very small handwriting (*fig.* 4) is that whose letters are short and small.

Angular handwriting (*fig.* 5) has its letters with angular bases.

Rounded handwriting (*fig.* 6) is where the curves are accentuated.

Temperate handwriting (*fig.* 7), where the strokes of the pen, particularly as regards the finals of letters and words, are restrained. This feature of handwriting is due to moderation and discretion in using the pen.

Handwriting containing pronounced movement (*fig.* 8) shows large and dashing strokes of the pen, either in the body of the words, in finals, or in the signature.

Hesitating handwriting (*fig.* 9) lacks cleanness of outline, its direction is more or less unsettled, and there is a feeble and wavering shakiness about it.[7]

Trembling Handwriting (*fig.* 10) differs from the preceding kind only by the persistence of the nervous and non-coordinated movements. It is found under diverse

[7] The letter, part of which, produced in facsimile, serves as our example, was written by the celebrated painter Prud'hon, to Wille the engraver (Fillon collection). It runs: " I am in doubt about the picture you ask to engrave," etc. This indecision shows itself prominently in this handwriting.

aspects, which vary as the cause to which it may be due varies.

Flourishing, ornate, affected handwriting (fig. 11) contains unnecessary flourishes, scrolls, etc.

Calligraphic or copper-plate handwriting (fig. 14) is the kind taught in many schools.   It is regular, clear, rounded, temperate, even, and moderately inclined, but without any original character.   We term it *official,*

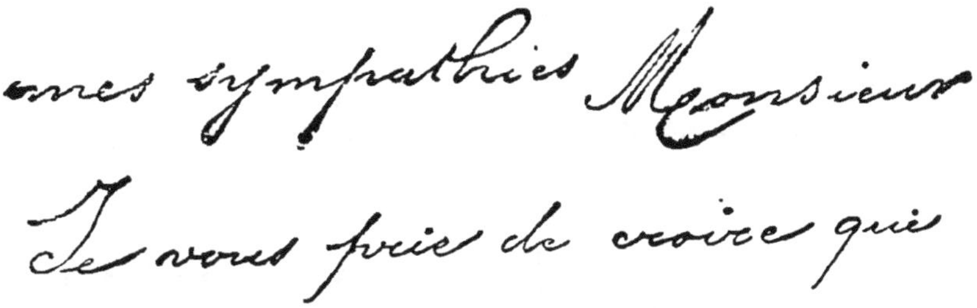

Fig. 14.—Calligraphic handwriting, termed official : insignificance, love of conventionality.

because it does not respond to individual character, but to conventional rules and regulations affecting its form.

Regular handwriting (fig. 15), with words and letters of equal height, the lines always in the same direction, letters not varying in their degree of inclination, and finally presenting the same characteristics in many specimens by the same writer.

Irregular handwriting (fig. 16) is unequal in height, in inclination, in the direction of the lines, or else as regards different specimens by the same writer.

Orderly handwriting (fig. 17) shows tokens of arrangement and order in margins, punctuation, etc.

Disorderly handwriting (fig. 97), on the contrary,

NOTE :—Fig. 13 is given on p. 66. For the explanation of the non-observance of consecutive numerical order in this instance, and in some others, see the reference table of illustrations at the end of the book.

shows no sign of attention to such details as margins, spaces between words or lines, nor to such accessory details of handwriting as punctuation and the bar of the small *t*.

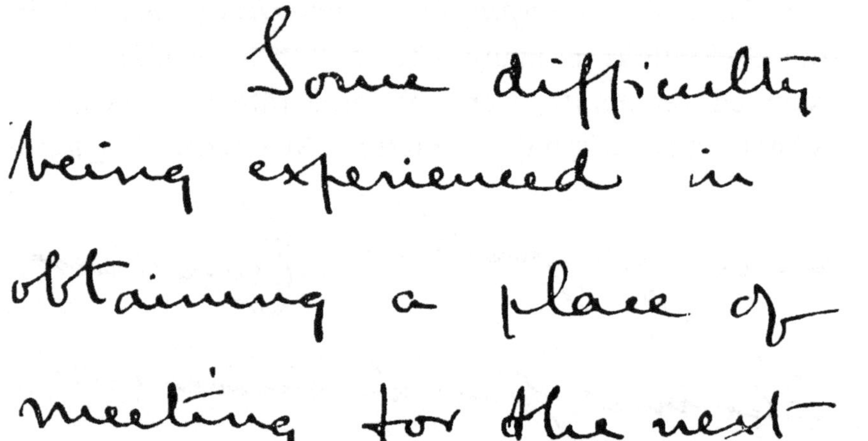

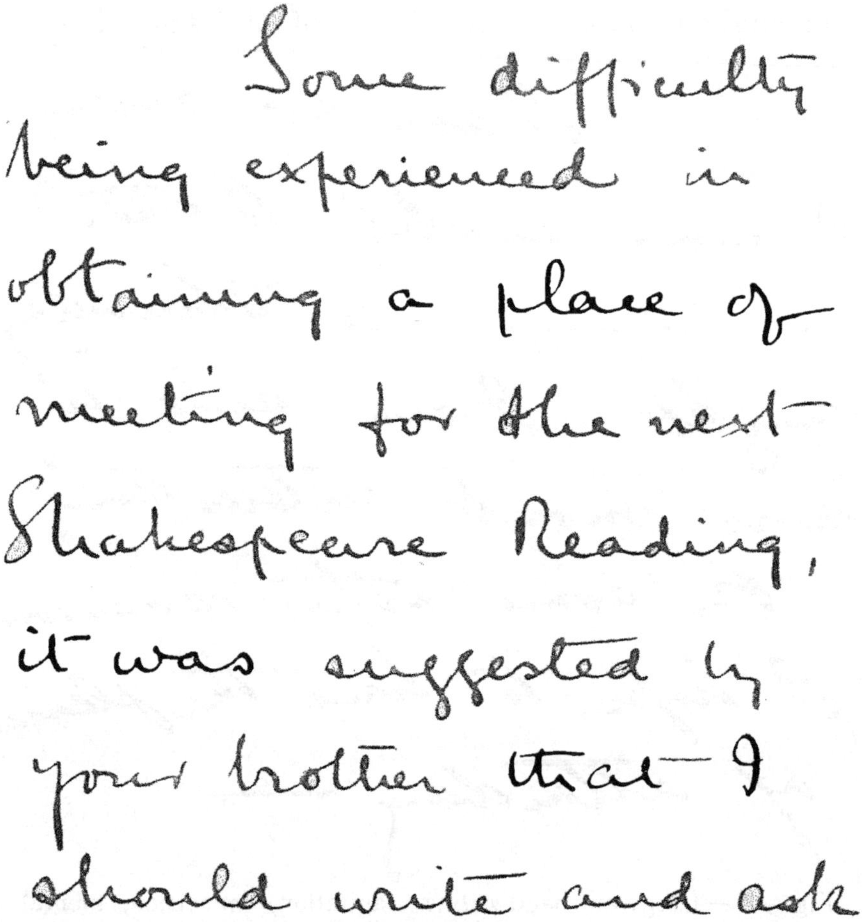

Some difficulty being experienced in obtaining a place of meeting for the next Shakespeare Reading, it was suggested by your brother that I should write and ask

Fig. 15.—Regular handwriting: constancy, firmness.

Clear handwriting (*fig.* 18) is specially to be recognized by the definite space between line and line.

Confused handwriting (*fig.* 96), where the words or the lines are confused and muddled as to their respective positions ; the up and down strokes of the small etters, or the capitals, may project into neighbouring lines, or the lines themselves may be too crowded either vertically or horizontally.

Rectilinear and rigid handwriting (*fig.* 19).   This is in straight lines, and the bases of the small letters

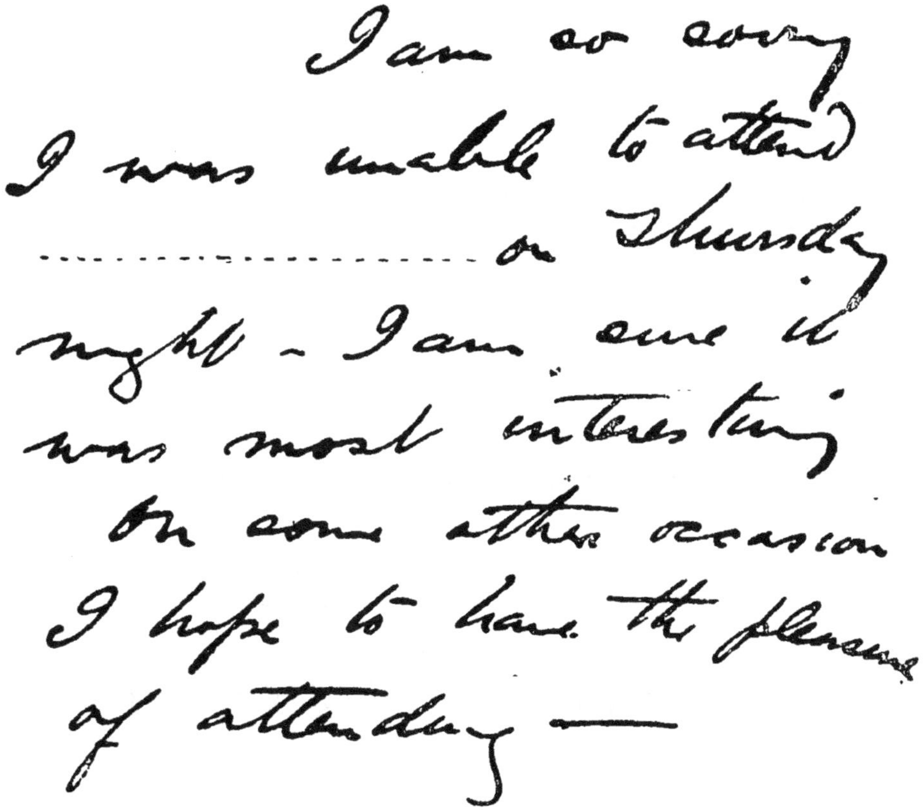

Fig. 16.—Irregular handwriting: agitation, indecision, mental activity, sensibility.

would touch a straight line ruled immediately below them.[8]

Serpentine handwriting (*fig.* 20) ascends or descends

[8] Such straight line might run in an ascending, horizontal, or descending direction across the page, but it would be non-undulating.

in the same word, or from one word to another, so that the lines of the writing are not straight.

Vertical handwriting (*fig.* 21), where the letters are upright.

Reversed handwriting (*fig.* 22) is where the letters lean backward to the left.

Inclined handwriting (*fig.* 12) leans to the right, in the ordinary way of most handwriting.

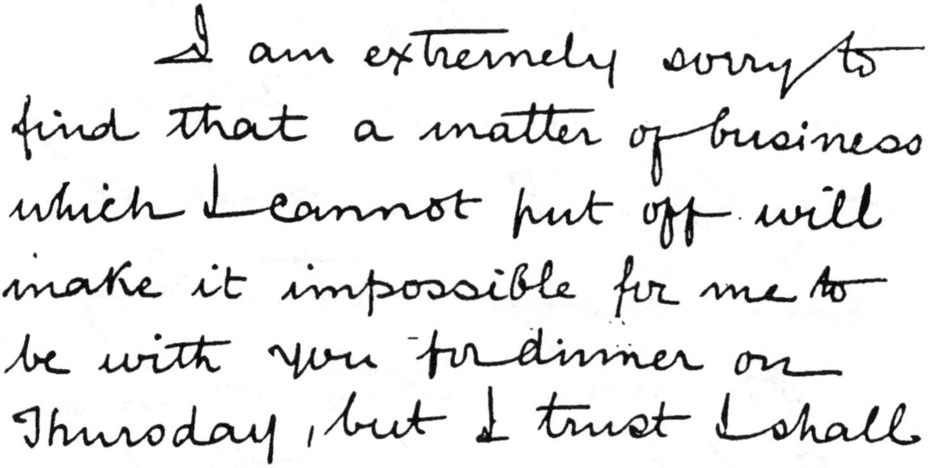

Fig. 17.—Orderly handwriting: order, classification.

Crowded handwriting (*fig.* 23) has its words or lines very near together.

Spaced-out handwriting (*fig.* 24) has considerable space between the words.

Simple handwriting (*fig.* 13) is writing which comprises just what strokes are needed to express the writer's meaning, without unnecessary flourishes or excrescences of any kind.

Bizarre handwriting (*fig.* 25) contains strokes and forms outside of those which are commonly used in writing, which we are unable to connect with any quality of the writer other than his eccentricity, and which must not be confused with merely abbreviated handwriting.

Light handwriting (*figs.* 4 and 13) is fine (not coarse), slender, delicate.   It is contrasted with

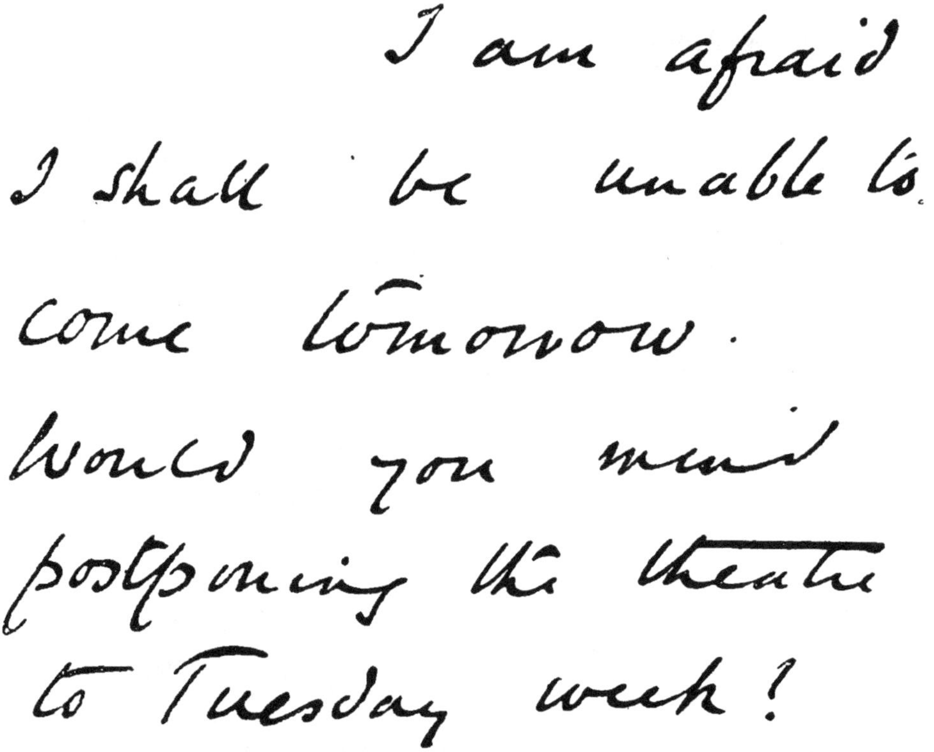

I am afraid I shall be unable to come tomorrow. Would you mind postponing the theatre to Tuesday week?

Fig 18.—Clear handwriting (see pp. 30 and 58): a clear conception, love of order.

Muddy, heavy handwriting (*fig.* 26), which shows signs of heavy pen-pressure. and is thick and coarse.

Cleanly-formed handwriting (*fig.* 7) is where the outlines are traced with precision.

Agitated handwriting (*fig.* 27) is a variety of irregular handwriting with a more pronounced unsteadiness and agitation.

Complicated handwriting (*fig.* 25) is formed by more strokes of the pen than are needed in tracing the letters.

Simplified handwriting (*fig.* 88), on the contrary,

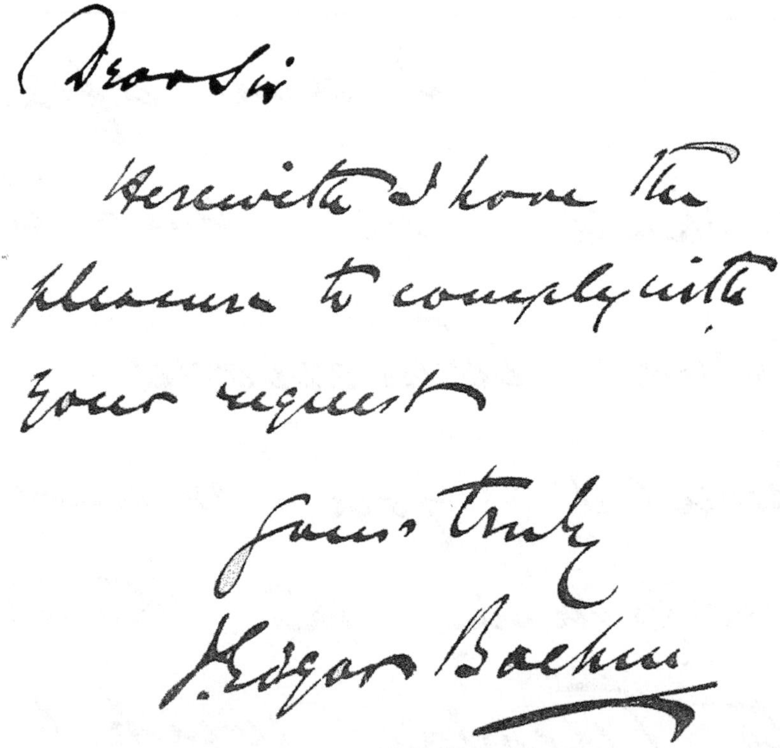

Dear Sir

Herewith I have the pleasure to comply with your request

Yours truly

J. Edgar Boehm

Fig. 19.—Rectilinear and rigid handwriting (see p. 59): firmness.

contains less strokes than are needed to form each letter correctly.

Touched-up handwriting (*fig.* 28) is that which has undergone corrections. The writer may either suppress or strike out useless parts, or he may add other strokes, etc., so as to make his writing clearer. But in either case this is touched-up handwriting.

Slow handwriting (*fig.* 97) shows no sign of being

rapidly traced ; it seems to hang fire owing to laboured thought.

Rapid handwriting (*fig.* 29) is that which is actively traced.

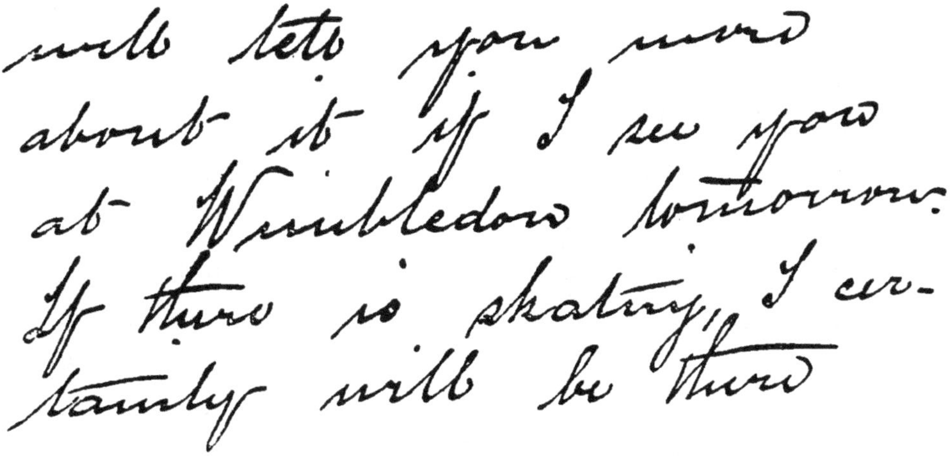

Fig. 20.—Serpentine handwriting : mental flexibility.

Handwriting which varies in size according to the size of paper used.   Such writing is large if the paper used

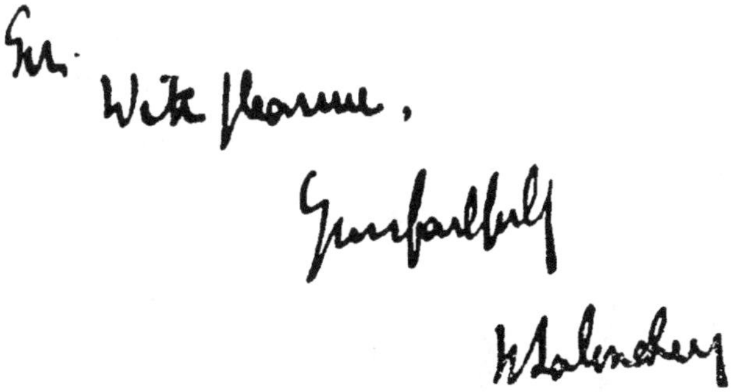

Fig. 21.—Vertical handwriting : little sensibility, reason.

be large, and smaller if the paper be of less dimensions. For example, we sometimes see post-cards written in a much smaller hand than that generally used by the writer ; while in other cases, on the contrary, rather

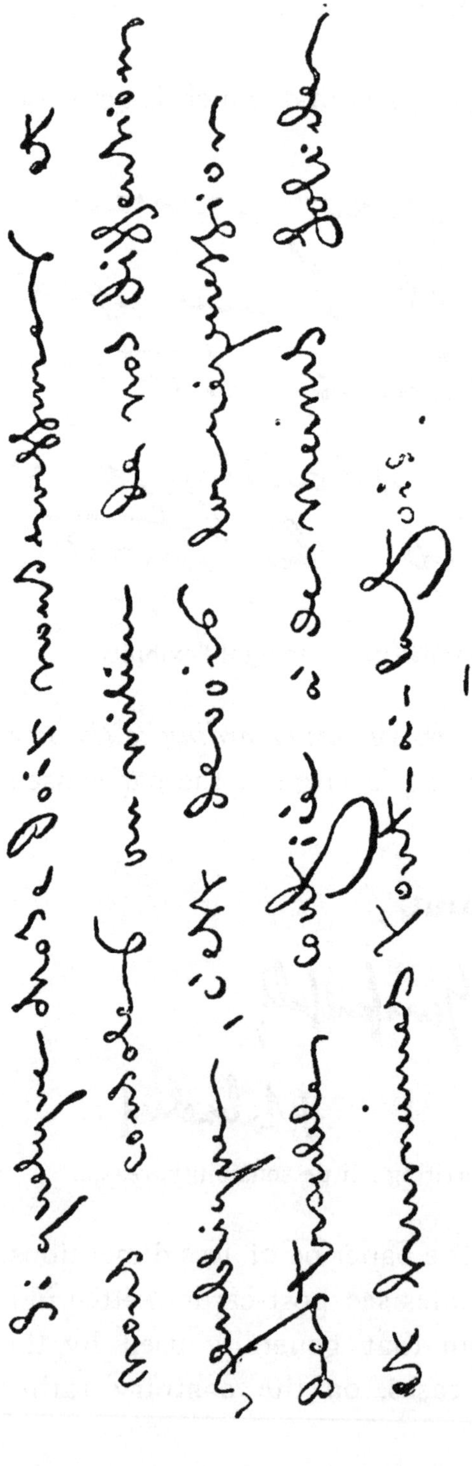

Fig. 22.—Reversed handwriting (see p. 60): distrust.

than modify the size of his letters, a person will write across what he has already written, **or** will abbreviate **his** text.

PARTICULAR SIGNS.

We shall not give here a verbal description of each of these detailed signs, because in nearly all cases, the mere indication of each given in the table which follows, is a sufficient description of its appearance.

Words ending in a point (fig. 30) are also called *gladiated,* because in form they resemble a pointed sword.

They are composed of letters larger at the beginning than at the end of a word.

Words becoming larger (*fig.* 30 *a*) commence with letters which are smaller than those at the end of the word.

Fillformed words (*fig.* 106) are legible only in the first part of the word; the last portion is formed by a stroke more or less long and sinuous.

Letters in juxtaposition (*fig.* 33 *a*) are placed side by side, but are not connected.

The Lasso signature-flourish (*fig.* 79) goes from right to left and then has a stroke returning to the right-hand.

The Lightning signature-flourish (*fig.* 80) resembles a flash of forked lightning.

The Arachnoid signature-flourish (*fig.* 81) is interwoven something after the fashion of a spider's web.

The Snail-like signature-flourish (82 *a*) is when the name is completely surrounded by the flourish.

The Signature-flourish resembling fig. 82. The name is here quite surrounded by the flourish, except a small portion.

The enclosing signature-flourish (*fig.* 83). The name is here fenced in, confined between two strokes, one formed by the flourish proper, the other placed above in addition. The bar of the small *t* often serves for the latter, and in such cases the bar is considerably augmented.

The Corkscrew signature-flourish (*fig.* 84) consists of a series of hoops or rings diminishing in size. We have found this sign beneath the name, above it, and at the side.

The Wavy signature-flourish (*fig.* 85) is formed by a curved stroke running horizontally.

The Intricate signature-flourish (*fig.* 86) consists of a profusion of accessory strokes. This is not a combination of various characteristic signs, but a sort of voluntary complication, as if the writer sought to render the forgery of his signature impossible.

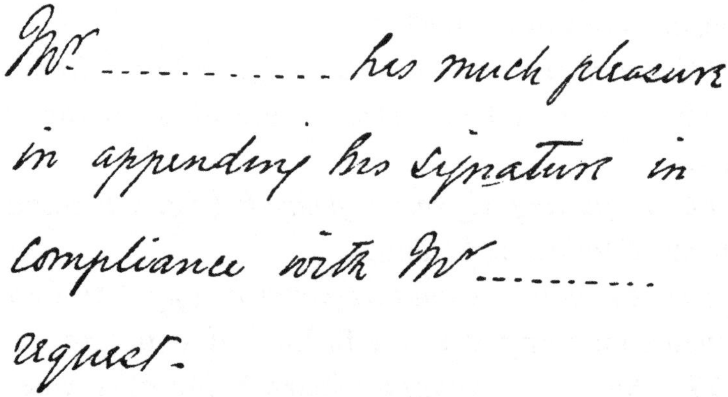
Mr. .... has much pleasure in appending his signature in compliance with Mr. .... request.

Fig. 13.—Simple, unaffected handwriting: simplicity and integrity of nature.

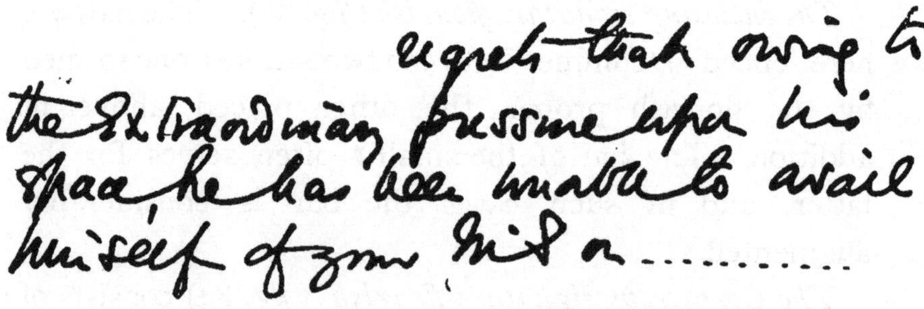
regrets that owing to the extraordinary pressure upon his space, he has been unable to avail himself of your MS. on ....
....

Fig. 23.—Crowded handwriting: economy.

NOTE:—For the explanation of the non-observance, in some cases, of consecutive numerical order of the illustrations, see the reference table at the end of the book.

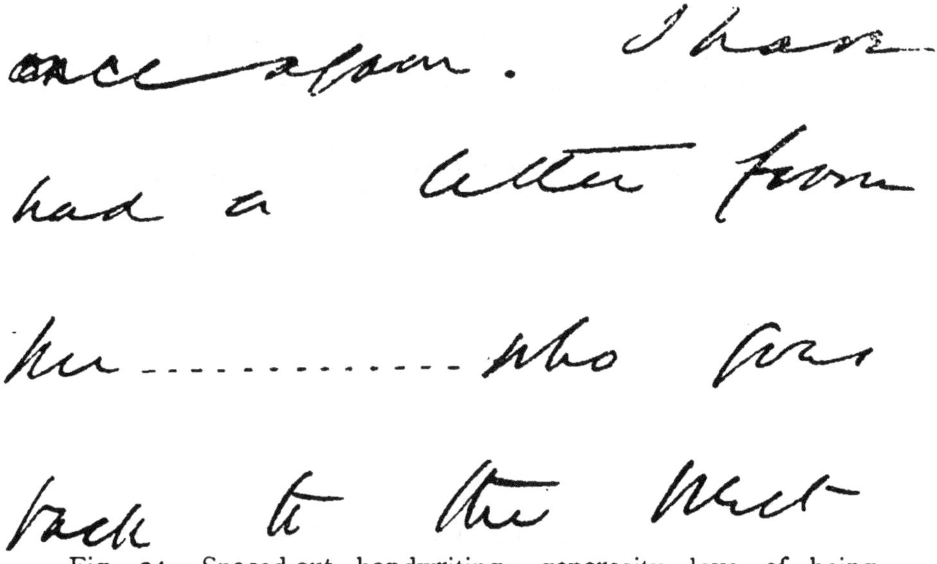

once again. I have had a letter from her .... who was back to the West

Fig. 24.—Spaced-out handwriting: generosity, love of being comfortable.

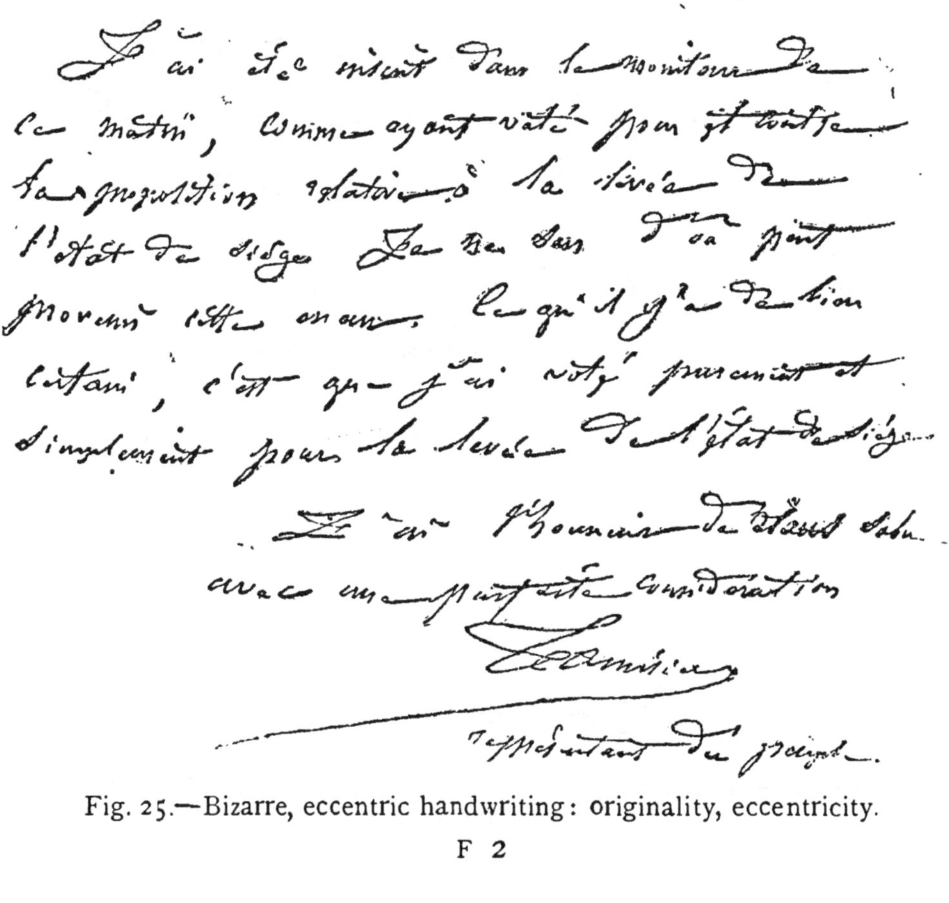

Fig. 25.—Bizarre, eccentric handwriting: originality, eccentricity.

F 2

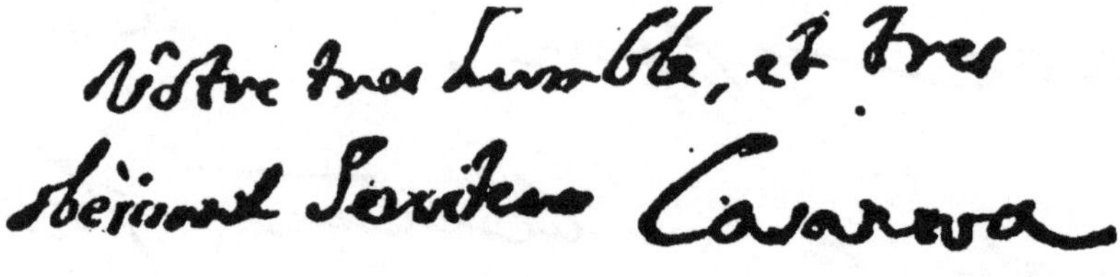

Fig. 26.—Thick, muddy handwriting: sensuality, gluttony.

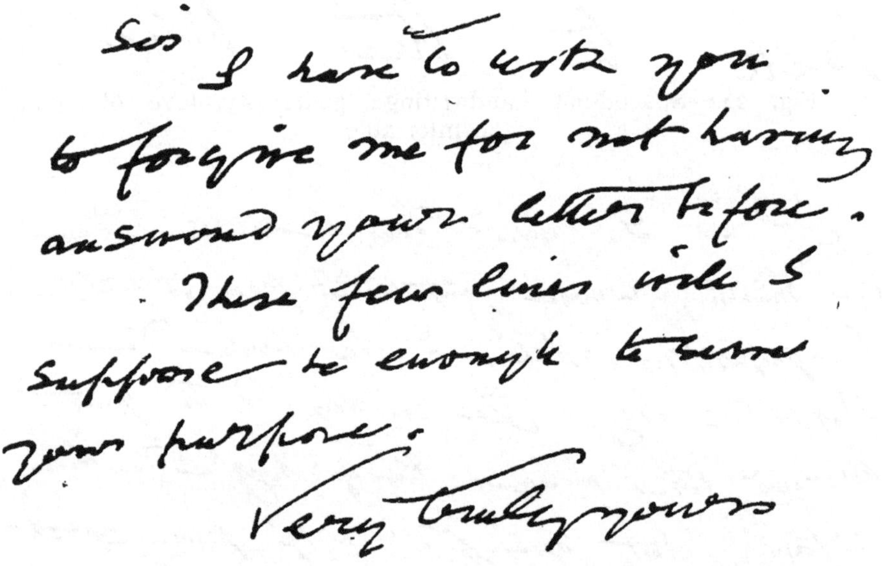

Fig. 27.—Agitated handwriting: nervousness, mental agitation.

Fig. 28.—Touched-up handwriting (notice the *r* in *esprit*): desire
for improvement.

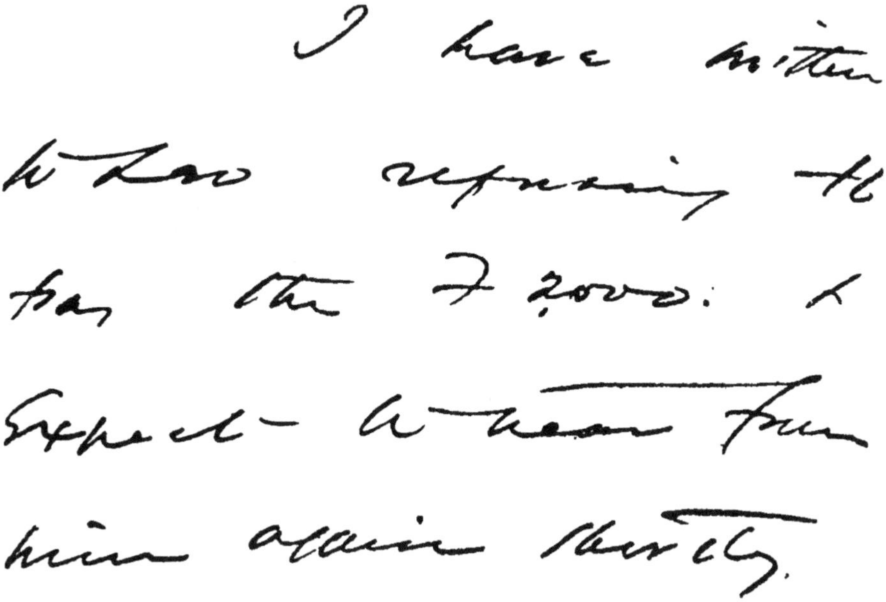

Fig. 29.—Rapid handwriting : activity, quick intelligence.

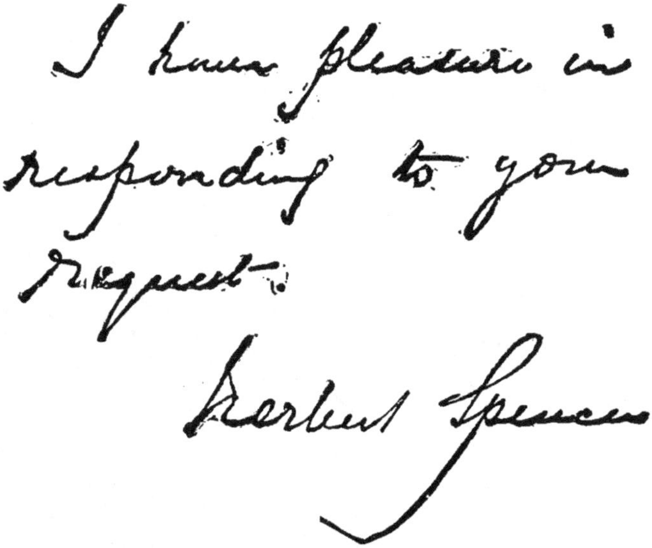

Fig. 30.—Words whose letters gradually become less in height, i.e. *gladiated* words : mental perspicuity.

Fig. 30 (*a*).—Letters becoming larger towards the end of the word : candour.

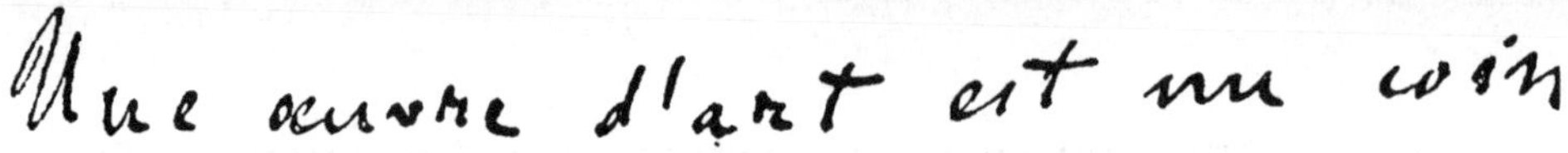

Fig. 33 (*a*).—Letters not connected, but placed side by side : intellectual capacity.

Fig. 79.—The " lasso " signature-flourish : defensiveness becoming aggressive.

Fig. 80.—The signature ending with a stroke like forked lightning: great activity.

Fig. 81.—The signature accompanied by a *cobwebbed* flourish : skill in affairs.

NOTE:—For the explanation of the non-observance, in some cases, of consecutive numerical order of the illustrations, see the reference table at the end of the book.

Fig. 82.—A signature-flourish of this kind
shows selfishness (?).

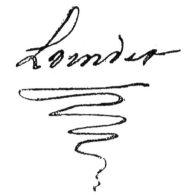

Fig. 84.—The corkscrew signature-flourish: finesse, skill in
practical affairs.

Fig. 82 (*a*).—Signature-flourish
like the shell of a snail: personal
instincts.

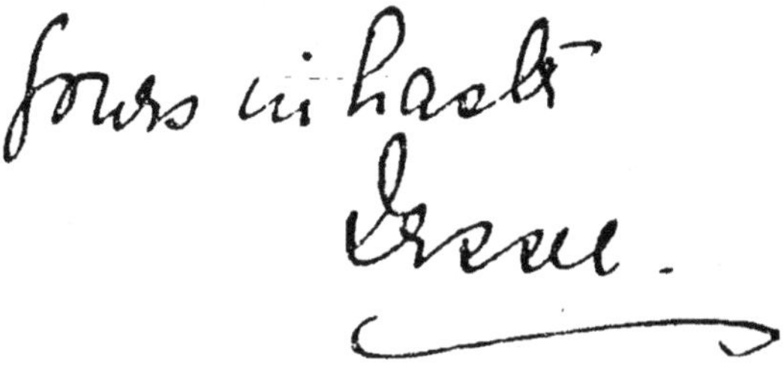

Fig. 85.—A wavy curve accompanying the
signature: gaiety.

ig. 83.—The signature *fenced in* by a line at
top and bottom: a reasoning selfishness.

Fig. 86.—The complicated signature-flourish: distrust.

...phologic Sign.	Ordinary Significance.	Significance more specially relating to a state of personal—		Accompanying and Accessory Significance.
		Superiority.	Inferiority.	
...riting which— ...ls (fig. 1)	Ardour, ambition	Ardour, ambition	Ardour or foolish vanity	...t..., hope, chance mirth, good temper.
...ds (fig. 2)	Sadness, want of ardour			Physical degeneration, fatigue, ext...me dejection, want of self-confidence, melancholy, a ...ous nature, uneasiness, sloth, an ...ic condition, discouragement.
e (fig. 3)	High aspirations	Much pride	A slow intelligence [1]	...ty, magnanimity, aristocratic pride, a presbyope,[2] imagination.
ll (fig. 4)	Pettiness	Acuteness	Pettiness	A narrow mind, the ...se faculty, a cheerful nature, spirituality, ...ht-sightedness.
...ular (fig. 5)	Obstinacy	Firmness	Hardness	Selfishness, a positive person.
...nded (fig. 6)	Gentleness	Gracefulness	A weak will	Imagination, ...nt of vigour, the æsthetic sense.
...perate (fig. 7)	Moderation, reserve, reflection	Prudence	Distrust	...on, desire of approval, perspicacity, positivism, judgment, bashfulness, ...roy, dignity, ...ty, timidity.
...ns pronounced ...vement (fig. 8)	Imagination	Imagination	Mental agitation	G...ty, ...es, animation, ...d-...es, a ...ative nature, ex-...kity, ...want of judgment, ...ns, pride.
...itating (fig. 9)	Hesitation	Indecision	Hesitation	Fear, timidity, ; ...nt.

NOTE.—For a more detailed description of the *graphologic sign* see p. 55, *Verbal description of the signs.*
[1] See p. 40.
[2] *Presbyopia* is far-sightedness accompanied by indistinct vision of near objects.

GENERAL SIGNS, *continued.* (See note to p. 38 of *The Signs.*)

Graphologic Sign.	Ordinary Significance.	Significance more specially relating to a state of personal—		Accompanying and Accessory Significance.
		Superiority.	*Inferiority.*	
Handwriting which—				
is trembling (fig. 10)	Old age	Old age	Old age	Fatigue, agitation, alcoholism, personal excesses, cold, apprehension, fright, indignation, anger, paralysis agitans.
is ornate (fig. 11)	Studied effect	Grace or pretension	Vulgar conceit	Vanity, coquetry, the æsthetic sense, insignificance, pettiness.
is simple and un-affected (fig. 13)	Simplicity	Modesty	Insignificance	Integrity.
is calligraphic (fig. 14)	Insignificance	An inclination for *posing*	Insignificance	Love of official affairs, of conventionality, of received practices, a narrow mind.
is regular (fig. 15)	Constancy	Steady logic	Equable character	Firmness, exactness, calmness.
is irregular (fig. 16)	Mobility	Impressionability	Variableness	Eclecticism, caprice, an unequable and fanciful nature, agitation.
is orderly (fig. 17)	Order	Order in ideas	Material order	Classification, detail.
is unorderly (fig. 97)	Want of order	Want of material order	An unorderly mind	Want of precision, want of care, thoughtlessness.
is clear (fig. 18)	Clearness	A clear conception	A clear mind	Love of order.
is confused (fig. 96)	Confusion	Want of clearness	A confused mind	Disorder, madness.
is rectilinear and rigid (fig. 19)	Firmness	A steadfast mind	Firmness	Inflexibility, routine, severity.
is serpentine (fig. 20)	Mental flexibility	Finesse	Untruth	Diplomacy, tact, agitation, mental effort, inconsistency, impressionability, hesitation, diseases of the eye.
is vertical (fig. 21)	Slight sensibility	Reason	Slight sensibility	Energy, coldness, selfishness.
inclines backward (fig. 22)	Distrust	Distrust	Distrust	Exaltation, restrained sensibility, dissimulation, reserve, gaucherie.

Graphologic Sign.	Ordinary Significance.	Significance more specially relating to a state of personal—		Accompanying and Accessory Significance.
		Superiority.	*Inferiority.*	
Handwriting which— inclines forward (fig. 12)	Sensibility	Sensibility	Sensibility	Passion, impressionability, irritability morbidness, desire of approval, affe tion.
is crowded together (fig. 23)	Parsimony	Economy	Stinginess	Reserve.
is spaced out (fig. 24)	Prodigality	Generosity	Disorder	Love of being comfortable.
is bizarre (fig. 25)	Oddness	Originality	Madness	Caprice.
is light (figs. 4 and 13)	Delicacy	A delicate mind	Feebleness	An unhealthy nature, sensibility, weakness.
is thick and muddy (fig. 26)	Sensuality	Sensuality	Bestiality	A heavy and common mind, gluttony.
is cleanly traced (fig. 7)	A cultivated mind	A cultivated mind	A cultivated mind	Precision in ideas, perspicacity.
is agitated (fig. 27)	Nervousness	Mental agitation	Exaggeration	Fatigue, fear, alcoholic excitement.
is complicated (fig. 25)	Want of precision	Want of precision	Want of precision	Folly, insincerity.
is simplified (fig. 88)	Precision, clearness	Mental culture	Mental culture	Fairness, good management, simplicity.
is touched up (fig. 28)	Desire for improvement	Desire for improvement	Desire for improvement	The habit of reverting to the first idea.
is slow (fig. 97)	A slow intelligence	Timidity, calmness	A slow perception	Inactivity.
is rapid (fig. 29)	Activity	A ready wit	Animation	Ardour.
varies in size according to the size of paper used in writing	Mental flexibility	Mental flexibility	Mental flexibility	Taste, intelligence.

PARTICULAR SIGNS. (See note to p. 38 of *The Signs*.)

Graphologic Sign.	Ordinary Significance.	Significance more specially relating to a state of personal—		Accompanying and Accessory Significance.
		Superiority.	Inferiority.	
Words— the letters of which are of equal height	Rectitude	Rectitude	Rectitude	Justice, calm judgment, decorum.
the letters of which are of unequal height	Mental pliability	Sensibility, indecision	Hesitation, weakness, untruthfulness	Untruth.
finishing in a point (fig. 30)	Finesse	Mental acuteness	Ability	Integrity, simplicity, clearness.
becoming larger towards the end (fig. 30a)	Naïveté	Candour	Credulity	Inattention.
omitted from the text	Heedlessness	Absence of mind	Thoughtlessness	Distrust, hypocrisy, agitation, precipitation.
whose final letters are illegible (fili-formed words, fig. 106)	Impenetrability	Subtleness	Dissimulation	
which are emphasized by an increase in size instead of by underlining (fig. 31)	Exaltation			
which are crowded together in the line (fig. 23)	Parsimony	Economy	Stinginess	Niggardliness, reserve.
well separated (fig. 24)	Lavishness	Generosity	Disorder	Love of being comfortable.
whose letters are not near together, although they may be connected (fig. 32)	A person easy of access	Kindness	A person easy of access	Generosity, love of being comfortable.
whose letters are crowded together, the words themselves not being crowded (fig. 33)	An ungracious man	Hardheartedness	A disagreeable nature	Reserve, economy.
Letters— which are connected throughout the word (fig. 1)	A practical and reasoning mind	Logic, order in ideas	Faulty reasoning	Insignificance.

PARTICULAR SIGNS, *continued.* (See note to p. 38 of *The Signs*.)

Graphologic Sign.	Ordinary Significance.	Significance more specially relating to a state of personal—		Accompanying and Accessory Significance.
		Superiority.	*Inferiority.*	
Letters :—				
...ed in groups of three or four (fig. 5)	Assimilation	Assimilatio...nd comparison	Assimilation	Eclecticism, an encyclopaedic mind.
...nt ...nd, but placed side by ...de (fig. 33*a*)	The intellectual sense	T...ly, cre...ite faculty, intuition	A visionary	A systematist, paradoxicalness.
...pn at ...he ...p (*o, a,* etc.) (fig. 113)	Open-heartedness	..., c...lour	...ant	Effusiveness.
usually ...ed (fig. 13)	Accuracy	...in,	...racy	...re.
...pn at ...le ...bttom (*o, a,* etc.) of typo...raphical form (figs. 109, 110, 111)	Dissimulation Taste	Dissimulation Art	Hypocrisy Art	Ling. M...ml cul...re, grace, ...tn (as opp. to insignificance).
of vulgar form (figs. 96 and 97) of the *copperplate* order (fig. 14)	Want of taste Insignificance	Want of taste Want of originality	A common mind Insignificance	Coarseness. A passive ...nd, love of ...ful ...rs.
...wh ...re t ...rk ...nd ...ly, or where the ...tokes are swollen in the middle (fig. 26)	Sensuality	Sensuality	Bestiality	Gluttony.
...r ...is inclined, sometimes up-...ght (fig. 8)	Mobility of feeling	Mobility of feeling	Caprice	Agitation.
commencing with a h ...dk ...commencing by a ...nd ...nd ...pid ...de of ...he pen (fig. 34)	Desire of acquisition Gaiety			Egoism. Good humour, high spirits.
commencing by a ...nd ad ...ght ...de of ...le ...gn (fig. 35) ...pital, being larger ...hn ...ls (...sually *a, r, s*) (...gs. 131, 132, 133)	Spirit of contradiction Imagination	Spirit of contradiction	Cavilling	Madness (?)

PARTICULAR SIGNS, *continued.* (See note to p. 38 of *The Signs*.)

Graphologic Sign.	Ordinary Significance.	Significance more specially relating to a state of personal—		Accompanying and Accessory Significance.
		Superiority.	*Inferiority.*	
Letters—				
...only in the form of a db (fig. 31)	Resolution	Resolution	Violence, brutality	
nt ... fid off ... bt wit but a db form (fig. 7)	Irresolution Restrained force	Prudence, reserve		Order, economy.
...e up nd ...n strokes ...d of straight stroke (fig. 101) ... by ...e	Mental culture			Simplification, purity.
...e up nd ...n ...es ...w an ...e up nd dp (fig. 133)	...igation			Exaltation.
...e up ...s ...e longer t...n the ...n ...s (fig. 36)	Neglect of bodily ...r... ...l labour(?) ...e of walking ...d tilly ...e (?)			
...e up ...es are ...r ...n the ...n strokes (fig. 37)	L...y imagination ...dima imgition	Imagination	Exaggeration	Pride, ...k imagination.
tall ...ils medium ...ed ...itals	Dissimulation Al ...n	Humility Benevolence	Hypocrisy Kindness	A man ...ily ap-... ...d.
dw ...ils ...s joined to he let ...r following (fig. 1)	Altruism ...stricted to family, or to ...e Exaggerat...on, ...ss			Party spirit.
...ials joined to he ...tter ...llowing ...r making a l op (fig. 38) capitals ...d ...d of small				Enthusiasm, ...nt of judgment.
capitals replaced by small letters capitals used correctly	Negligence Order	Simplicity Moderation, judgment	Disorder Moderation	...n.

PARTICULAR SIGNS, *continued.* (See note to p. 38 of *The Signs.*)

Graphologic Sign.	Ordinary Significance.	Significance more specially relating to a state of personal—		Accompanying and Accessory Significance.
		Superiority.	*Inferiority.*	
Letters :—L (capital)— raised up from the base (fig. 39) with a large base (fig. 40)	Pride of comparison Self-complacence, boasting	Pride of comparison	Pride of comparison	
M (capital)— the first stroke higher than the ... (fig. 41)	Pride of comparison	Aristocratic pride	Pride of comparison	Dignity, distinction
the first stroke l ... than the ... (fig. 42)	Envious pride (?)		Vulgar pride (?)	Humility (?)
... strokes are of ... height (fig. 43)	Calm mind			Order, reason.
with three strokes, ... being ... than the ot... (fig. 44)	Pride in honours			
... strokes ... apart (fig. 45)	Presumption Constraint	Self-complacence Timidity		Pride. Uneasiness.
... being ... together (fig. 46)				
the ... of ... stroke being exaggerated (fig. 47)	Common vanity (?)		Common vanity	
P (capital)— surmounted by a flourish (fig. 48)	Vanity	Pride	Vanity	
a (small) in form of the Greek alpha	Mental culture	Want of originality	Insignificance	Arrested developm[ent]
d (small) made with an *o* and a vertical stroke (fig. 49)	A passive spirit			
with a curved stroke from right to left	Mental culture			

Graphologic Sign.	Ordinary Significance.	Significance more specially relating to a state of personal —		Accompanying and Accessory Significance.
		Superiority.	Inferiority.	
Letters :—*d* (small), *biassed*— with t his stroke curling itself in a spiral (fig. 51)	Affectation, pretension			Vanity, coquetry, selfishness
with a ... loop returning to the right (fig. 52)	Imagination			
with the ... dp (fig. 53) ... forming a	Lively imagination	Enthusiasm	Exaggeration	Deductive faculty.
with a ... loop returning to the right ... joined to the letter following (fig. 54)	Mental cultivation	Sequence in ideas	Mental cultivation	
with a long and low ... stroke going from ... right to left (fig. 55)	Constraint	Reserve	Constraint	Reserved imagination.
with a ... st ... be from left to right (fig. 56)	Constraint	Constraint		Inferiority.
e (small) formed like ... in "the" of fig. 29.	Acquired benevolence			
g and *g* (small) ... as in fig. 100	Mental cultivation	Benevolence and goodness	Kindness and *bonhomie*	Love of form, love of comfort, kindness, sensuality.
m and *n* (small) in form of the *u* (fig. 107*a*)	Natural benevolence	Contemplation, gentleness	Nonchalance	
r (small) in form of the *u* (fig. 108)	Inactivity			
r (small) in form of the *i* with a little stroke made above it (fig. 28)	Desire for improvement			The habit of reverting to the first idea.

PARTICULAR SIGNS, *continued.* (See note to p. 38 of *The Signs.*)

Graphologic Sign.	Ordinary Significance.	Significance more specially relating to a state of personal —		Accompanying and Accessory Significance.
		Superiority.	*Inferiority.*	
inals (of letters or words)— short (fig. 7)	Discretion, reserve, reflection	Prudence	Distrust	Economy.
long (fig. 107*a*)	Imagination	Imagination	Mental agitation	Generosity, liberality.
with very little hooks (fig. 12)	Tenacity			Insignificance or mediocrity (if the handwriting be of calligraphic form).
with fairly pronounced curves returning to the left (especially in capital letters, and in the small letters *x* and *e*) (fig. 140)	Selfishness			Selfishness, a positive [person.
stretching out to the right hand formed by a horizontal stroke (fig. 93)	Altruism	Love of justice	Obstinacy	Imagination, softness, aesthetic sense.
which are angular (fig. 112)	Firmness	Firmness	Hardness	
which are rounded (fig. 6 and 113)	Obstinacy / Sweetness of disposition	Graciousness	Feeble will	
of a letter gliding under the word (fig. 6)	Self-complacence	Self-complacence	Pretension	Vanity.
of a letter covering the word formed by a returning curve which is higher than the letter it is part of (fig. 132)	Spirit of protection / Want of judgment	Self-complacence	Pretension	Vanity.
ascending straight, and nearly or quite vertically above the letters (fig. 140)	Mysticism	Religious sentiment	Love of the marvellous	
ars of the (small) t— regular in form and size (fig. 15)	Equable will	Stability		Calmness, moderation,

Bars of the (small) t—

Graphologic Sign.	Ordinary Significance.	Significance more specially relating to a state of personal—		Accompanying and Accessory Significance.
		Superiority.	*Inferiority.*	
irregular	Non-equable will	Versatility	Fickleness	
absent, and the final stroke curved (fig. 57)	Want of will	Want of will	Want of will	Negligence, want of spirit.
absent, and the final stroke angular (fig. 58)	Want of initiatory will-power, obstinacy			
long	Animation			
short	Energy			
slender	Want of vigour			
strong	Vigour			
long and slender (fig. 59)	Small will-power			Inability.
long and strong (fig. 60)	Ill-considered effort			
short and strong (fig. 61)	Great energy			
short and slender (fig. 62)	Feeble will	Feeble will	Indecision	Submission, a passive [nature.
placed above the *t* (fig. 63)	Authoritativeness	Authoritativeness	Despotism	Enterprise.
placed very low down (fig. 64)	Obedience	Humility	Obedience	
placed in front (at the right-hand side) (fig. 65)	Initiative faculty			
placed behind (at the left-hand side) (fig. 66)	Tardy resolution			Weakness, hesitation.
ascending from left to right (fig. 67)	Cavilling	Spirit of contradiction	Wrangling	Resolution.
descending from left to right (fig. 68)	Obstinacy			Causticity, wit, repartee, aggressiveness, irritability, vivacity,
short and ending in a point (fig. 69)	Critical mind	Critical mind	Cavilling	

PARTICULAR SIGNS, continued. (See note to p. 38 of *The Signs*.)

Graphologic Sign.	Ordinary Significance.	Significance more specially relating to a state of personal—		Accompanying and Accessory Significance.
		Superiority.	Inferiority.	
Bars of the (small) t—				
long and ending in a point from a thick start (fig. 70)	Maliciousness			Weakness, criticism.
ending in a club (fig. 71)	Resolution			
like the lash of a whip (fig. 72)	Unconstraint	Resolution	Violence	Imagination, vivacity.
in a curved shape (fig. 73)	Constraint			Sweetness, kindliness, weakness, irresolution.
in a serpentine line (fig. 74)	Gaiety	Liveliness	Joviality	Grace.
hooked on the bottom part of the *t* (fig. 75)	Tenacity			
with a hook at the start (fig. 76)	Tenacity in passive resistance			
with a hook at the end (fig. 77)	Tenacity in action			
A Stroke—				
between two sentences (fig. 108)	Order in ideas	Clearness	Distrust	Prudence.
at the end of a line of writing to fill up the space	Distrust			
horizontal, straight (apart from its position)	Reason	Justice, fairness	Firmness	A positive mind.
wavy (apart from its position)	Tact, gaiety			Grace.
Punctuation—				
neglected	Negligence			Absence of mind, forgetfulness, thoughtlessness.

PARTICULAR SIGNS, *continued.* (See note to p. 38 of *The Signs.*)

Graphologic Sign.	Ordinary Significance.	Significance more specially relating to a state of personal—		Accompanying and Accessory Significance.
		Superiority.	*Inferiority.*	
Dots—				
varying in emphasis	Animation			
placed very high	Religious spirit			
placed in advance of the letter	Spontaneity			Mysticism (?)
				Initiative faculty, vivacity.
placed behind the letter	Want of ardour			
very slight	Delicacy	Delicacy	Weakness	Timidity.
emphasized	Materiality			Firmness.
placed after the signature	Prudence	Prudence	Distrust	
placed frequently where not needed	Constraint in breathing, obesity			
placed where not needed, but light and scattered (fig. 126)	Constraint in breathing			Asthma, shortness of breath.
placed where not needed at the commencement of sentences	Hesitation			A fastidious choice of words.
Mis-use—				
of notes of exclamation, of interrogation, of suspension	Exaggeratio	Enthusiasm	Want of judgment	Imagination, exaltation, madness.
Frequent underlining	Exaggeration	Enthusiasm	Want of judgment	Imagination, exaltation, madness.
Margins—				
absent	Want of taste			
regular	Taste			Economy.
at both sides of the writing	Delicate taste			Artistic feeling.
Signature—				

PARTICULAR SIGNS, continued. (See note to p. 38 of The Signs.)

Graphologic Sign.	Ordinary Significance.	Significance more specially relating to a state of personal—		Accompanying and Accessory Significance.
		Superiority.	Inferiority.	
Signature—				
followed by a dot	Prudence	Prudence	Distrust	
followed by a line accompanied with dots	Distrust			
with a straight line underneath	Pride of name			
with a curved line underneath	Self-complacence			
Signature Flourish—				
with a stroke from right to left (fig. 77a)	Defensiveness			
with a stroke from left to right (fig. 78)	Aggressiveness			
like a lasso (fig. 79)	Defensiveness becoming aggressive			
like forked lightning (fig. 80)	Great activity			
cobwebbed (fig. 81)	Skill in affairs			
like the shell of a snail (fig. 82a)	Personal instincts	Skill in affairs	Finesse	Distrust. Selfishness, reserve.
like the jaws of a wolf (fig. 82)	Selfishness (?)			
fencing-in the signature (fig. 83)	A reasoning selfishness			
like a corkscrew (fig. 84)	Finesse			
in a wavy curve (fig. 85)	Gaiety			Dissimulation.
formed by intertwined lines complicated (fig. 86)	Intrigue / Distrust			

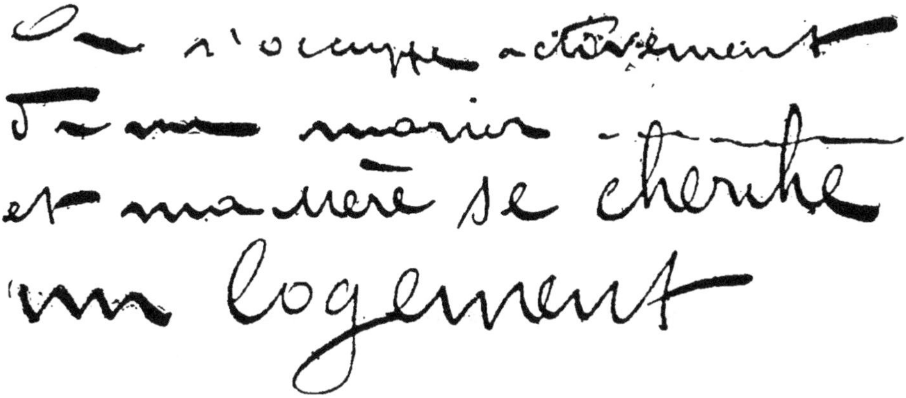

[handwritten specimen]

Fig. 31.—Words accentuated by an increase in size instead of by underlining : exaltation.

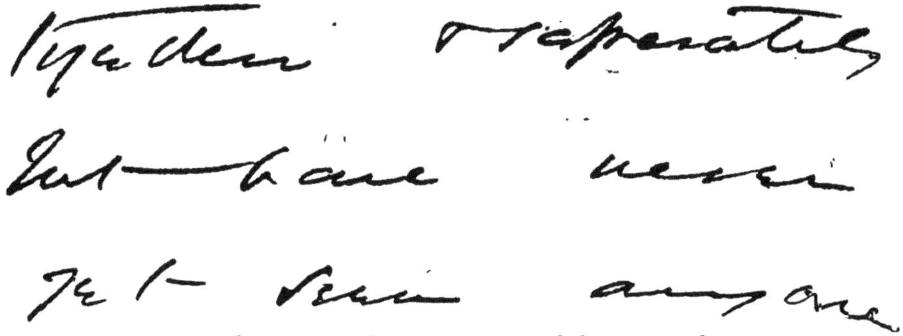

[handwritten specimens]

Fig. 32.—Words whose letters are widely formed : a person easy of access.

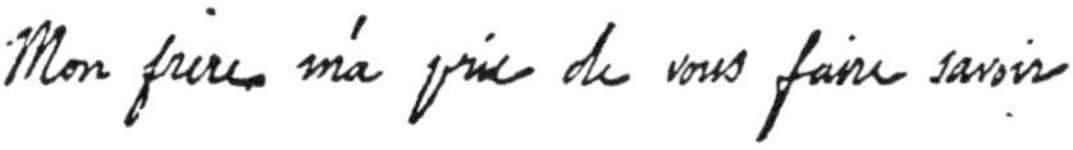

[handwritten specimen]

Fig. 33.—Words whose letters are crowded together : a disagreeable, ungracious nature.

[handwritten signature]

Fig. 34.—A letter commencing with a rounded and rapid penstroke : gaiety, good-humour.

NOTE.—The above illustrations relate to the Table of Graphologic Signs.

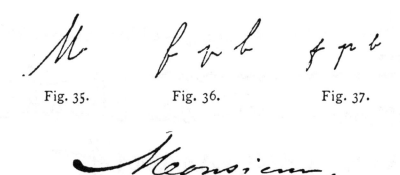

Fig. 35.   Fig. 36.   Fig. 37.

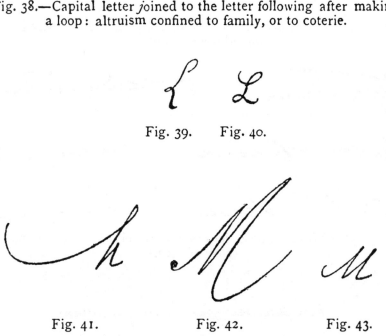

Fig. 38.—Capital letter *j*oined to the letter following after making
a loop: altruism confined to family, or to coterie.

Fig. 39.   Fig. 40.

Fig. 41.   Fig. 42.   Fig. 43.

Fig. 44.    Fig. 45.    Fig. 46.

NOTE.—The above illustrations relate to the Table of Graphologic
Signs.

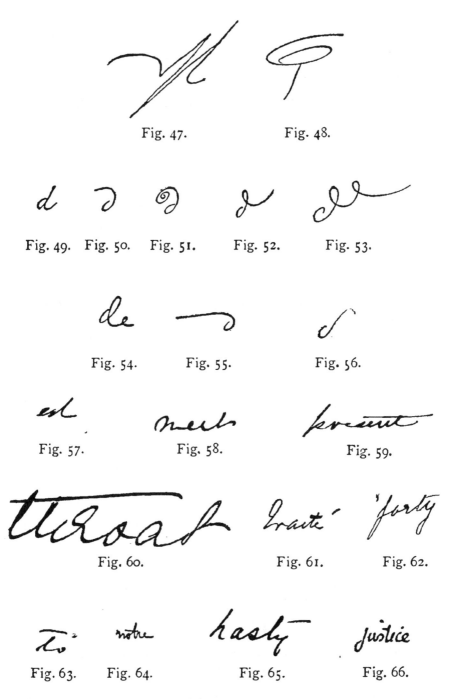

Fig. 47.   Fig. 48.

Fig. 49. Fig. 50. Fig. 51.   Fig. 52.   Fig. 53.

Fig. 54.   Fig. 55.   Fig. 56.

Fig. 57.   Fig. 58.   Fig. 59.

Fig. 60.   Fig. 61.   Fig. 62.

Fig. 63.   Fig. 64.   Fig. 65.   Fig. 66.

NOTE.—The above illustrations relate to the Table of Graphologic
Signs.

Fig. 67.   Fig. 68.   Fig. 69.   Fig. 70.

Fig. 71.   Fig. 72.   Fig. 73.

Fig. 74.   Fig. 75.   Fig. 76.   Fig. 77.

Fig. 77 (a).—The signature ending with a stroke from right to left hand: defensiveness.

Fig. 78.—The signature ending with a stroke from left to right: aggressiveness.

NOTE.—The above illustrations relate to the Table of Graphologic Signs.

PRINCIPLES OF GRAPHOLOGIC INTERPRE-TATION.

RESULTANT CHARACTERISTICS.

I.

WHEN we have extracted several personal traits from a specimen of handwriting, we can often draw deductions from them, by the aid of a special calculus, which may modify one or more of the traits obtained, or which may lead to a fresh characteristic.

Thus, if (say) the faculty of finesse be doubly shown in a specimen, a modification would ensue causing this quality to be emphasized.

Gladiated words . . *finesse* ⎫
Small handwriting . . *finesse* ⎬ *much finesse.*

A double indication of sensibility works similarly.

Inclined handwriting . . *sensibility* ⎫
Letters being separated . . *sensibility* ⎬ *great sensibility.*

Such cases as these increase the *intensity* of the original trait.

If, now, we discover finesse and also mental suppleness, we obtain *diplomacy*, which is a different trait from its two factors, neither of which disappear, but which, being co-existent, produce this new feature.

Gladiated words . . . . *finesse* ⎫
Serpentine handwriting . *mental suppleness* ⎬ *diplomacy.*

Notwithstanding the superiority of graphology over all other methods of practically studying character, its scope would be much limited if we could not, by the aid of psychology, elucidate and co-ordinate the immediate results of graphologic analysis. There are but few characteristic traits which may not be modified or combined by this calculus of resultants ; nearly all vary in significance according to the writer's degree of intelligence, and reflect each other after the manner of bright colours, some of which modify or absorb others, thereby giving new tints.

It is probable that a law of combinations of characteristics exists, but it is at present unknown. Perhaps graphology may be on the road to discovery in setting out such combinations as are most frequently met with. But meanwhile it must endeavour to establish its facts, which are sometimes very nice (delicate), and which are so numerous that in this matter of resultant signs there is no limit to graphology. M. Michon drew attention to this phase of the science, which as yet is less advanced than any other section.

This method of resultants throws light upon the singular contrasts to be met with in the same individual and upon his varying action under given conditions. Precise knowledge of the chief characteristics of a man allows of a certain amount of prediction as to his actions. Some such results can be readily obtained in connection with two individuals: for example, we may be fairly sure that an energetic and choleric man will not be on very good terms with a woman who is irritable and liable to fits of passion. We may fairly safely predict of two business partners, one of whom is simple and generous, and the other scheming and selfish, that the former will be duped. In many little strifes and contests between two men, when one tries to oppose the strength of mind and tenacity of the other by a more or less direct appeal to his feelings, an on-looker who knows the main characteristics of both men, can predict the final result, thereby achieving a true psychological *resultant.*

The study of resultants based upon graphologic analysis will be very interesting to those of our readers who may become graphologists in the true sense ; we shall, therefore, develop it to some extent.

We shall first consider, with the necessary detail, the most important of all resultants, namely, the condition as to superiority or inferiority of the writer of any specimen of handwriting. Hitherto but slight attention has been given to this by graphologists, and no clear idea of character has been expressed on this important question. M. Michon's journal, *La Graphologie*, contained graphologic portraits of all sorts of celebrities, but they are not classified by personal superiority or the reverse. The subjects are there stated to be refined, ardent, ambitious, etc., and if we except their signatures, and if we put on one side the traits in these graphologic portraits which refer to the acquired reputation of the subjects, there is very little real significance in what is left, composed, as it is, of a string of bare general faculties, instead of being a record of the special powers and weaknesses that all possess.

Practical psychology is not possible if we confound personal superiority and inferiority, because the same quality varies according to individual condition in this respect. We have, therefore, given much attention to the elucidation of this matter, and we believe that we have obtained pregnant results upon what is the basis of differentiation of character.

II.

CONCERNING INTELLIGENCE AND NON-INTELLIGENCE.

Degrees of General and Special Superiority and Inferiority. The Signs of Culture.

(*The Intellect.*)

LET us take a graphologic sign: for example, words whose last letters are higher than the first letters, which M. Michon tells us is the sign of sincerity and of naïveté.

Now, Lavater's words had this peculiarity, but his acute observation of physiognomical expression and his penetrative judgment do not admit of the latter of the two qualities being ascribed to him. But the purity of his life and his religious convictions allow us to say that he was *candid.* And this non-application of naïveté applies to Schliemann and some other eminent men, whose handwriting shows the sign stated, but whom it would be absurd to call naïve.

If we found this sign in the handwriting of uneducated men, we should say rather that the writers were *credulous ;* and if in the handwriting of a man of the middle class, with a fair amount of education, we might then apply the term naïve.

Thus we have formed three different opinions as to the significance of the same sign.

For another illustration we will consider handwriting the lines of which are undulating or serpentine, and which M. Michon interprets as the sign of *diplomacy*.

Compare the handwriting of Talleyrand with that of a common peasant. By means of ruled black lines placed underneath each specimen, we find the intensity of this sign to be (say) equal in both cases. Now, we could scarcely call this peasant a great diplomatist; his friends would not believe us if we did, but they might agree with us that he was stupid and *addicted to lying*.

Again, these serpentine lines with the man of middling station would not cause us to waste our time in convincing his family that he was a diplomatist, and they might, quite rightly perhaps, not consider him a liar. But they would probably think with us that he has a certain mental suppleness.

Such distinctions as the preceding apply to nearly all graphologic signs, and they show that a connection should be formed between the general value of a man and the special traits of his character. We see also that typical graphologic signs should represent faculties at a medium intensity. Therefore, in considering from the absolute (non-relative) standpoint, the fact of *words becoming larger towards the end*, we say it is a typical sign of naïveté, and that *serpentine lines* in handwriting form a typical sign of *mental suppleness*.

Candour and credulity, diplomacy and lying, are the derivatives from these signs.

1ST FACTOR.	2ND FACTOR.	PRODUCT.
Words becoming larger	Superiority	*Candour.*
idem	Mediocrity	*Naïveté.*
idem	Inferiority	*Credulity.*
Serpentine lines	Superiority	*Diplomacy.*
idem	Mediocrity	*Mental suppleness.*
idem	Inferiority	*Lying.*

We must bear in mind that graphologic signs have an absolute value only when regarded as *typical signs.* In a whole specimen their significance is relative, for, *to make a graphologic portrait is to establish a nearly un-intermitted resultant between the general value of the writer and the special traits of his character.*

But we ought not to confine ourselves merely to superiority or inferiority. There are evidently important grades in both these intellectual conditions, and we here define six of them, viz :—

Three conditions of superiority :

Genius, which is creative.
Talent, which realizes, criticizes, and appreciates.
Intelligence, which assimilates, and which appreciates, specially by comparison.

And three conditions of inferiority :

Mediocrity, the indication of a commonplace or little developed intelligence.
Absence of any special character, viz.: insignificance.
Intellect of a low order.

Superior Men.

I. Men of high superiority or of genius.

II. Men of talent.   Critics.

III. Intelligent and appreciative men.

Inferior Men.

I. Mediocrities.

II. Insignificant men.

III. Men of a low type.

We may now advantageously define, with some detail, each of these six distinctive grades.

Men of a low order of intellect are to be met with under various appearances, but they are easily recognized. As a rule—but not always—they fill the inferior places in the social scale ; they may be unskilled workmen, agricultural labourers, servants, etc., and one noticeable trait in them is that they can never give a proper reply to any question that may be asked of them. They have no mental precision, no differentiation, they experience considerable difficulty in any connected thought and their comprehension is slow. They work entirely by routine and resent hints as to better methods of working, and will view the same phenomena day after day without any fresh idea occurring to them. Those included in our lowest scale are also frequently characterized by violent actions and touchiness, or by sluggish apathy and a total absence of self-respect. There are but few men who show all the signs of this low order of mind. Usually some better qualities exist which modify their character and render them at least supportable to those who are better endowed. Thus it is that they are sometimes capable of attachment, of fidelity, even of devotion to an approved leader or patron. Nevertheless, we must remember that greediness, thievishness, lying and cruelty are special attributes of an inferior intellect. Anyone who has seen much of our French peasantry, especially of those living in poor villages far away from large towns, can testify as to the mixture of jealousy, malice, and selfishness, which is there to be found.

Insignificant men are people apparently filled with all sorts of fine qualities and whom no one thoroughly knows, because there is really nothing to know in them, and of whom people say that they never do harm to anybody, for the reason that such persons are incapable of doing either good or harm. Their silence passes for modesty, their calmness for sagacity, and their lack of initiative for timidity. They are the source of many of our disillusions, for appearances are in their favour, especially if they be fairly well educated, and the older they may be the less susceptible are they of any development.

Mediocrities, while they are not without intelligence, have too often an alloy of the common-place and vulgar, which places them under the head of inferior men. They have but little culture and are very susceptible to prejudice and routine, and they do not admit of much development; their taste lacks purity and refinement, their ideas are narrow and without originality, and they are wanting in mental vigour.

When such men have plenty of obstinacy they often endeavour to force their opinions upon others. There are a good many men of this kind in the French Chamber of Deputies, some of whose handwriting we possess, and which confirms their already too evident mediocrity. And given a supple mind and a little finesse, this class will sometimes engage in commerce and make large fortunes.

We define a man as *intelligent* when he can engage

in intellectual pursuits with a fair amount of ease, and this shows that he possesses the faculties of accurate appreciation and useful assimilation of facts. When these faculties have a wider scope and are more pronounced, we arrive at the condition which we have designated as *talent*.

The main difference between talent and intelligence consists in the greater facility with which men of talent can realize and express their own conceptions or those of others. Intelligent men reflect and judge, but they lack power. They judge by comparison and they fall back upon authorities. If they write, their works are rather compilations than new thoughts, and their fiction has a languid style ; if they paint, they copy the works of masters, and their landscapes contain the inevitable castle in ruins, a windmill, or a flock of sheep. But, nevertheless, such action in early life helps on their evolution towards talent.

For, little by little, as the mind of an intelligent man becomes stronger, he begins to think on his own account instead of merely following the thoughts of others. Yesterday he appreciated, to-day he criticizes, and soon he will find himself able to do something that has not been done before : he will realize his conceptions. And some day he will arrive at talent.

On the whole, an intelligent man appreciates rather than criticizes and produces, while a talented man criticizes with ability and produces with ease.

Genius is still more clearly differentiated from talent than is the latter from that which we have defined as intelligence. A man has genius when he stamps the individuality of his talent upon his work ; the origin-

H

ality of talent being the source of creation in arts and sciences alike.

Many people consider a genius a man who is illus‐trious. But circumstances, especially in such spheres of life as war and politics, may render men illustrious who are gifted with but very ordinary talent, and sometimes even quite mediocrities may thus be advanced by circum‐stances. Now, an illustrious man is not a man of genius unless in his rise he has shown original powers. For it is the *personality of talent* which makes a genius.

Men of genius are not perhaps quite so rare as may be popularly supposed. But the very originality of those who possess genius sometimes causes them to be considered mad, or at least to be deemed unsatisfac‐tory persons for advancement by those who dispense honours and places. And it must be admitted that when genius does err, it commits most singular errors.

And now, by what graphologic signs are we to deter‐mine in which of the preceding classes a man should be placed ?

The handwriting of men of superior intelligence will possess as distinctive signs, clearness (see p. 30), sim‐plicity of form, absence of ill-regulated movements of the pen. We say that such handwriting is *harmonious*.

RESULTANT OF HARMONIOUS HANDWRITING.

Simplicity of form   .   .   .   . *Simplicity* ⎫
Temperate[1] handwriting   . *Reflection, discretion* ⎬ *Intelligence.*
Clear handwriting (see p. 30)   . *A clear mind* ⎭

The handwriting of inferior men will be confused, more or less badly arranged, of vulgar form, with large and ill-controlled pen movement. And such handwriting we designate as *inharmonious*.

[1] See p. 56 for detailed description of temperate handwriting.

RESULTANT OF INHARMONIOUS HANDWRITING.

Vulgar form . . . . . *Vulgarity*		
Large and ill-controlled { *Thoughtlessness, or*		*Non-intelligence.*
pen-movement { *irrational enthusiasm*		
Confused handwriting . *A confused mind*		

Our definition of harmonious and inharmonious hand-writing being new, it is well to remark that we must not solely consider as harmonious handwriting that which complies with the three conditions just stated. There is a beauty of form in some handwritings which are quite different from any specific model, but which, however, may be very harmonious. M. Michon applied the words "harmonious handwriting" in another and more restricted sense than ourselves. He defined as harmonious, handwriting which expresses the æsthetic sense and artistic faculty.[2]

His works show that M. Michon did not attach much importance to his definition, for, as he was acquainted with several special signs relating to the æsthetic sense, he did not much concern himself with a general sign which seemed to him less easy to appreciate than his more detailed traits. In fact, a truly superior intelligence cannot express itself without a certain grace and without clearness. Painters, poets, and musicians cannot attain a sure degree of talent without a considerable personal development of taste for the beautiful. Authors of great ability cannot avoid clearness of expression ; simplicity is one of the signs of their genius, and the imagination which they must possess gives a natural grace to their intellect. Mathematicians, again, are necessarily addicted to a high degree of accuracy and

Journal *La Graphologie.* Article on *Harmonious Handwritings*, 15th May, 1876.

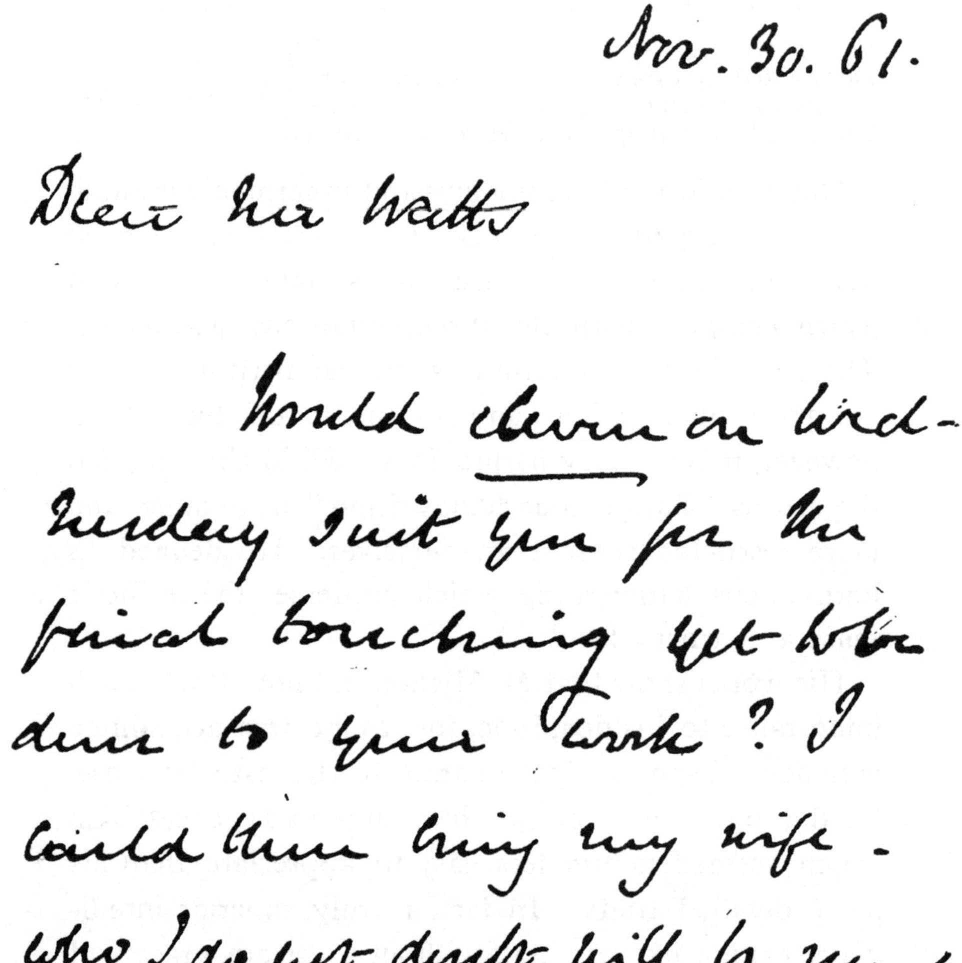

Nov. 30. 61.

Dear Mr Watts

Would eleven on Wed-
nesday suit you for the
final touching yet to be
done to your work? I
could then bring my wife.
who I do not doubt will be much
pleased. I remain

My faithfully yours

Fig. 87.—Temperate, firm, and clearly traced handwriting: harmonious to the first degree (see pp. 98 and 101).

NOTE.—We have seen handwriting of the writer of Fig. 87 of a more recent date than 1861. These later specimens do not entirely match the above definition of this illustration.

clearness of expression ; one who was obscure in his mode of expression would fail in the very essence of his work.

This distinction between harmonious and inharmonious handwriting is fundamental, and by aid of it we now set out the graphologic signs of superiority :—

Genius.—Harmonious handwriting of the first order, very clear, remarkable for its vigour and the simplicity

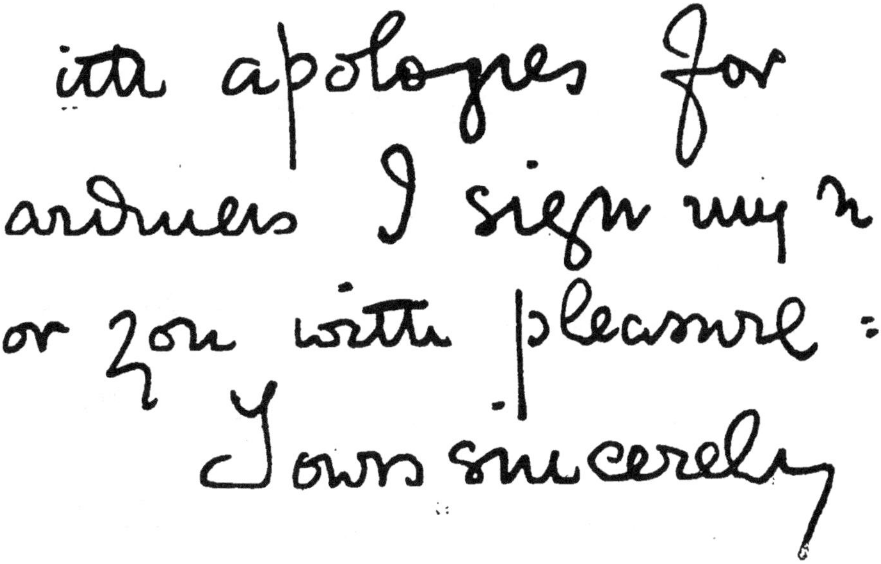

Fig. 87 (*a*).—Temperate, firm, and clearly traced handwriting: harmonious to the first degree (see p. 98).

of its form, and often original by this very fact, with a total absence of vulgar traits. (*Figs.* 87 and 87*a*.)

Talent.—Harmonious handwriting of the second order, with all the signs of the preceding but with less character and power in the whole. (*Figs.* 88 and 89.)

Intelligence.—Harmonious handwriting of the third order. A less degree of clearness and simplicity in its form than in the preceding. Indications of will power

less evident and less purely shown (*i.e.* in the vigour of
the outlines, and in the bars of the small *t*), especially

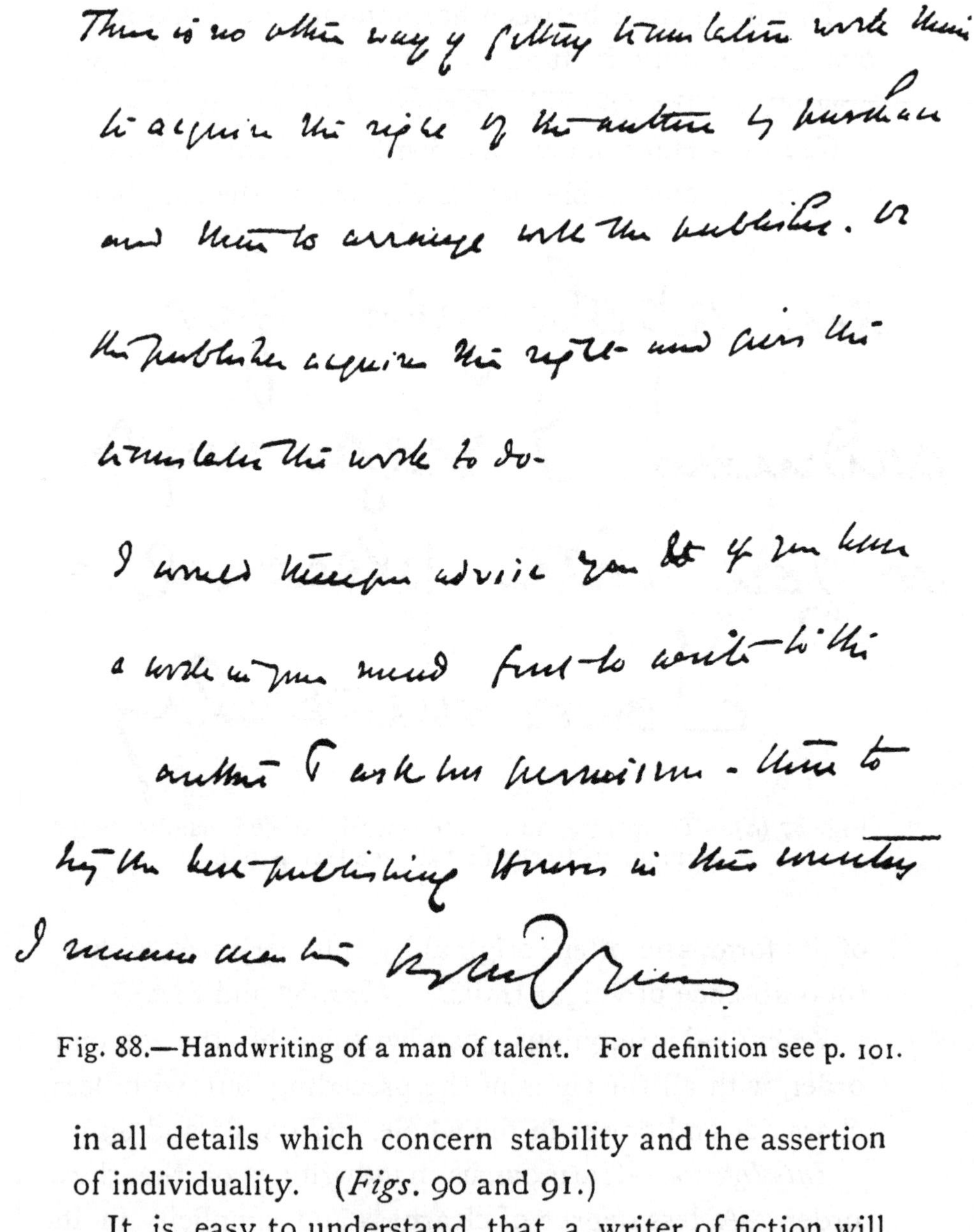

Fig. 88.—Handwriting of a man of talent.   For definition see p. 101.

in all details which concern stability and the assertion
of individuality. (*Figs.* 90 and 91.)

It is easy to understand that a writer of fiction will
have the sign of imagination more pronounced than will

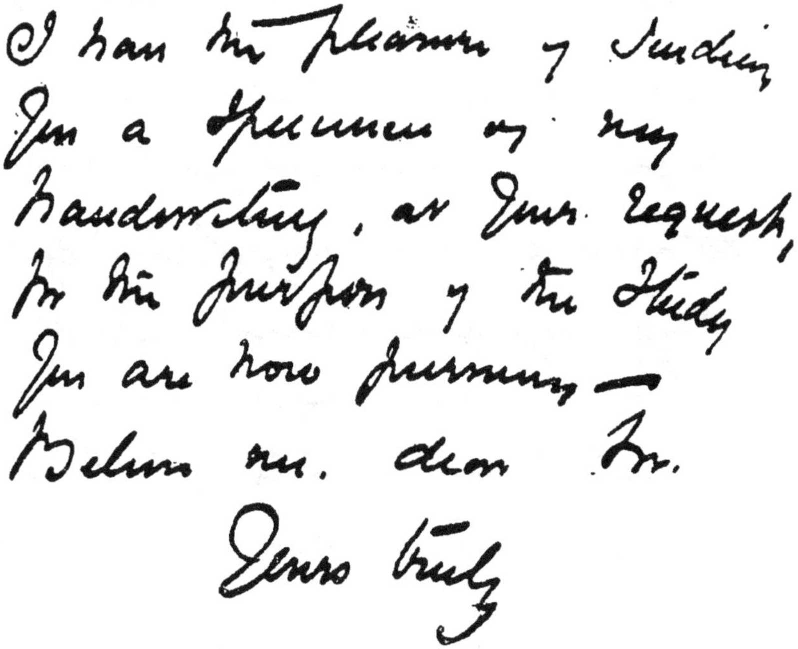

Fig. 89.—Handwriting of a man of talent.   For definition
see p 101.

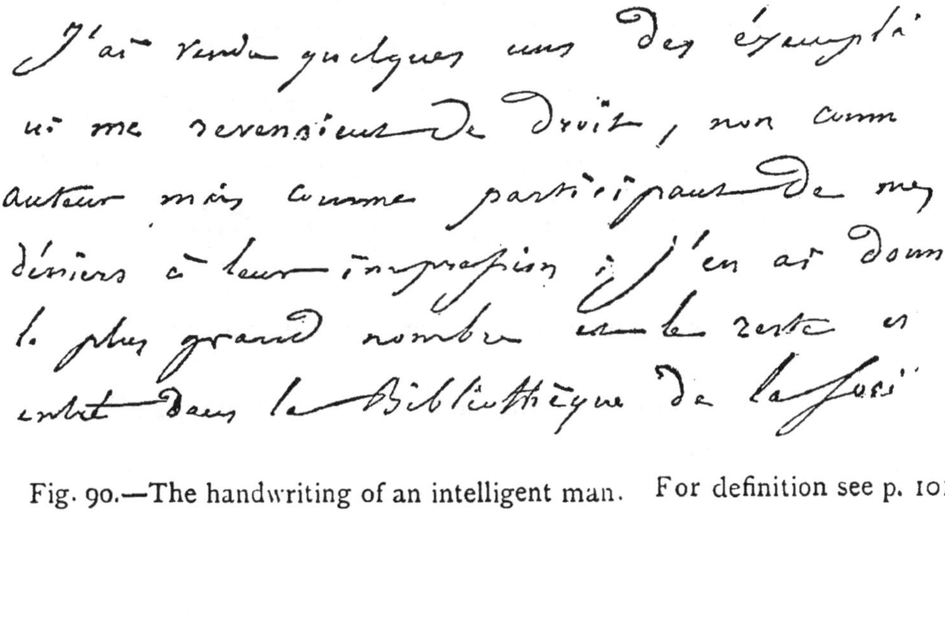

Fig. 90.—The handwriting of an intelligent man.   For definition see p. 101

a mathematician. But such differences are not always so obvious. Practically, however, the greater the degree to which handwriting is clear, simple, vigorous, and free

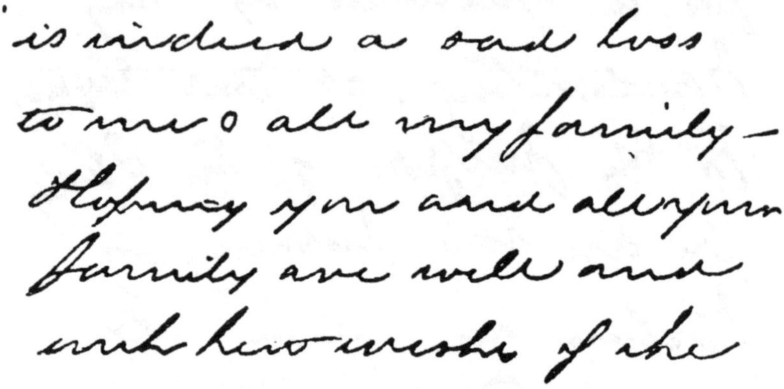
is indeed a sad loss
to me & all my family—
Hoping you and all your
family are well and
with kind wishes of the

Fig. 91.—Handwriting of an intelligent man. For definition see p. 101.

from large pen-movements, to the exclusion of other signs, the greater is the genius of the writer; the less exclusive these four characteristics are, the more special is his genius.

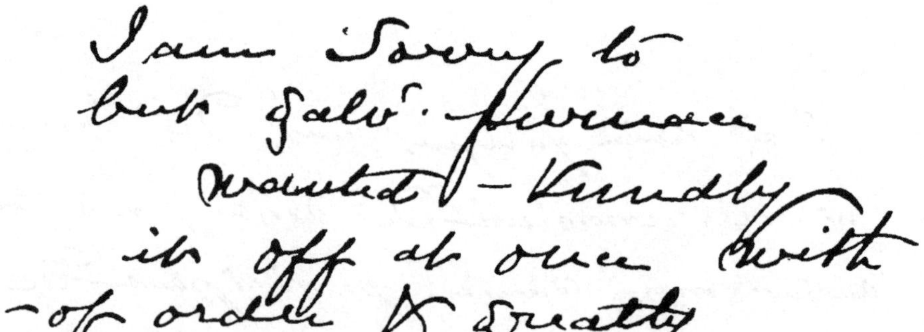
I am sorry to
but Galv. Furnace
wanted — Kindly
it off at once with
of order & greatly

Fig. 92.—Handwriting of a mediocrity. For definition see p. 104.

We now come to the signs of our three grades of inferiority:—

Mediocrity.—Clearness leaving much to be desired,

form lacking in simplicity or touching upon vulgarity, the frequent use of calligraphic handwriting; with such

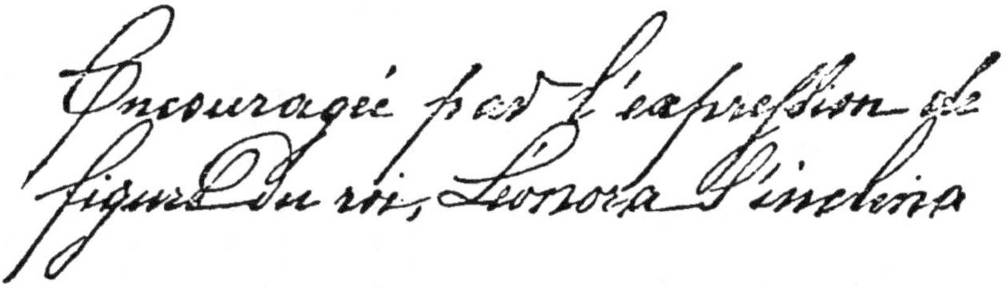

Fig. 93.—The handwriting of a female mediocrity. For definition see p. 104.

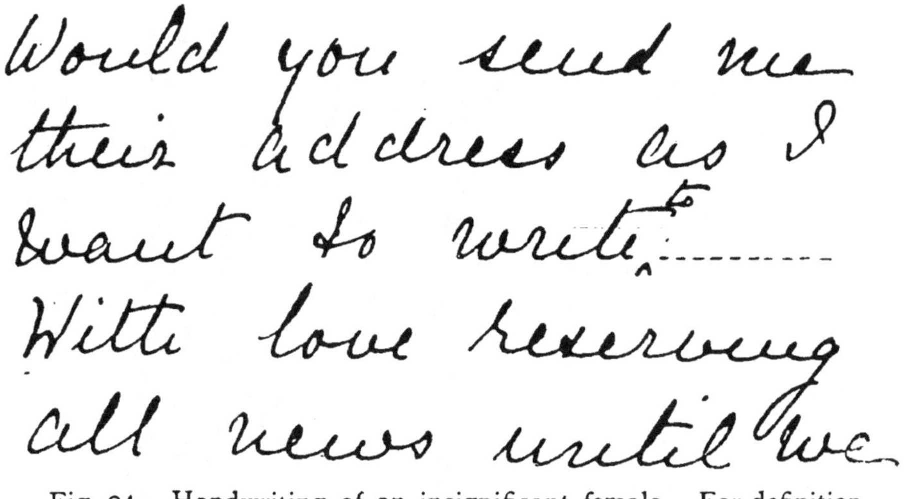

Fig. 94.—Handwriting of an insignificant female. For definition see p. 106.

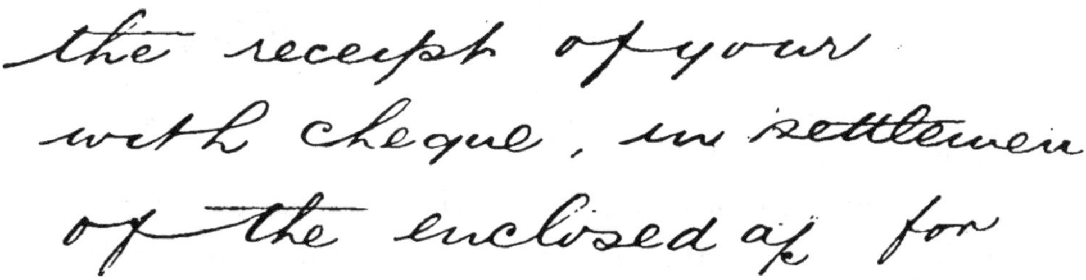

Fig. 95.—Handwriting of an insignificant male. For definition see p. 106.

men the faculties are but little developed, and it is in this class that we most often find the marks of pettiness, vanity, and pretension, but never do we find here a gracious originality of character. We give two different illustrations of this grade. (*Figs.* 92 and 93)

Insignificance.— Handwriting which at first sight presents some of the characteristics of superiority, notably clearness and simplicity, but it entirely lacks originality, vigour, and the signs of culture. (*Figs.* 94 and 95.)

Intellect of a low order.—Large movements of the pen, confusion or vulgarity in the form of the handwriting. (*Figs.* 96 and 97.)   This last kind is relatively rare, because people in our lowest grade do not always know how to write, or they write but seldom.

The determination of harmonious handwriting may often be facilitated by looking for some special signs

Fig. 96.—The confused and ill-managed handwriting of a distinctly inferior man. For definition see p. 106.

Fig. 97.—The laboured and disorderly handwriting of a distinctly inferior woman. For definition see p. 16.

which we may term *signs of culture*, and which we have recently discovered. Intelligence and intellectual culture are two very different things. A man who has not an exceptionally powerful intellect will never become a genius; but there is so great a difference between two young men both naturally well endowed, one of whom has developed his intellect by study, while the other has not, that we are led to admit that intellect is of small value without cultivation. A man's qualities are of real account only so far as they may be employed. For it is of little use for a man to possess an intellect of considerable potential activity, if, owing to his general ignorance, he is incapable of applying himself to such work as superior men engage in. Several of the signs of culture are concomitants of the signs of intelligence, which is readily understood, since even the fact of knowing how to write denotes some amount of cultivation. Thus cleanness or precision of tracing in handwriting shows the clearness of the writer's mental perception, and is a sign of intelligence. It also shows facility in the transmission of thought by the agency of handwriting ; in this case it is a sign of culture. But we may find one without the other. We have seen the handwriting of a man whose intelligence was by no means of the first order, but which, nevertheless, possessed most markedly this cleanness of finish ; but it was a specimen of his personal correspondence, which was considerable, and it seemed that in writing to his friends this man had acquired a quite original turn of mind. Again, the handwriting of some talented men is

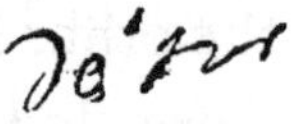

Fig. 98. 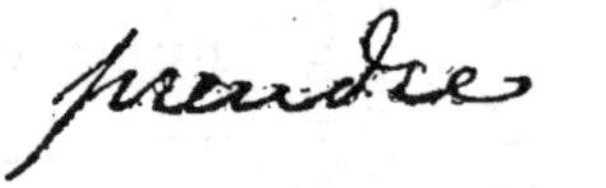   Fig. 99. 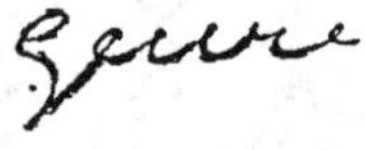   Fig. 100.

devoid of the signs of culture ; this may be met with where the writers have devoted themselves to a branch of study specialized to excess.

We do not pretend to have ascertained all the graphologic signs of culture ; we now give those which we believe to be reliable.

Cleanness and precision of finish in handwriting. (*Figs.* 7, 87, 87*a*, 88, and 89.)

The small *d*, whose upper part takes the form of a curve going from right to left. (*Figs.* 50 and 98.)

The small *d*, whose upper part is connected with the letter following. (*Figs.* 54 and 99.)

The small *g*, the *o* portion of which is curved like that in *fig.* 100.

The small *b, f, g, h, j, l, y, z,* whose looped up or down strokes are replaced by one simple stroke. (*Fig.* 101.)

All small or capital letters of typographic form (this is also a sign of the æsthetic sense). (*Figs.* 98, 102, 110, and 111.)

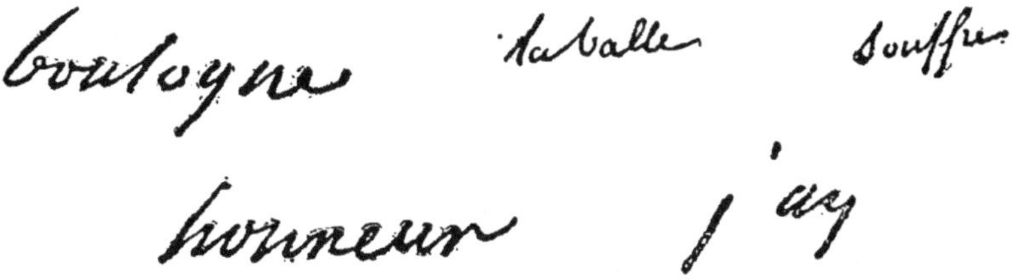

Fig. 101.

The small *a,* formed like the Greek alpha.

The small *p,* whose second part is open at the top. (*Fig.* 103.)

And, in fact, all abbreviations or modifications of the normal forms of letters or words which indicate to us some special knowledge, may be considered as signs of

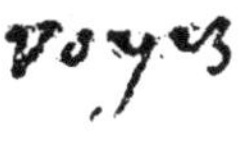

Fig. 102.    Fig. 103.

mental culture. (The small *e* formed thus ε, like the Greek, for example.)

Distinctions concerning harmonious handwritings will appear at first to be rather fine, but a moderate amount of practice will remove any difficulties in appreciating them. It is certainly necessary to acquire a special kind of mental *touch* for this work, and the student must not be surprised if he goes wrong at first for want of it. When we see how uncertain the tyro is in his application of even the most definite signs, it is not surprising that accurate discernment of a general state of personality resulting from several signs, is not attained without some trouble. This procedure is complex, but not of necessity complicated ; it is a sort of synthetic survey, thanks to which, considerable aid is obtained in accurate and detailed interpretation of graphologic signs. The most difficult part of the study is not in seeing if the handwriting be clear or not, or regular or confused, but in determining what should result from such ascertained facts. For example, it is not very difficult to find that a specimen belongs (say) to a mediocrity, but it then becomes necessary to gauge the condition of mental quality and will-power appertaining to this state of being, when we are giving meanings to such graphologic signs as we may have discovered in the handwriting.

In the summary which follows on p. 113, we have indicated the signs of moral faculties and will-power, as well as those of the intellect. This complement is necessary, for a survey which referred character to intellect alone would fall short of the truth. The distinctions of superiority and inferiority apply equally to morality and volition as to intellect. *Simplicity, moderation*, and *distinction*, for example, are qualities of general superiority of character. Manifestations of intellect, morality, and will-power are all the better for simplicity in expression. Moderation in judgment is a high quality, and is of great use to our moral side in excluding the passions, while a will of moderate power is perhaps the most constant and certain in its action.

And a natural or acquired distinction of character throws up and dignifies such qualities, activity tending to their development.

The predominance of special signs belonging to each of these three divisions of character indicates the existence of intellect, morality, or will. For instance, the signs of reflection, of clearness, and of mental pliability as regards *intellect*, of altruism and rectitude for *morality*, of energy and constancy for the *will*, are traits whose influence is decisive upon character. And it is expedient, moreover, to discriminate between handwriting which is harmonious, from the standpoint of intellect, or morality, or will ; the signs of general superiority apply to each of these orders of handwriting.

The qualities which we have just referred to are very susceptible of combination, especially altruism and activity, and they have great influence upon character ; but in all doubtful cases a graphologist will not run much risk of deceiving himself, in attributing to people ranked as inferior from the intellectual side, the less favourable shade of any trait which may be in doubt. As regards the justification for this procedure, we appeal to those who have experienced something of life's troubles, who will, we think, agree with us that those of our friends by whom we have been the most disillusioned, have usually been the least intelligent.

Men of common or vulgar minds are the most lacking in resources, and we should avoid them as much as possible. Their *absorbent* power is of the first degree. There are many such men to be met with who pass very well in society, whose actions are dishonest or cruel, and who sometimes cause irreparable misfortunes.

owing to their obstinacy or want of judgment. We cannot say too often that this is a condition of intellectual inferiority.

A sound understanding, on the contrary, gives fertility to a man's faculties, and in some degree makes up for those that are wanting. Without some amount of intelligence there can be no substantial virtue, but with it defects of character become less, or they are checked from developing into action. Often they almost disappear, and remain only as tendencies against which the man of sound mind is quite on his guard. Even want of will-power itself may be remedied by such men. An idea occurs to them, reflection points out the way for action, and reason forces them along in spite of a defective will-power. And thus results a special form of stability, which takes the place of native force of will. We have laid stress on the influence of intelligence upon moral action, but we do not deny that men of superior intellect may have a deplorable moral nature. But such men directing their powers morally, would obtain results far superior to those of a hundred insignificant men animated by the most praiseworthy intentions.

The use of our method of graphologic interpretation of character, ought to render flattery out of the question, putting as it does each person in his place in the intellectual scale. This is an advantage, for, by a more general use of the art, we may lose the habit of paying compliments to public men who do not deserve them, compliments which are sometimes expressed so effusively that there are not sufficient words left in the dictionary for use towards those who do deserve such expressions of admiration from others.

SUMMARY.

[The left-hand column denotes signs of superiority ; *the right-hand, signs of* inferiority.]*

Psychological Signs.

GENERAL SIGNS

(Applying equally to the intellect, the morals, and the will-power).

1. Simplicity.	14. Absence of simplicity.
2. Moderation.	15. Passion.
3. Distinction.	16. Vulgarity.
4. Activity.	17. Inactivity.

SPECIAL SIGNS.

Intellect.

5. Imagination (controlled).	18. Imagination (ill-controlled, or nil).
6. Reflection.	19. Want of reflection.
7. Clearness of mind.	20. Mental confusion.
8. Mental pliability.	21. Obstinacy.

Morals.

9. Rectitude.	22. Want of rectitude.
10. Altruism.	23. Selfishness.
11. Sensibility.	24. Coldness.

Will-power.

12. Constancy.	25. Instability.
13. Energy.	26. Weakness.

NOTE.—*For the explanation of the numbers* 1 *to* 26 *see below.*

Graphological Signs.

1. Simple, natural, spontaneous handwriting.
2. Temperate handwriting (see p. 56), absence of large movements of the pen, handwriting moderately inclined.
3. Absence of vulgar traits, art.

4. Rapid handwriting, ascending handwriting, simplified handwriting, the bars of the small *t* placed
in front of it.

5. Large pen-movement which is harmonious and easily
traced.   Handwriting which grows larger, either
as a whole or in parts.

6. Temperate handwriting (see p. 56), absence of large
movements of the pen, the signs of order, of
calm, of care and attention.   Well-arranged
punctuation.

7. Very legible handwriting, words and lines spaced
out.

8. Handwriting more or less unequal in its formation
and in its direction upon the paper.   Curved
handwriting.

9. Letters and words of equal height, the lines of
writing straight, non-serpentine, regular handwriting, handwriting which is cleanly finished,
simple, natural and very legible.

10. Capital letters joined to the letter following, finals
running from left to right-hand, the small *n*
and *m* made like the small *u*, inclined handwriting, curved (non-angular) handwriting, the
small (final) *e* made thus ⌒— (see *fig.* 29,
"the.")

11. Sloping handwriting (to the right-hand), handwriting which varies, especially if variation occur
in the same document, handwriting which shows
much movement, letters composing a word
varying in their slope, words made up of
separate letters or of separate little groups of
letters.

12. Uniform and regular handwriting, the bars of the small *t* uniform and regular in shape and position. Firm and active handwriting.

13. Firm handwriting, or that which is slightly angular, not too slender, the bars of the small *t* and any under-lines well marked, the direction of the lines of writing being non-hesitating.

14. Needless ornamentation, complicated letters, affected, non-simple, and eccentric forms, the various signs of pride, pretension, etc.

15. Large movements of the pen, very inclined hand-writing, and the various signs of irrational enthusiasm and of excessive activity.

16. Coarse and vulgar strokes, absence of art, ridiculous and pretentious ornamentation.

17. Too pronounced curves, rounded handwriting, the bars of the small *t* absent, slow handwriting, descending handwriting.

18. Large pen-movement causing confusion. Inhar·monious and considerable enlargement of the handwriting as a whole, or merely the exaggeration of certain letters or parts of letters. While small handwriting, and handwriting lacking movement or grace, are indications of imagination being *nil*.

19. Very agitated handwriting, large pen-movements, inequalities in the absence of the signs of intellectual superiority.

20. Words and lines of the handwriting which are intermingled; confused handwriting, and that which is badly placed upon the paper.

21. Angular handwriting, and regularity carried to

rigidness. The base of the small *t* forming an acute angle.

22. Serpentine or undulating lines of handwriting, handwriting which is irregular or sloping backward, or badly formed and confused, filiformed words, affectation, want of cleanness and simplicity in the pen strokes.

23. Capital letters and finals of words returning towards the letter, signature-flourishes like figs. 82a, and 83, handwriting crowded together, and very angular handwriting.

24. Vertical, uniform, regular handwriting with but little movement.

25. Handwriting which is irregular and non-uniform in shape. The bars of the small *t* irregular and non-uniform in shape and position, and sometimes absent. Rounded handwriting.

26. Slender handwriting. The bars of the small *t* slender or absent. Serpentine handwriting, the curves too pronounced, a lack of firmness in the pen-strokes.

III.

TYPICAL RESULTANT SIGNS.

Sensibility.—Phenomena arising from this condition of sensitiveness to impressions, sensations, or feelings, are very numerous and varied, but the only sign of general sensibility at present known graphologically is the inclined action which produces sloping handwriting, and perhaps there are no other graphologic signs of sensibility.[1] We may state that each different manifestation of different kinds of sensibility corresponds to different resultants. In the study of resultants, those signs which are directly connected with sensibility are called *modifiers;* those which re-act against this faculty are termed its *moderators;* and those which tend to increase its intensity are called *multipliers.* For example, intuition (letters separated and placed side by side) is an accompaniment of sensibility (inclined handwriting), because the fact of perception without demonstration shows a quick conception, which implies a condition ready to receive impressions. When these two traits meet, they combine, owing especially to their similarity, to form a resultant of intensity, at the same time that a modifying action is also effected, for intuition contains an element of intelligence.

The chief moderators of sensibility are the signs of reason, of reflection, and of calmness. There are some which have but small effect; indecision amongst others will hardly moderate the activity of sensibility, although it may sometimes cause irregularity in its action.

These different kinds of resultants apply to all elements of character, and we will now illustrate some of them.

Moral, combined with intellectual sensibility, gives us two parts of sensibility to one of intellect. And in all characters, without exception, these two kinds of sensibility give a resultant of intensity. But the general resultant varies according to character when we consider the factor of intellect only.

Given a vivid moral and intellectual sensibility. With a very well endowed man we then have a very quick

Since these lines were written, we have discovered that handwriting showing inequalities, of whatever nature, is an important sign of sensibility.

moral and intellectual sensibility.   In a superior nature
these two traits support each other and unite to produce
the personality of talent which causes genius.

Very harmonious handwriting .	. *Superior mind*	*Very quick*
Letters separated, but side by side	*Intellectual per-*	*moral and*
	ception	*intellectual*
Inclined handwriting .	. *Moral sensibility*	*sensibility.*

With a man of mediocrity the two kinds of sensibility also combine to produce vivid sensibility.   But
mediocre instead of superior faculties now being its
accompaniments, a mental effect is produced analogous
to the effect of an electric light flashing into the eyes of
a man who is emerging from darkness.   This vivid
sensibility will now cause serious errors of judgment, it
will lead to passionate rather than to moderate actions,
and should circumstances over-excite it, it may become
the cause of many errors and serious evils in a man's life.

Handwriting middlingly harmoni-	*A mediocre in-*	*Very quick*
ous	*tellect .*	*sensibility,*
Letters separated, but side by side	*Intellectual per-*	*passion,*
	ception .	*want of*
Inclined handwriting . .	*Moral sensibility*	*judgment.*

These faculties are not found together in people who
are insignificant, or of a very low order of mind.
Sensibility they may possess, but not intellectual perception, for the reason that a man of quick intellectual
sensibility, is not insignificant, nor can he be classed
among those whose intellect is almost nil.

Passion, as we have seen, is the undue exaggeration
of feeling of some kind, and it is the more vivid as those
faculties which act as moderators are weak.   Passion
may be obtained as a resultant from numerous combi-

nations of various graphologic signs.   Those most often
found in handwriting, are the following :—

Inclined handwriting .	*Sensibility* .	} *Passion.*
Large pen-movements .	*Vivid imagination*	
Inclined handwriting . .	*Sensibility* .	} *Passion.*
Inharmonious handwriting .	*A common mind*	
Inclined handwriting . . .	*Sensibility*	} *Passion.*
Ascending handwriting, or long		
bars to the small *t* . . .	*Animation*	

It is important to know the working of these resultants.   Sensibility increased by imagination results in
passion.   In fact, a sensitive man has a natural tendency towards enthusiasm, towards fixed conclusions,
towards all that may be the consequence of his great
receptivity of impressions ; if such a disposition chances
to possess imagination also, passionate speech or action
of some kind is an almost necessary result.

A low type of nature, lacking that ability for
judicious self-control which is so essential for keeping
sensibility in check, has nothing to prevent the development of passionate action.

Sensibility coupled with hastiness of thought or
action, is affected thereby in much the same way as by
imagination.   This hastiness modifies a keen sensibility
so much, that the latter degenerates into passion.

Want of judgment accompanies passion in all cases
when the two factors of the resultant are in a state of
activity.   A man is not always thus sensitive and imaginative ; some particular excitation is needed to put
these two elements in play.   *Thus a mediocrity who
possesses sensibility and imagination, is not always
faulty in his judgment,* but whenever these two traits of
his character are excited at the same time, as for ex-

ample in organizing a work of charity, in political fight-
ing, in love affairs, or in gambling, passion will lead him
to extremes, and want of judgment to impracticable
suggestions for proper action.

Passion may also be obtained as a resultant from a
combination of signs in which sensibility or imagination
could not produce it unaided.   For instance, a sensitive
egotist is jealous (Michon, *Méthode*) because he desires
the whole of an affection to be centred upon himself,
and his jealousy being worked upon by any trivial fact
which excites his imagination, creates a passionate state
of mind.

Inclined handwriting   .   .   .   *Sensibility*⎫
Any of the signs of selfishness   ⎬*Jealousy.*
   (See p. 116, No. 23)   .   .   *Selfishness*⎭

Jealousy [1]   ⎫
Imagination [2] ⎬ *Passion.*

But moderated sensibility is a source of some very
fine qualities.   Coupled with intelligence, it produces
kindness; and kindness emphasized by being doubly
shown in handwriting becomes tenderness, while devotedness and generosity are the outcome of sensibility
and intelligence, with benevolence and a broad mind
assisting them.

Intelligence   .   .   .   .   ⎫
Sensibility   .   .   .   .   ⎬ *Kindness.*

Intelligence   .   .   .   .   ⎫
Sensibility   .   .   .   .   ⎬ *Tenderness.*
Kindness   .   .   .   .   ⎭

Intelligence   .   .   .   .   ⎫
Sensibility   .   .   .   .   ⎬ *Devotedness.*
Benevolence   .   .   .   .   ⎭

[1] and [2] We do not propose to repeat any further for each resultant, the sign in handwriting which corresponds to this or that
trait of character.   For those who study resultants may be sup-
posed to know the graphologic alphabet.

Intelligence . . . . ⎱ *Generosity of*
Sensibility . . . . ⎰ *thought and act.*
A broad mind . . .. .

Opposite resultants may be obtained thus :—

Mediocrity . . . . ⎱ *Great coldness.*
A cold nature . . . . ⎰

Mediocrity . . . . ⎱
Little sensibility . : . ⎬ *Selfishness.*
Little benevolence . . . ⎰

Mediocrity . . . . ⎱ *Moral pettishness.*
Little sensibility . . . ⎰

Mediocrity . . . . ⎱
Selfishness . . . . ⎬ *Envy.*
Sensibility . . . . ⎰
Little benevolence . . .

Now coldness of nature is akin to hardness, personal
feeling to selfishness, moral pettiness to stupidity.
These failings result from coldness, slight sensibility,
and a narrow mind, being allied to a condition of non-
intelligence.   Thus :—

Non-intelligence . . . ⎱ *Hardness.*
A cold nature . . . . ⎰

Non-intelligence . . . ⎱ *Selfishness.*
Little sensibility . . . ⎰

Non intelligence . . . ⎱
Little sensibility . . . ⎬ *Stupidity.*
A narrow mind . . . ⎰

Hardness of heart and pride produce disdain.[1]   When
a man has no sensibility, and wishes to ascend high in
the social scale, it is natural to him to scorn those he
thinks beneath him.

Pride . . . . . ⎱ *Disdain.*
Hard-heartedness . . . ⎰

Sensibility, pride and kindliness give on the contrary
the spirit of protection.[2]

[1] and [2] These resultants are communicated by Dr. Paul Helot.

$$\left.\begin{array}{l} \textit{Pride} \\ \textit{Sensibility} \\ \textit{Kindliness} \end{array}\right\} \textit{Spirit of pro-}\atop\textit{tection.}$$

Preponderance of feeling over reason produces a condition of weakness which influences the development of irritability. This defect of character is also shown by a particular graphologic sign, viz.: very inclined handwriting.

Irritability and *touchiness* are specially to be found in a condition of personal inferiority. The lower classes as a rule are very *touchy*, while superior men restrain their irritation and often convert it into dignity.

$$\left.\begin{array}{l} \textit{Superiority} \\ \textit{Quick sensibility} \end{array}\right\}\begin{array}{l}\text{in the face}\\\text{of a taunt,}\\\text{produce}\end{array}\left.\right\} \textit{Moderation, dignity.}$$

$$\left.\begin{array}{l} \textit{Inferiority} \\ \textit{Quick sensibility} \end{array}\right\}\begin{array}{l}\text{in the face}\\\text{of a taunt,}\\\text{produce}\end{array}\left.\right\} \textit{Anger, irritability.}$$

Irritability allied to treachery produces malice.

$$\left.\begin{array}{l} \textit{Irritability} \\ \textit{Self-concentration or treachery} \end{array}\right\} \textit{Malice.}$$

Irritability and touchiness may be obtained as resultants from moderate, instead of from quick sensibility, by a combination with the latter of the signs of pride, vanity, pretension, etc.

$$\left.\begin{array}{l} \textit{Sensibility} \\ \textit{Pride} \end{array}\right\} \textit{Irritability.}$$

$$\left.\begin{array}{l} \textit{Sensibility} \\ \textit{Vanity} \end{array}\right\} \textit{Irritability.}$$

$$\left.\begin{array}{l} \textit{Sensibility} \\ \textit{Self-complacence} \end{array}\right\} \textit{Irritability.}$$

$$\left.\begin{array}{l} \textit{Sensibility} \\ \textit{Pretension} \end{array}\right\} \textit{Irritability.}$$

Sensibility	*Irritabilit͵,*
Ambition	*desire of ap-*
	probation.

More vivid sensibility and ambition produce an un-healthy condition of mental irritation and susceptibility. We once met with the case of a lady who called her-self the most unhappy of women. She wished to die, but she was not a melancholist, as might be thought, but a very susceptible woman with a great need of ad-miration and tenderness. Her handwriting was very inclined, with lines which were very ascendant across the page.

Very inclined handwriting .	*Vivid sensibility*	*An unhealthy*
		susceptibility
Very ascending handwriting .	*Great ambition*	*to impressions.*

Imagination and feeling both equally weak, and combined with vanity, also give susceptibility.

Weak imagination . . .	*Susceptibility to*
Little sensibility . . .	*impressions.*
Vanity . . .	

Imagination animated by vanity excites moral sen-sitiveness. But a man under these conditions will evince moral sensitiveness only when the object of his vanity is despised. We have no hesitation in repeating that the product or *resultant* of two traits of character can only be obtained when such are in absolute co-operation, that this or that resultant is manifested only when the special kind of excitation is produced that is essential for the existence of any specific resultant sign of character.

Imagination.—The preceding observations concern-ing sensibility have shown us that imagination is an

important factor in the play of feeling ; the latter is
nearly always increased by imagination, as in the various
illustrations of passion, and it is sometimes modified, as
was shown in the *resultant*, jealousy.

Inspiration is a resultant of sensibility and imagination, but only when these latter are found in the
handwriting of superior men, for inspiration is incompatible with a state of inferiority.

Imagination . . . . . ⎞
Sensibility . . . . . . ⎬ *Inspiration.*
Harmonious handwriting . . . ⎠

It is important to state that sensibility allied to imagination gives grace to the intellect. But the more
dense the intelligence, the less is this effect produced ;
in fact these two qualities in the handwriting of a quite
inferior man, would indicate not grace but rather
errors of judgment, and sensibility itself would then be a
weakness.

Imagination . . . . ⎞
Sensibility . . . . . ⎬ *A graceful mind.*
Intelligence . . . . ⎠

Imagination . . . . ⎞
Sensibility . . . . . ⎬ *False judgment.*
Non-intelligence . . . ⎠

Imagination and sensibility strongly dispose a man
towards objective admiration, and given a motive-
power, admiration is produced. The nature of this
motive-power may be beautiful or ugly, vulgar or dis-
tinguished, commonplace or delicate, moral or immoral.
For as vice is not always punished, nor virtue rewarded,
so we cannot say that it is only the beautiful and the
true which generally excite admiration. There is hardly
a murderer without some admirers, and if he be

specially notorious, some will even envy him : some men will gainsay beauty or truth and may never dream about either, they are content to follow the tastes and customs of their neighbours. Voltaire once said that for the toad, beauty consists in the she-toad. Thus it is not surprising that admiration should often be aroused by things or circumstances which may be repugnant to many people.

Imagination and sensibility . . .	*Admiration* for beautiful things.
The æsthetic sense	
Imagination and sensibility . . .	*Admiration* for truth.
Integrity or sincerity	
Imagination and sensibility . . .	*Admiration* for vulgar or ugly things.
No æsthetic sense	
Imagination and sensibility . . .	*Admiration* for things dainty and delicate.
A delicate mind	
Imagination and sensibility . . .	*Admiration* for the marvellous.
Mysticism	
Imagination and sensibility . . .	*Admiration* for craft and falseness.
A mediocre or common mind . . .	
Finesse and untruth	
Imagination and sensibility . . .	*Admiration* for things pure.
Modesty	
Imagination and sensibility . . .	*Admiration* for things impure.
Sensuality or gluttony	
A vulgar mind	

Admiration becomes enthusiastic when allied with animation or ardour.

Imagination	*Enthusiasm.*
Animation	
Imagination and sensibility . .	*Enthusiastic admiration.*
Animation or ardour . . .	

We now proceed to give some other resultants in which imagination, allied to various traits, plays the chief part, which always has the effect of *increasing the intensity of a faculty, until becoming excessive it is converted into some other characteristic.*

Thoughtlessness and imagination combine to produce frivolity. The former is a mental state which imagination is always exciting, and repetition of thoughtless words and acts produces a condition of frivolity.

Words being omitted from
 the handwriting .   .   *Thoughtlessness* } *Frivolity.*
               Imagination

Exaggerated by imagination, subtleness becomes roguery ; hesitation changes to perplexity ; prudence to distrust, etc.

Gladiolated words (*fig.* 30), and
 serpentine lines .   .   .   *Subtleness* } *Roguery.*
Large movements of the pen .   *Imagination*

Letters being shaky .   .   *Hesitation* } *Perplexity.*
               Imagination

Temperate handwriting, moderate
 animation, etc.   .   .   .   .   *Prudence* } *Distrust.*
               Imagination

The small *t* weakly barred   .   *Feeble will* } *Indecision.*
               Imagination

Calm and slender handwriting .   *Timidity* } *Cowardice.*
               Imagination

Ascending handwriting   .   .   *Ambition* } *An enterprising*
               Imagination *mind.*

Very ascending handwriting   .   *Vivid ambition* } *A strong desire*
               Imagination *for power and dignities*

Final strokes of letters glid-
 ing under the words .   .   *Self-complacence* } *Self-conceit.*
               Imagination

Words being omitted   .   .   *Thoughtlessness* } *Temerity,*
Ascending handwriting .   .   *Ardour*   .   *rash enter-*
               Imagination . *prises.*

Inharmonious handwriting and
 serpentine lines   .   .   .   *Untruth* .
Final strokes of capital and small } *Swindling.*
 letters curved inwards .   .   *Selfishness*
               Imagination

Curved handwriting . . .	*Indolence* } *Imagination* }	*Contemplation idleness, reverie.*
Spaced-out handwriting . .	*Liberality Imagination* }	*Extravagance.*
Variable handwriting . . .	*Mobility . Imagination* }	*Caprice.*
Words becoming larger towards the end	*Naïveté . Imagination* }	*Superstition.*

Will.—Psychological phenomena are so closely connected among themselves, and their accompanying traits are so numerous, that if ever the laws governing the composition of character should be definitely settled, it would suffice to know only the principal traits of a man's mind in order to build up the whole therefrom.

Right through character we see intellect, feeling and will associating or combining for development or for change among themselves.

We here ask ourselves whether will is really something outside the intellect. What is activity but a faculty of the mind? What is firmness but a form of mental attention to an object? And of what avail is energy itself, which is a force and not the will, when it is not used as a servant by the intellect?

We have already indicated by our heading on p. 113 "*General signs*" of "*Superiority*" and of "*Inferiority*," that we believe in the oneness of character, and if we preserve something of the traditional classification, it is only as a transitory heading, for we are persuaded that the various sides of human nature are so intermingled, that they must be considered relatively to the character and not in any absolute manner.

As a rule, initiative will power stimulates intellect, and resistive will power moderates feeling.

Intelligence *Vivacity*	} *Quick-wittedness.*
Intelligence *Activity*	} *An active mind.*
Firmness *Sensibility*	} *Moderated sensibility.*
Tenacity *Imagination*	} *Moderated imagination.*

Mild shades of will-power produce weaknesses even when they are associated with the signs of morality. Nevertheless a good intellect always favourably modifies the resultant.

Bright intelligence *A calm mind.*	} *Perseverance.*
Gentleness *Kindness* *Intelligence*	} *Amiability.*
Feeble will *Sensibility* *Want of ardour*	} *Timidity.*
Gentleness *Calmness* *Inferiority*	} *Placidness.*
Intelligence *Calmness* *Constancy*	} *Patience.*
Feeble will *Gentleness* *Imagination*	} *The mind of a dreamer.*
Feeble will *Gentleness* *Imagination* *Non-intelligence*	} *Idleness.*
Feeble will *Sensibility* *A commonplace mind*	} *Tame-spiritedness.*

A strong will is one of the factors of success; but as we have pointed out to M. Henri Marion, this latter term has been graphologically abused. Success is a fact, a temporal result; it is not a trait of character, nor a graphologic resultant sign. Activity is always modified in association with a state of common or non-intelligence; great nervous activity produces useful effects with a superior man, but is a source of disorder in common minds.

Great activity	. .	} *An enterprising mind.*
Intelligence .	. .	
Great activity	. .	} *Unprofitable and dan-*
A common mind .	. .	*gerous mental agitation.*

Of all voluntary indications, hastiness or ill-considered action affords the most dangers to inferior minds. If very prominently shown in a handwriting, this trait itself is a sign of inferiority. Temperament may give a man this defect, but, given a certain degree of superiority, its manifestations are restrained, ruled, and therefore moderated. Thus, in describing graphologic signs (see p. 43), we have mentioned calm and temperate handwriting as one of the chief signs of superiority, as indicating restraint, moderation, and diseretion.

Moderated hastiness	.	} *A quick intelligence,*
Superiority .	. .	*good judgment.*[1]
Hastiness	. .	} *Moderate intelligence,*
Mediocrity .	. .	*and judgment.*[1]
Hastiness	. .	} *Non-intelligence,*
A common mind .	. .	*and no judgment.*[1]

Obstinacy, and hasty, ill-controlled action are very important elements of character; they cause most of the misfortunes we witness or perhaps may suffer from.

A hasty act or an obstinate persistence is the usual source of original error; pride and vanity confirm the

---

Relatively to the circumstances when hastiness may be so excited as to take the lead in action.

mistake, or render obstinacy more stubborn.   Thus the various kinds of pride and self-love cause in this connection a considerable access of faulty judgment, which is then an accompaniment of self-love and will-power.

Obstinacy . . . } *Very great persistence*
Self-love . . : } *in error.*
Lack of intelligence .)

Self-love . . . } *Very great persistence*
Hastiness of action : } *in error.*[1]
Lack of intelligence .)

This hastiness combined with force is the producer of anger, violence, brutality, revenge.   Combined with weakness it causes rage and spite.

Malice, cunning, and hypocrisy are certainly born of weakness.

Intelligence . . . }
Hastiness . . . } *Momentary bad temper.*
Kindness . . .)

Hastiness . . . }
Force . . . . } *Anger.*
Imagination . . .)

Hastiness . . }
Great force (club-like } *Violence.*
    pen-strokes) . . }
Imagination .)

Hastiness . . }
Force . . . } *Brutality.*
A low mind . . .)

Irascibility . . . }
Hastiness . . . } *Revenge*
Imagination . . .)

Hastiness . . . }
Sensibility . . . } *Spiteful anger.*
Weak will . . .)

Sensibility . . . }
Untruth . . . } *Hypocrisy.*
Weak will . . .)

[1] With, also, a strong tendency to give unasked-for advice, even upon matters of which such a man knows little or nothing.

Sensibility . . . ⎫
Want of principle . . ⎬ *Badness of character.*
Feeble will . . . ⎭

Feeble will . . . ⎫
Mental suppleness . . ⎬ *Cunning.*
⎭

Hastiness of temperament combined with activity gives ardour, and but a slight degree of nervousness is wanted to change the latter into agitation.

Activity. . . . ⎫
Hastiness ⎬ *Ardour.*
⎭

Hastiness ⎫
Activity. . . ⎬ *Agitation.*
Nervousness . . . ⎭

But agitation may exist as a resultant without ardour, if activity be less pronounced. For example, nervousness and non-equable hastiness result in agitation.

Non-equable hastiness . ⎫
Nervousness . . . ⎬ *Agitation.*
⎭

This agitation applied to mental affairs can produce peculiar results. Assimilation [1] with activity gives curiosity. This resultant varies considerably according to the condition of the writer as regards intelligence or non-intelligence. The Abbé Michon, the bibliophile Jacob, Littré, Louis Figuier were curious and very intelligent men. They engaged successfully in many different subjects, and their handwritings show the signs of activity and assimilation.

Assimilation. . . ⎫
Activity . . . ⎬ *Intellectual curiosity.*
Superiority . . . ⎭

This mental restlessness cannot be so favourably con-

___

[1] Graphologic sign—words separated into syllables, or nearly so —thus :—*as sim il ation.*

strued in the case of inferior men. Their curiosity
leads them rather to listen at closed doors and to ferret
out other people's affairs. Their faculty of assimilation
must have pabulum, and, in default of intellectual food,
it contents itself with coarser matters or it leads to the
study of (so-called) occult arts, such as astrology,
chiromancy, etc.

Assimilation .   .   .
Agitation   .   .   . } *Vulgar curiosity.*
Inferiority   .   .   .

Indiscretion resulting from excessive curiosity may
attach even to a superior man. With mediocrities it is
frequent and walks abreast with quickened curiosity,
and in inferior men the two are always co-existent.

Excessive curiosity   . } *Indiscretion.*
Superiority .   .   .

Considerable curiosity . } *Indiscretion.*
Mediocrity . .   .

Curiosity   .   .   . } *Indiscretion.*
Inferiority   .   .   .

Mental restlessness, feeble energy, and imagination
produce caprice.

Agitation   .   .   .
Feeble energy   .   . } *Caprice.*
Imagination   .   .

The same factors without imagination give indecision.

Imagination, feeble or
  nil .   .   .   . } *Indecision.*
Agitation   .   .   .
Feeble energy   .   .

A man at once agitated and hasty is irritable, a resultant which in this case is an irritation of the will.

Agitation . . . } *Irritability.*
Hastiness . . .

The same signs less pronounced cause impatience. Mental agitation is wanted for irritability, but nervousness suffices for impatience. In the latter case the excitement which produces irritability is lacking, but the slightest thing working upon nervousness gives impatience.

Nervousness . . . } *Impatience.*
Hastiness . . .

Substituting energy for nervousness, we obtain authoritativeness and the love of ordering others.

Hastiness . . . } *Authoritativeness.*
Energy . . . .

Hastiness, resistive will-power (notably obstinacy), and ignorance are the chief factors of the spirit of contradiction, but are not quite sufficient to cause it. Pretension, vanity, or pride is also wanted. We may mention the case of a young man who had been to hear a violinist of decided merit, but who did not deserve nearly such a high place as this man wished to give to him, who, while backing up his opinion very strongly, accidentally mentioned that he had received a flattering letter from the said violinist. Being a rather vain man, he wished the flattery to come from as great an authority as possible, and there was no altering his exaggerated statement of the musician's merit.

Hastiness . . .
Obstinacy . . . } *The spirit of contradiction.*
Vanity . . . .

In cases similar to the above, the resultant quality

comes into play each time that vanity gives the motive power, and obstinacy affords the necessary persistent force.   But contradiction would not be chronic in such cases, as it necessitates certain conditions not always existing.   For contradiction to be habitual, we require a man to be hasty, ignorant, and pretentious, so that the most trivial cause will produce it.   We have probably all met with young men possessing a remarkable facility for contradiction, who will say white if another says black, or black if you mention white ; and who readily take the measure of our great men, being perhaps good enough to award to them a certain talent.

But a man who merely contradicts is not a critic. He does not know his subject ; he seeks to work off his mental restlessness by siding with some one or something ; he sticks to his opinion because the desire for abstract truth, which requires a flexible and not an obstinate mind, is unknown to or is uncared for by him, and his pretension renders a confession of error out of the question.

Hastiness	.	.	.
Obstinacy	.	.	.
Ignorance	.	.	.
Pretension	.	.	.

} *The spirit of contra-diction always ready.*

Many fine qualities are based upon firmness, which plays an important part in character.   Its absence engenders laxness, idleness, and is a source of moral and material disorder, such as cowardice, which we have already seen connected with a feeble will.   But being present, firmness strengthens and fertilizes the character.   Calm firmness gives us constancy ; active, it produces perseverance ; and spirited firmness leads to persistence in the face of difficulties.

Firmness
Calmness . . . } Constancy.

Firmness
Activity . . . } Perseverance. ·

Firmness
Ardour . . . . } Persistence.

Courage is due to firmness allied to tenacity. It may be animated by imagination, but firmness sustains courage, and tenacity makes it heroic.

Firmness
Tenacity . . . } Resistance.

Imagination .
Firmness . . . } Courage.
Tenacity . . .

Imagination .
Great firmness . . } Heroic courage.
Great tenacity . .

Firmness and energy give opinionativeness, which with inferior minds degenerates into mere obstinacy.

Firmness
Energy . . . . } Opinionativeness.

A common mind . . } Obstinacy.
Opinionativeness . .

Decision comes from firmness and ardour; add tenacity, and resolution follows.

Firmness
Ardour . . . . } Decision.

Firmness
Ardour . . . . } Resolution.
Tenacity . . .

The Philosophy of Resultant Signs.—To draw up resultants, to harmonize them, and to set out the knowledge gathered from them, is to do the most advanced part of a graphologic portrait. The number of possible combinations becomes greater as the factors drawn from

graphologic analysis are more numerous. We now give an example, by no means one of the most complex, to show what scope the study of resultant signs offers to the student of graphology.

First resultant.—Gaiety may be the consequence of grace allied to imagination and to a lively mind.

Second resultant.—If the handwriting which produces the first resultant shows activity also, its vivacity becomes ardour.

Now, these two resultants, gaiety and ardour combined, give high spirits.

```
Grace        .    .    .   ⎫
Imagination  .    .    .   ⎬ Gaiety ⎫
A lively mind.    .    .   ⎭        ⎬ High spirits.
Vivacity .   .    .    .   ⎫        ⎟
Activity .   .    .    .   ⎬ Ardour ⎭
```

Gaiety may be connected with other traits of character with the following results :—

```
Kindliness   .    .    .   ⎫
Joviality    .    .    .   ⎬ Bonhomie.
Mediocrity   .    .    .   ⎭

Gaiety   .   .    .    .   ⎫
Causticity   .    .    .   ⎬ Mockery.
A critical mind   .    .   ⎭

Gaiety   .   .    .    .   ⎫ Punning, far-fetched
Pretension   .    .    .   ⎬ jocularity, a would-
Mediocrity   .    .    .   ⎭ be funny man.

Gaiety   .   .    .    .   ⎫ Gaiety which does not
Delicacy     .    .    .   ⎭ appreciate vulgar jokes.

Gaiety   .   .    .    .   ⎫
Æsthetic sense    .    .   ⎟
Delicacy     .    .    .   ⎬ Wit, smart repartee.
Vivacity     .    .    .   ⎭

Gaiety   .   .    .    .   ⎫ A capacity for
A common mind     .    .   ⎭ coarse jokes.
```

IV.

Happiness as a Resultant.—A meteorologist predicts a rainy to-morrow by observing previous atmospheric phenomena ; a physician who knows the normal succession of organic disorders caused by an illness foresees such and such consequences to his patient : these are predictions likely to be true, as resulting from careful observation of the various facts as well as of their environment.   Upon foreknowledge of this kind only, we shall now offer some remarks to our readers.

To begin with, we venture to state that serious study of a man's character authorizes, to some extent, a prediction of his future, as this depends mainly upon himself.   Graphology affords the means for this study, and by its aid we can obtain deductions as to the future, which are the more probable as the insignificance of the character is small and the prominence of its outlines well-marked.   Here are a few examples.   We find in a man's handwriting (say) the following sign : Letters very much inclined, which fact indicates a morbid sensibility.   This in itself is a source of disturbance, and if we also observe an absence of will-power, which being present would check this unhealthy sensibility, we can hardly say of such a man that his character is likely to lead him to happiness.   For his want of will (which tends to inaction), and his extreme sensibility (one of the elements of dreaming), will make him lazy ; they will also give his passions too much play, and his conduct as much as his character then becomes an improbable source of happiness.

Descending handwriting is a fact of much importance

when considering the probable future.   This sign shows us melancholy, sadness, want of self-confidence ; and to lack self-confidence is to be the servant of circumstances.

Future welfare is not for those who constantly mistrust themselves, and melancholy leads a man to discouragement and may, as it not infrequently does, induce suicide. Thus a man whose handwriting descends is not a happy man. If the cause of the depression be passing and accidental, and apart from his character, this will be shown by its grapholgic sign being merely exceptional and not normal to his handwriting, and it cannot then be viewed as a menace to his future.   But if, on the contrary, the cause for sadness be found in the character itself, it being (say) a morbid sensitiveness, it is but too probable that such a man will never be happy.

On account of external circumstances, which are often the causes of transitory sadness or joy, we can state only probabilities in this respect, and we must be content with this result, which is, however, of fair importance, for any indications concerning our happiness are of value.   A man's future is under his control to a certain degree only ; but that this degree is very considerable, observation of life plainly shows.   For we see that prolific sources of unhappiness are mental laxity, idleness, dissipation, want of will, selfishness, extreme sensitiveness, undue imagination and hastiness, impatience—all or most of which defects admit of remedy or of restraint.

But, on the other hand, reason, enlightened honesty, perseverance, energy, kindness, and a moderate degree of sensibility, are qualities which, found in handwriting, would render probable the future happiness of the writer.

Disregarding exceptional cases, it is to virtuous men that happiness belongs. But let us add the important corollary, that the more intelligent men are, the more probable is their happiness and the more complete.

There is, in fact, a marked difference between the happiness that belongs to men of a low order, and that which men of intellect seek. A cultivated mind, at once upright, firm, and of delicate appreciation, will find in life a number of inward sources of joy that a common stamp of man will know nothing about, however kind, active, and honest he may be. Absence of intelligence renders happiness more difficult of attainment, for, if a man be good but stupid, he will be capable of unconscious wrong-doing ; he may be energetic, but he will not know how to use his efforts to good advantage ; his honesty will make him respected by some, but, if he be stupid, he will be duped by others.

Pride is the greatest enemy to tranquillity of life for a man who is both intelligent and good. Ambition itself, which is so powerful an element of progress, which stimulates scientists in their researches, philanthropists in their humanitarian projects, and without which civilization would never have existed—ambition is often a hindrance to individual happiness. Look at those directing governmental affairs. At first sight it seems scarcely possible that an intelligent man, in good health, with an adequate fortune, and pleasant domestic surroundings, can to a great extent relinquish these advantages in order to throw himself into political strife,

thereby destroying his peace, and letting his honour be
at the mercy of the public; and yet this has been done,
and still is done, by some members of the French
Chamber of Deputies. Such men are too ambitious,
and they enter the political arena to be mixed up with
vexatious intrigues, from which they cannot so readily
withdraw when they wish. Their too ascending handwriting would point to this defect in their character,
which causes the chagrin they experience. It is true
that the feeling of duty in private life may sometimes
produce a similar chagrin and disappointment ; but if so,
it is attended with a much less degree of irritation of
personal vanity.

To be happy let us be wisely modest and unpretend-
ing, and we shall see disappear from our handwriting
the capital *M* whose strokes are too wide apart, and
that whose middle or last stroke rises much above the
other two, both very characteristic signs of undue pride ;
the capital *L* raised up high above its base, which
shows pride in self-admiration, and those large signatures with extravagant flourishes which so clearly indicate the absurd pretentiousness of their writers.

Now, we may be asked to describe the handwriting
of those destined to happiness. We will reply that
there is no type of handwriting special to such men.
There merely exist in the handwriting of each individual
certain signs of powers and weaknesses which can combine in numerous ways, and which can give a general
result which is *always different,* and from which we can
draw conclusions more or less certain regarding the
future of the writer. It is not necessary to be a graphologist to know that intelligent and good men are in the

long run more happy than those who are non-intelligent and bad. Let us then salute handwriting which is harmonious, cleanly traced, graceful, slightly ascending, without flourishes, somewhat angular, and with consistent bars to the small *t;* for happiness and a future probably await its writer, even if they be not already achieved.

THE PRACTICE OF GRAPHOLOGY.

BEFORE commencing a graphologic analysis of character, we ought to satisfy ourselves that the material supplied to us allows of the portrait being drawn. The first condition to obtain is a sufficient amount of data for investigation ; but in this, as in many other studies, the scope of our inquiry may be limited by necessity. If the materials at our disposal be numerous, the conditions are very favourable, and observation becomes more easy, certain, and complete. The graphologist can then readily determine the question of intentional falsification of the writing, the impressionability of the writer, his inequalities, and those sides of his nature easily influenced by various emotions ; in short, he can clearly discern the fundamental character apart from its accidental variations.

It must, moreover, be apparent that a character is not set out in the tracing of a single line ; a man's nature shows itself in its entirety only in a large number of his written acts and gestures, and not in merely a few strokes of the pen. Thus it is rash to express an unreserved opinion based upon the name and address on an envelope. For although some accurate deductions can be drawn from an envelope, it is easy to exaggerate the number of indications thereby afforded, and few men are ready to say *I do not know ;* vanity

urges us on, and, even in face of a document whose insufficiency should afford us a ready excuse for silence,
we cannot bring ourselves to say that our observations
are neither reliable nor to the point.

A letter with its envelope will usually suffice for a
sketch of character, while some pages of written
matter with a couple of letters of different dates will
allow of a detailed portrait of individuality being made.
In default of either of these opportunities we advise
much discretion in giving an opinion.

There are several kinds of unreliable specimens of
handwriting considered from the graphologic standpoint.
For example, the handwriting may be purposely
rendered false, either by the writer imitating that of
another, or by distorting his natural hand. Such falsification, be it well done, can at the worst lead only to an
erroneous analysis, which brings no discredit to the
graphologist. There is no need to particularize here
the method of such analyses, which are sometimes very
difficult, but which in such cases soon show the graphologist, by comparison of data, the inconsistency and the
contradiction of the written signs, and enlighten him as
to the unreliability of the specimen under analysis.
The kind of modified document which concerns us is
that of mediocre value for our purpose, even though
it may be presented in good faith ; such as copper-
plate handwriting, studied handwriting, and sometimes
vertical handwriting. Handwriting may also be very
materially modified by accessory circumstances, such as
personal irritation, a strong momentary impression,
etc., or by a bad pen, defective paper, muddy ink, an in-
convenient position for the arm of the writer, fatigue, etc.

When several of these causes unite, a handwriting results that is not only modified, but which is actually false, and the graphologist must be able to recognize such specimens. As a general rule, we consider of doubtful utility as data, handwriting which is very disorderly, or very slowly traced, unduly regular, or calligraphic.

Very disorderly handwriting is due either to some special pathologic condition of the writer, or to anger, mental agitation, haste, etc. It is a passing handwriting which is worthless for determining the normal character.

If *very slowly traced* handwriting may be regarded as a lifeless drawing.

If *unduly regular*, especially when it is also vertical, or nearly so, handwriting indicates a studied, non-spontaneous mode of expression, and it blends with insignificant handwriting, of which it is one form. Insignificant persons with some education write thus, *and they have no other hand*. They exaggerate the distance between the lines, and they write without animation and spontaneity, using angles more readily than curves ; but in either case individuality and force are lacking.

Calligraphic handwriting is almost valueless as an exponent of character.

Now, given a natural and spontaneous specimen of handwriting, does it suffice to look in our table of graphologic signs for those which exist in the specimen under analysis ?

Certainly not. It would be a strange illusion to suppose that a novice, without any preparatory study, could successfully apply himself to the delicate observation and the subsequent deductions which graphology

entails.   The possession of an English dictionary does
not enable a Frenchman to speak English, nor is a man
a chemist because he possesses works upon that science.
Yet there are many men who, quite as a matter of course,
assume a competent knowledge of psychology, and it
appears to us that many people also attribute to themselves graphologic knowledge, without in any way
grasping the spirit of the art, and the principles upon
which it is founded.   Yet, in fact, no study is more
difficult than that of character, at least when we wish to
pass beyond mere crudity of opinion, and to determine
clearly and precisely the real worth of a man.   Our
readers can scarcely have failed to observe this ; but, by
studying with method, the initial difficulties may be considerably reduced.   In graphology, as in everything
else, success depends upon the special fitness of the
student.   Yet, strangely enough, but few men admit
incapacity for judging others, although most of us do
not lay claim to be designers, musicians, mathematicians,
or naturalists, unless we can show some reason for our
inclinations tending in this or that direction.

In delineating character from handwriting, the first
step is to examine the general traits of the specimen.

A physician who sees a patient for the first time,
observes him, questions him, and seeks to understand
him, and to ascertain his general temperament, before
making up his mind upon the more detailed aspect of
the case before him.   And thus should a graphologist
proceed.   Handwriting is a whole which has a special
physiognomy, and it is very important to accurately
determine these special traits relatively to the general
character.

We obtain from such preliminary examination an impression which aids us in giving a true graphologic portrait. This impression relates to this or that type of man which is to be met with in life. When we have to judge the handwriting of a man of different nationality from our own, or who lived in a former age, we must bear in mind his general environment if we wish to form a sound opinion. If we look through a good collection of old autographs, we shall see that what we have defined as *general* graphologic signs show the least

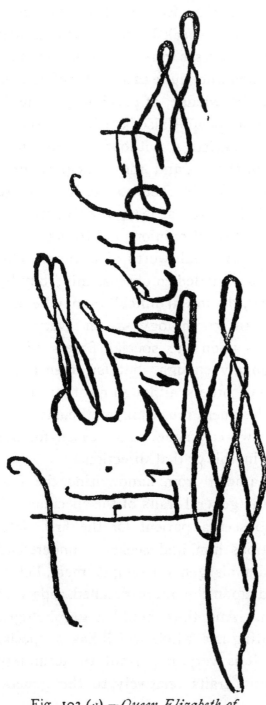

Fig. 103 (*a*).—*Queen Elizabeth of England.*

variation from modern specimens of the same class.
The *special* signs, on the contrary, differ considerably,
and the more so the farther back we go. Voltaire, had
he lived now, would certainly not have written as did
the Voltaire of the eighteenth century. *Autres temps*,
autres mœurs. Thus, to graphologically understand
Voltaire, we must imagine the time in which he lived.
Also, in the sixteenth century people signed their
names with an amount of elaboration and studied
care, which now-a-days would be rightly enough
ascribed to the eccentricity of a madman. The sig-

Fig. 104.—*Lord Bacon.*

nature of Queen Elizabeth of England is an example
of this (*fig.* 103, *a*), and that of Bacon (*fig.* 104),
although less extravagant in form, is very different from
the signature of a man of equal power and knowledge,
who might live in our own time. Such gross exaggeration is probably due to the official and conventional
powers and dignities which played such an important
part at that epoch.

When the mind has received the impression of the
physiognomy of a handwriting, we should then look
for the traits which denote a general condition of

superiority or inferiority, which as regards superiority are signs of simplicity, moderation, distinction, and activity, as contrasted with insignificance. This result being obtained, we have then to settle the degree of intellectual superiority, then that of the moral side, and then that of the will-power, having due regard to their reciprocal effect upon the character, as shown by the predominance of this or that side of the personality. Finally, we look for the signs of artistic sense. Then, when we have arrived at some sure basis of general character, we may proceed to investigate the more detailed traits, grouping them around the preceding lines of character, and blending the minor traits with the general cast of the nature. When experience has shown the student how to determine with certitude the dominant traits of character, the psychological development of minor traits can be achieved without much difficulty. The way to become a good graphologist is to make progressive studies of handwriting, at first crude, later on becoming more detailed.

Tyros in graphology ought at first to confine themselves to delineating merely the rough sketch of a character, for the endeavour to attain minuteness of detail will only hinder them and lead to a general confusion of opinion upon the personality of the writer of the specimen they may be analysing.

In setting out a graphologic portrait, it is well to avoid formal and technical expressions. For example, the words *intuition* and *deduction* have been abused. Many men attach no definite meaning to such terms, although they have a distinct significance; and, as a matter of fact, these two terms do not denote fundamental characteristics, but rather two different channels in which the intellect works.[1]

Beginners are liable to go astray by expatiating in an absolute, non-relative way upon a few characteristics, such as selfishness, pretension, truthfulness, etc., although,

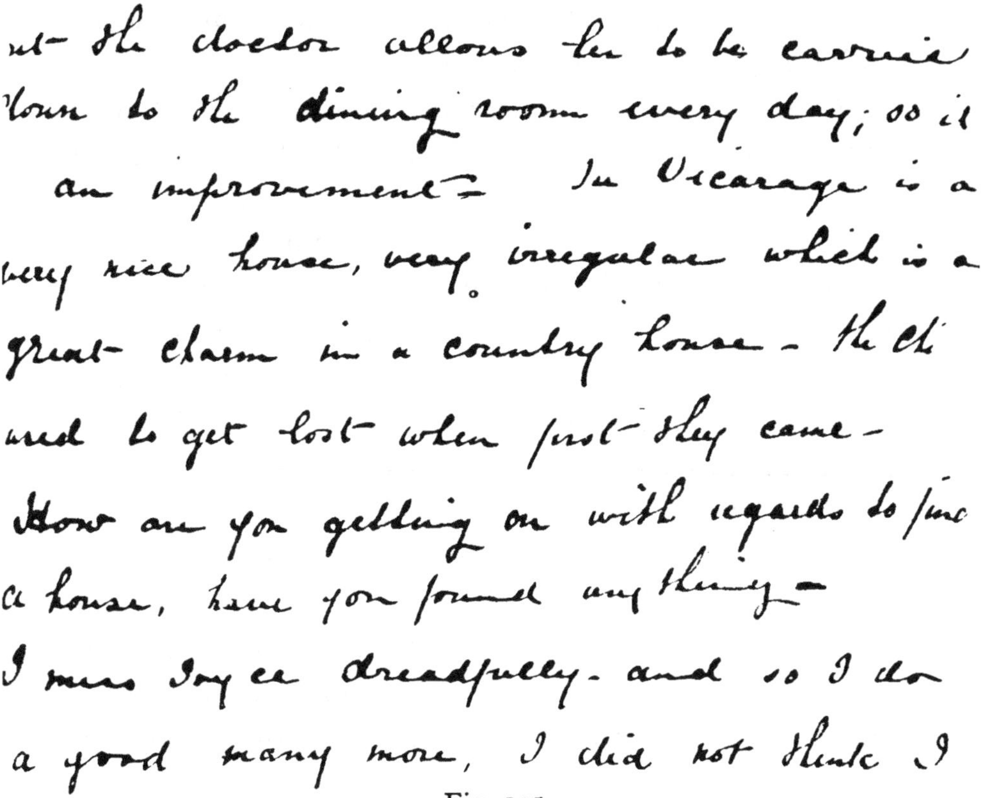
at the doctor allows her to be carried
down to the dining room every day; so it
an improvement = The Vicarage is a
very nice house, very irregular which is a
great charm in a country house - the ch
used to get lost when first they came -
How are you getting on with regards to find
a house, have you found anything =
I miss Joyce dreadfully - and so I do
a good many more, I did not think I

Fig. 105.

not infrequently, the handwriting they may be deciphering does not contain the signs relating to these traits. The graphologist does not need to review the whole gamut of psychology in order to draw a portrait. His chief purpose is differentiation of character, and if this

[1] This remark relates to the works of the Abbé Michon, who, in his graphologic portraits, considered these two traits of the first importance.

or that specimen show to him the insignificance of its
writer, the simple statement of such insignificance is
itself a portrait.   It is, moreover, very far from being
the case that all characters admit of equal graphologic
development ; some can be set out in a short statement,
while others necessitate a considerable amount of work
to investigate and express them.

We will now give some practical illustrations.   Notice
the handwriting shown in *fig.* 105.   How shall we
proceed to analyse it ?   The novice is always anxious
to know how to start, and here this is not very difficult :
we must begin by noting the most striking features of
the handwriting, putting on one side the minor traits.
Now, this specimen (*fig.* 105) possesses a characteristic
feature due to the slowness of the pen-strokes.   It looks
free from haste, and from nervous and agitated movements of the pen.   We see in this specimen a nature
which is inactive, timid, hesitating.   Thus, we have
arrived at the *dominant* characteristics, which should
always be most carefully looked for by the graphologist,
for they nearly always materially influence the other
traits ; they give a clue to the impulses and tendencies
of the writer.

Side by side with this slowness of the pen, we notice
that the lines and words are well spaced out, a feature
which tells us of clearness of thought.

The strokes of the pen are temperate and simple, a
sign of moderation and simplicity of nature, and the
specimen as a whole shows some elevation of natural
character, although it is not particularly *gracieuse.*
The letters are not very sloping to the right-hand, but we
notice considerable inequalities in their slope, which fact
is a sign of sensitiveness.

There is but little energy shown in these pen-strokes,
from which we infer that the will lacks force ; and the

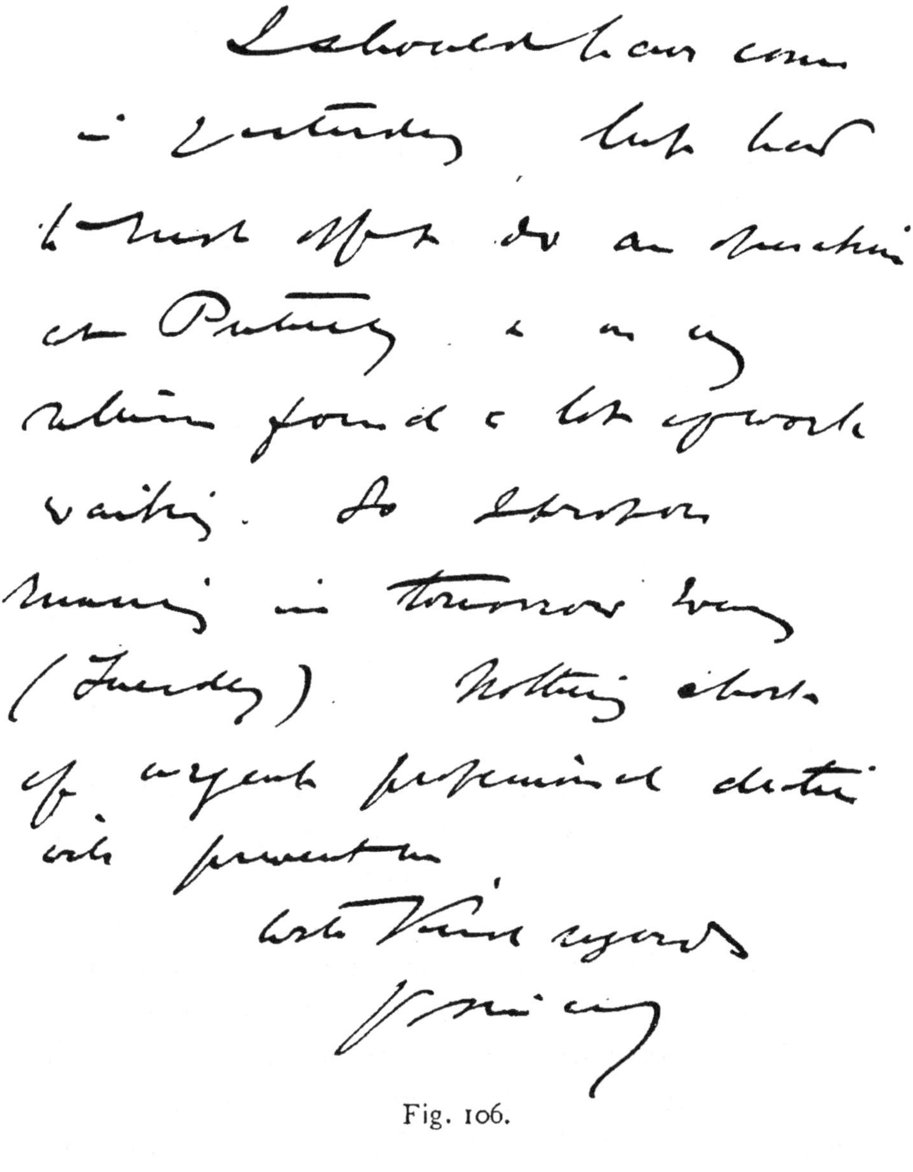

Fig. 106.

lines have a downward tendency, a sign of sadness and
want of ardour.

We might report the presence of other signs besides

those pointed out, but the latter are the main features of this specimen. It is always important to ascertain the activity or inactivity of a writer in order to give a good graphologic sketch. We are now able without further analysis to sketch the character of Miss ——. By bringing together the preceding observations we shall not unlikely be nearer the mark as regards Miss —— than her friends might be in estimating her nature ; for we are frequently judged by minor or even by accidental personal traits or acts, whilst the graphologist shows the basis of the character itself.

In this handwriting, which is both slow and descending, we have two signs which confirm each other, and from them we deduce a nature somewhat inactive, hesitating, prone to sadness. The writer is, moreover, unaffected and upright, but reserved and prudent, fairly sensitive, kind, and without much energy. There is a good disposition, lacking energy and broadness of mind, and we are reminded of a flower which has been deprived of the sunlight.

Let us 'now apply the method to another specimen, that of *fig.* 106, which was written by a man. The appearance of this handwriting is very different from the preceding, and we have purposely selected it because of this marked variation, in order to show that there is something more important to determine than the *minor signs* which are often looked for by some graphologists. The aim of these latter seems to be, not so much the determination of the nature of a given specimen, and deducing therefrom the general character of its writer, but rather to state categorically

the presence or the absence of certain signs—a procedure which may be compared to reading a book, not
in order to grasp its meaning, but to limiting one's self
to noting the presence of certain words on this page,
and of variously turned phrases on that.   But if all the
capital and small letters, the accents and the stops, etc.,
which make up the book be accurately specified, we do
not even then know much about its meaning.   Thus it
is a mistake to analyse a handwriting by passing over
the main features, which are most important to observe,
and by giving instead a large number of accessory
details concerning an object the chief outlines of which
have not even been sketched.   Nevertheless, this is
frequently done.

In *fig.* 105, the important feature to note was its
calm ; here, in *fig.* 106, activity is the key-note.   The
handwriting ascends, a sign of ardour ; it is rapid, a
sign of quick intelligence ; it is of simple form without
unnecessary pen-strokes, another sign of activity and
of mental culture.   It is also nervous and agitated,
showing mental agitation.   These traits support each
other, and, occurring in the same specimen, unite to
form a resultant which clearly shows the tendency of
the character, which, if necessary to define in a single
word, we might describe as very active.

We notice, moreover, signs of mental clearness (the
lines well separated), and of reasoning ability (words
joined to each other).

This specimen is scarcely adequate for us to express
an opinion as regards the rectitude of the writer ; we
should prefer to see one written at more leisure, in

order to truly appreciate the inequality of the height of the letters, and the illegibility of various words. However, we are favourably impressed by this specimen, and we believe that the inequalities to be noticed are due to haste in the act of writing, and to the great vivacity of its writer, and his spontaneity (quick, simple, and natural pen-movement). We are of opinion that he may perhaps be impulsive, but that he is straightforward and honourable. Being spontaneous and possessing feeling (handwriting inclined and varying in its inclination), we may conclude that the writer is altruistic, the more so as we see no signs of selfishness in the handwriting.

The strokes are energetic, firm, and very clearly defined ; the handwriting stands out well upon the paper ; the writer most certainly has a strong will, and his energy is supported by his great activity.

Our readers will see that a character may be gauged without it being necessary to investigate all the minor traits of the handwriting. The *general* signs give us the most reliable information, and great attention should be paid to these. Beginners are apt to get lost among the details, or *particular* signs, and we cannot too often point out that a man's character does not consist merely of four or five traits, such as care for minutiæ, a love of comfortable surroundings, and such-like.

We now pass to another handwriting which presents rather more difficulty, that of *fig.* 107. What is its chief characteristic ? The spacing out of the words and of the lines.

If we were to interpret these signs strictly in

accordance with the table of signs, we should obtain a
very clear intelligence and much generosity.   But this

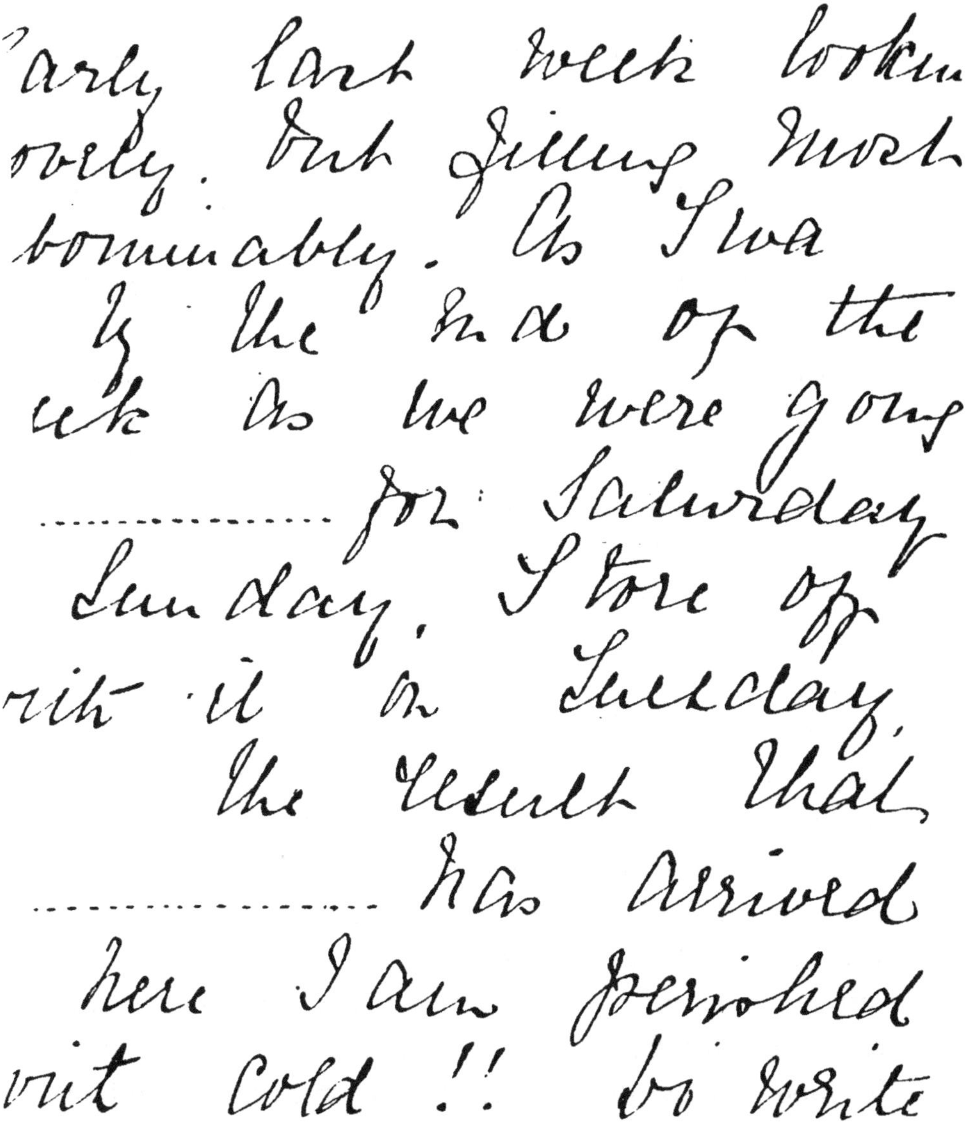

Fig. 107.

would be an *absolute* mode of treatment, and opposed to
the principle of the *relativity* of graphologic signs
according to their environment, upon which we have

previously laid so much stress. Now, this handwriting is not harmonious ; it does not accord with such interpretation ; it is neither ascending nor rapid ; it has a monotonous uniformity about it, and it is slightly angular—all signs which lessen the value of handwriting showing a clear intelligence, for a mind of superior order is scarcely allied with a character giving such evident tokens of mediocrity.

Nor does the spacing out of the words allow us to retain the trait of generosity, for the final letters are cut short, a sign of reserve (in this case, perhaps, distrust might be nearer the mark), or else they are curved inward towards the left hand, a sign of selfishness. There is a regular pause between each word, indicating a mind which is tardy in manifesting itself.

Having ascertained these leading traits of the handwriting, the rest of it appears to us rather insignificant and unfortunate. It is not without signs of culture, but culture does not take the place of a naturally frank disposition. The writing has too much sameness about it, which, with the words but slightly inclined, is a sign of a very moderate amount of feeling and sensibility. Energy is feeble, if we may believe the bars of the small *t*, which are thin and long. The words are formed of letters which are larger at the beginning than at the end of the word ; this a sign of finesse, which, however, is modified by this *deliberate* and temperate kind of writing (reserve, distrust), and by the signs of a weak will and of cavilling (bars of the *t* ascending, long and ending in a point). We obtain a resultant which shows a disagreeable and *rusé* character, perhaps even a cheat.

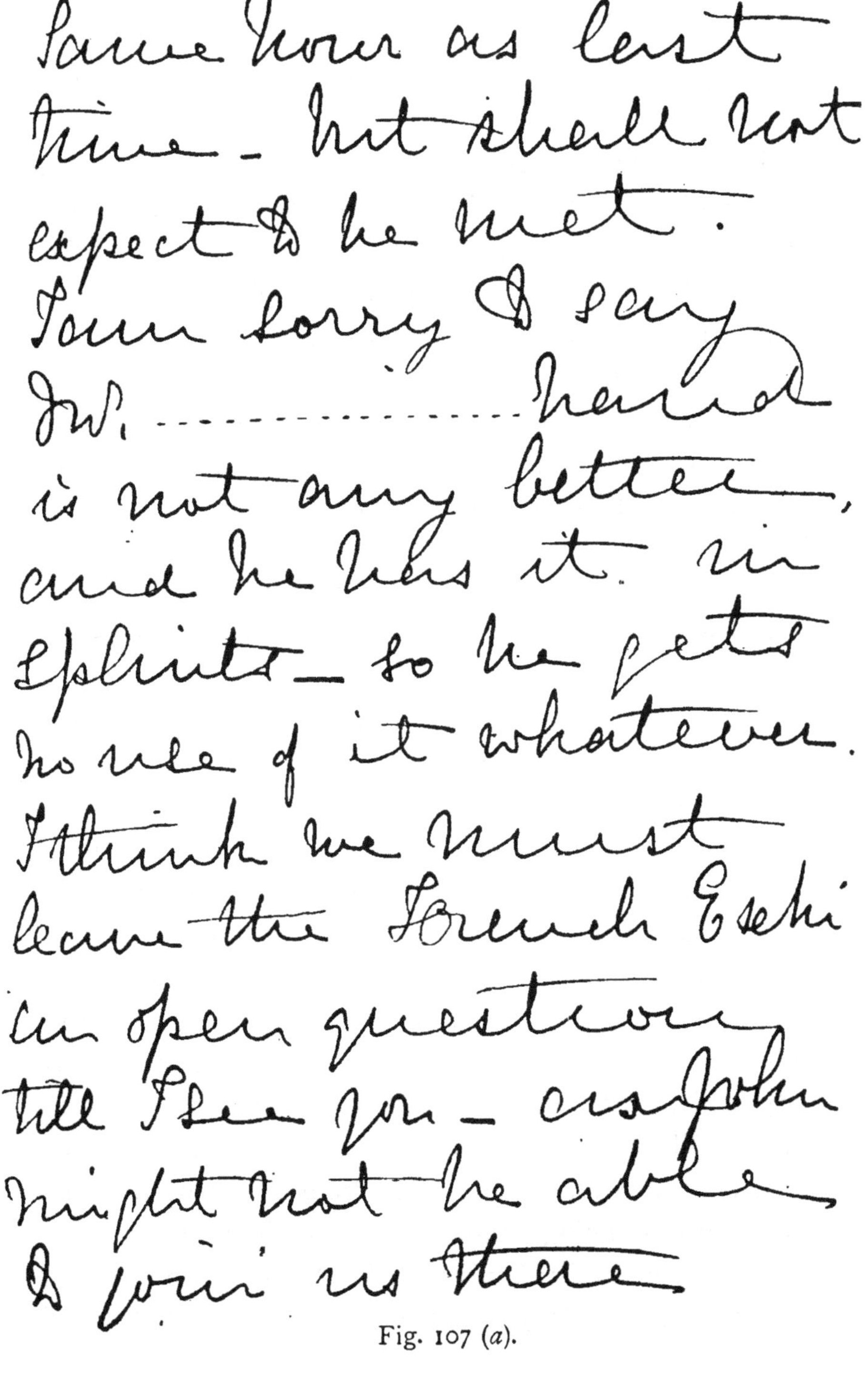

Same hour as last time — but shall not expect to be met. I am sorry to say JW. ———————— harried is not any better, and he has it in splints — so he gets no use of it whatever. I think we must leave the French Eski an open question till I see you — as John might not be able to join us there

Fig. 107 (a).

Gladiated words	*Finesse* . .	⎫ *An*
Temperate handwriting . .	*Reserve, distrust*	⎬ *unpleasant*
Bars of the *t* thin and long, and		*and rusé*
handwriting lacking activity .	*Weak will* .	*character.*
Bars of the *t* ascending. . .	*Cavilling* .	⎭

We can now sketch the character of Miss ——, who is of mediocre intellect, but which has been cultivated. She has ruse rather than its superior, finesse, and a capacity for cheating—we hope not employed—which is an inferior form of mental pliability. Miss —— lacks energy and activity, the want of which does not aid the development of her moral qualities. Her tendency to criticize and to contradict might pass unnoticed if her personal worth were greater than we can discern, but she wants the correct judgment and the active mind which direct criticism aright and give it force.

She has not much feeling, is selfish, distrustful, reserved, and capable of cheating others. We have here a nature of mediocre value, but slightly sympathetic, and whose tendencies might cause the writer of this specimen to become a very disagreeable person.

Figure 107 (*a*) represents a female handwriting which is again very different from the three preceding ones. Its aspect appears cold at the first glance and yet it is clear, lively, simple and of a superior type, notwithstanding a certain air of negligence and of taking things easily. This specimen contains indications of general superiority which soon enlighten us as to the nature of its writer. The signs of culture, and consequently of refinement, are numerous. The lines of the writing are pliant without being sinuous, an excellent sign, which shows us a mental pliability without which the intellect cannot be completely free and active. The letters of

the words are vertical (ability, good sense) or slightly
inclined. The inequality of this inclination is striking,
and shows a lively and sensitive disposition. The
small letters *m* are shaped like the *u* and tell us of kindness; this trait combined with the simple form of the
handwriting and its altruism (the finals of words stretch-
ing out to the right hand) allows us to deduce as a
resultant an amiable and kindly disposition. The
letters are practically of equal height, and the handwriting, besides being very legible, is clearly traced,
signs of an open and honourable nature.

The bars of the *t* are long and pointed, a sign of a
critical mind and vivacity. The signature [1] is underlined,
a fact which shows us that the writer is not unaware of
her personal worth.

Such are the leading traits of this handwriting, and
we can present the following sketch of character without much hesitation.

Mrs. —— is a superior woman, not only in mental
qualities, but also in matters of kind and good feelings
of the heart. Hers is a cultivated mind, clear, *gracieuse*
and lively, possessing also the critical faculty. Her
sentiment does not override her good sense, and thus
she has a correct judgment. She is kind and gentle,
that is to say amiable, and very simple and unaffected
in the distinction of personal worth that she possesses.
There is no selfishness, but there is a serene and intelligent benevolence. We have here an honourable and
reliable disposition, frank and trustworthy. Her energy
is less than her liveliness, but it suffices.

Mrs. —— has an excellent nature with full control of

The signature is not given in Fig. 107 (*a*).

herself. If her good qualities be not discerned upon first acquaintance, they will be fully appreciated when acquaintance ripens into friendship.

We will now show how handwriting can be more extensively analysed as a means of judging character, and for this purpose we shall use the autograph letters of one or two well-known persons.

PIERRE LOTI.

A GRAPHOLOGIC SURVEY.

OUR readers will probably remember that M. Julien Viaud, the young naval officer who has made his mark in literature under the *nom de plume* of " Pierre Loti," was elected in 1891 to take a place among the forty men who compose the French Academy, his predecessor being Octave Feuillet.

Pierre Loti became famous with his book " Le Mariage de Loti " ; and his other works, " Pêcheur d'Islande," a tale of Breton fishing-life; " Mon Frére Yves ; " " Ayéadé," an Eastern story ; " Le Roman d'un Spahis ; " " Madame Chrysanthéme," with its clever description of Japanese life, have rapidly secured for Pierre Loti a prominent place among the popular and appreciated authors of to-day. It may be remembered that M. Emile Zola ran him close for the votes, and this fact proves, as was mentioned by *Black and White* at the time,[1] " that there is plenty of room in France for good sane literature if only *les jeunes* could be made to see it."

[1] *Black and White.* No. 18, vol. i., June 6th, 1891.

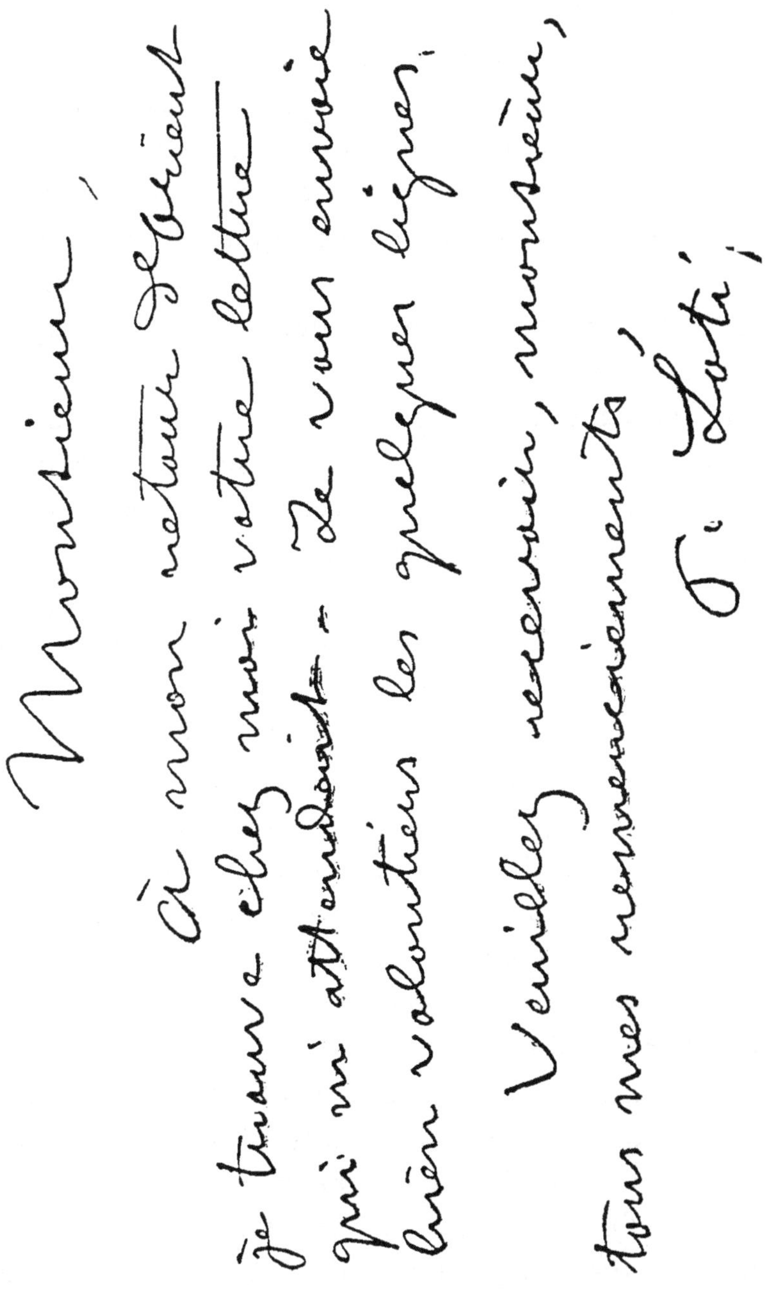

Monsieur,

à mon retour Sévrioul
je trouve chez moi votre lettre
qui m'attendait — Je vous envoie
bien volontiers les quelques lignes,

Veuillez recevoir, monsieur,
tous mes remerciements,

P. Loti;

Fig. 108.—M. Julien Viaud (*Pierre Loti*).

We will commence our study by ascertaining :

The Value of the Character.—Pierre Loti's handwriting (*fig.* 108) is simple ; it contains neither large unnecessary pen-strokes, nor signs of extravagant movement of the hand.   The words are well separated, and the lines are all clear of each other.   The firmness of the pen-strokes is rather striking, and we do not discern among them one which is vulgarly or coarsely formed.   By these signs we recognize a general superiority of character.

The Dominants.—The faculty of assimilation is very marked, and its power is increased because it is connected, let us state, with a very harmonious handwriting.   In the letter, a part of which only is here produced, there occur the words *que je*, *de faire*, *la plupart*, which are all written respectively as one word instead of two, and the word *Monsieur* is made by one continuous stroke of the pen (a sign of deductive power) ; but, on the other hand, the word *trouve* is written in three parts—*tr ouv e*—and similarly with other words (a sign of intuition).   Although the deductive faculty predominates, we may say that Pierre Loti has an eclectic mind.   He can both assimilate and reason, and we should say that he could treat successfully many different subjects.

A clear intellect and simplicity of nature certainly form part of the dominant traits of character, and these qualities are shown by the lines of the writing being so definitely separated from each other, and by the pen-strokes being merely adequate to express the writer's thoughts without any redundancy of pen-movement.   The value of these signs is not diminished by other and contrary indications, such as self-complacence, pretension, pride, of which there are no traces. On the other hand, if we take into account the superiority of the character under notice, we are justified in assigning to Pierre Loti a higher order of simplicity than might be due to a man of lower intellect ; the *distinction* of his character justifies this difference. The curve (a sign of gentleness) is very frequent in this specimen, and the letters *n* and *m* are formed like the *u*, which indicates kindness. This gentleness and kindness are so prominent in the character, that they cause the existence of another sign, of which we shall speak later on (the *r* made like a *u*).

Rectitude is well evidenced by the words being of equal height and by the lines of the writing being straight, non-serpentine. Trickiness forms no part of Pierre Loti's nature.

Sequence of ideas is shown by the *d* being joined to the letter following it ; altruism by the absence of final strokes curving backward towards the left hand, and by nearly all the capital letters being joined to the small letters which follow them.

Pierre Loti controls rather than encourages his impressionability. His nature is strong and courageous, traits shown to us by the letters of the words being nearly vertical, and by the general aspect of his writing ; but nevertheless, kindness and affection are indicated by the numerous letters which incline to the right hand, despite the vertical aspect of the writing looked at as a whole.

Secondary Traits.—Several kinds of will-quality

are shown, and all in unequal degrees. Gentleness
asserts itself fairly regularly with the curved strokes;
next comes hastiness of thought or action (bars of the
t long), stubbornness (angles, notice that of the *t* in
Orient), obstinacy (bars of the *t* descending from left
to right). Initiative will-power is fairly well marked
(bars of the *t* tending towards the right hand).

Pierre Loti is careful (the dots over the *i's* and *j's*),
but his handwriting has a certain negligence about it.
He would attend to details only in matters which
thoroughly interested him. We have another sign of
mental clearness and order of ideas in the little stroke
which is placed between two sentences.

The letters are spaced out and widely formed, thus
indicating a love of very comfortable surroundings.

The *r* made like a *u* is a sign which we believe has
not yet been observed by graphologists. In this form
of the *r* we have a little nonchalance, that of contemplative persons, of lovers of form[1] (indicated by widely-
formed letters and by a laziness of pen-strokes). We
shall see when we draw up our resultant characteristics, that the gentleness we have stated might become
tenderness, so that our opinion on this point agrees
in any case with the traits we observe in the rest of
the handwriting.

We can also state delicacy (by the absence of vulgar
signs), distinction (by the form of the *m* in *monsieur*),
originality (the curious shape of the small *z* and of the
capital *J*), a slight nervousness (some of the letters are
shaky), a lively but well-controlled imagination (some
of the loops of the *j, g,* and *l* are " fat," the finals brisk

[1] *I.e.* shape, configuration,—not ceremony.

but devoid of large pen-movement), and finally, much calmness, and an undefined sadness (the lines of the writing are not ascendant ; they rather tend downwards, but very little).

A few letters shaped typographically show the good taste of the writer, although the entire absence of any vulgar strokes has already enlightened us in this respect.

Resultants.—Graphology does not tell us as regards Pierre Loti of any other trait worth mentioning, but, by looking over and grouping the traits we have already deduced, we can use a kind of psychological calculus and thereby arrive at fresh results which we have termed resultants.[1]

As an instance, the great gentleness of Pierre Loti, his delicacy and sensitiveness, can scarcely exist in the same nature without causing a psychological condition which includes these three factors, and *tenderness,* we think, is the result.

$$\left.\begin{array}{l} \textit{Much gentleness} \\ \textit{Delicacy} \\ \textit{Sensitiveness.} \end{array}\right\} \textit{Tenderness.}$$

Bringing together the kindness and the altruism already noted, we obtain naturally enough the quality of *generosity.*

$$\left.\begin{array}{l} \textit{Kindness} \\ \textit{Altruism} \end{array}\right\} \textit{Generosity.}$$

By the same procedure we obtain sensuousness, which we refer to later on, and the other resultants which now follow :—

$$\left.\begin{array}{l} \textit{Sensitiveness.} \\ \textit{Love of form.} \end{array}\right\} \textit{Sensuousness.}$$

See the chapter *Resultant Characteristics.*

Sensuousness. . .	}	*Appreciation of beauty.*
Æsthetic sense . .		

A superior nature, recti-	}	*An entire and open straightforwardness, honour.*
tude		
Absence of ruse . .		
Simplicity . .		

Sensitiveness. . .	}	*A vague sadness, dreaminess, pessimism.*
Controlled imagination.		
Gentleness . . .		
Delicacy . .		

The man himself.—The works of M. Pierre Loti confirm our conclusions ; we believe that his readers will neither accuse us of being far from the mark, nor of having flattered their author ; they can check most of our opinions.

Although it may not be practicable for M. Pierre Loti's readers to express an opinion upon some of the characteristics deduced, they should nevertheless perceive that they have been given an insight as to the reliability of our assertions. It is difficult, for example, for M. Pierre Loti to show his honourable nature and his generosity in his writings ; but it will be recognized that these qualities are produced by the union of other traits of his character.

The *sadness* we have found is, we think, instinctive, innate, and to be attributed also to the childhood of this author, who was born in Brittany, and whose early thoughts lost themselves in the unlimited horizons of that country ; this trait, moreover, has been encouraged and engrained in the character by long watches out at sea, during slowly passing hours of vague reverie, by close contemplation of the dark waters under clouds and the blackness of night. This is the sadness of a contemplative mind which has compared the finite with the infinite, man with the universe, the puny atom with the vast whole, weakness with omnipotence, and which has thence derived a great store of tenderness for the weakness and finiteness of mankind. The *pessimism* is that of a kindly-natured and poetical man, who, with the simplicity of a superior nature, recognizes his own impotence as compared with the great problems of life, and who takes refuge in his surroundings, in all that is impressive and on a large scale, the earth, its trees, its wondrous oceans, the winds that come and go, and which great facts of nature engross him, and serve him as a prop and a protective stay to support the smallness of every-day life in our times. Whence we obtain his *sensuousness* and *love of the beautiful*, which have nothing of the material and gross in them, but which are, on the contrary, quite ideal. This is the sensuousness of a nature which looks for the mind inside its wrapping-up, for the soul in its fleshly covering, a nature which loves material things not for themselves, but for what they have hidden, for what animates them. With M. Pierre Loti, the *sunt lacrymae rerum* of Virgil is accurate and true ; with him the phenomena of nature live, a heart beats in them—and the heart is that of M. Pierre Loti.

This is the philosophy of generous natures, and one which shuts out egotism. With M. Pierre Loti, this absence of regard for self is so marked that we may say he avoids investigating his own personality, and descrying its mortality and its boundaries, and that he loses sight of himself in vast scenery, in the roar of rushing winds and in dreamy reveries.

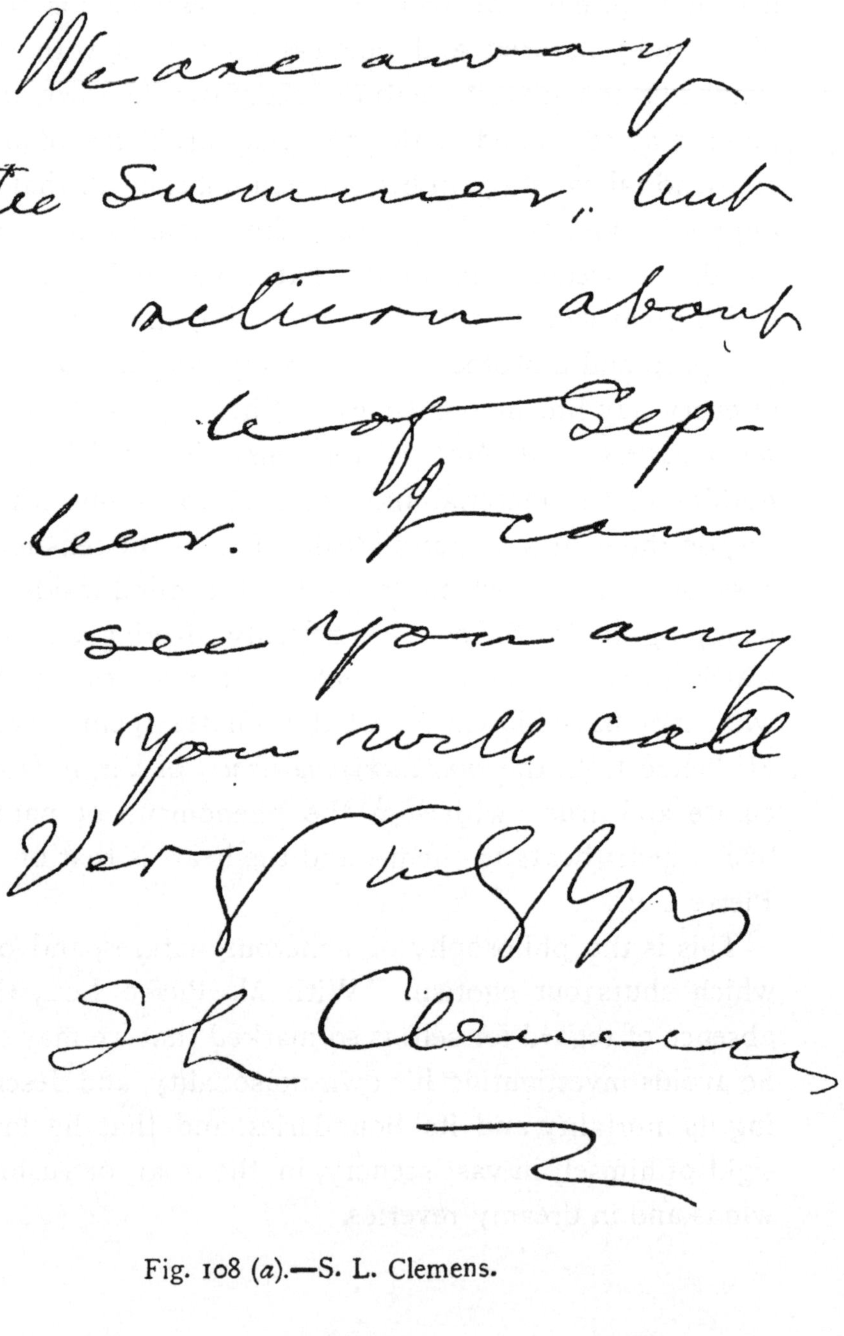

Fig. 108 (a).—S. L. Clemens.

MARK TWAIN (*Samuel Clemens*).

A GRAPHOLOGIC PORTRAIT.

The handwriting that we now proceed to analyse (*fig.* 108*a*) is pleasant to the eye; it is sufficiently legible although quickly traced. The negligence of some of the words is agreeable, because it is here due to the personal activity of the writer. Moreover, all the strokes are so delicate and graceful, that the graphologist is at once led to form a favourable opinion of their writer. There is sympathy expressed here, which is undoubtedly a characteristic of the man.

The talent which Mr. Clemens possesses is clearly enough shown by the absence of vulgar strokes and by the simplicity and brightness of the handwriting, signs which show distinction, simplicity and clearness of intellect, all qualities of personal superiority. Moderation is not wanting: in the liaison of the words *the middle of Sep-* we see very great activity, but which is, however, well regulated, and which must not be confounded with the ill-controlled pen-movement indicative of a lack of moderation and control, which is usually one of the signs of inferiority. Many of the letters also are formed simply and tersely, signs of culture which heighten the preceding qualities. The letters akin to a typographical form show more especially an artistic feeling.

The intellectual abilities of Mr. Clemens are various. He proceeds as much by deduction as by intuition. The capital letters separated from the words they commence, indicate his mental cast. They show us a sudden movement due to intuition, followed by the

working out of the idea, which latter trait of deductive
ability is evidenced by the liaison of the letters and even
of the words.

In the affairs of life our subject pauses for a moment
to make up his mind, and then boldly follows the course
decided upon, and he brings feeling into play before he
acts. In our experience this trait of character is not
usually found in an inferior type of man.

Mr. Clemens is true and honourable ; witness the
letters of his handwriting, which are of equal height.
And although some of the lines of the specimen are
sinuous, the presence of signs showing moral superiority, tells us that it is rather his mind and talent which
are pliant and versatile, and not that his moral side is
too lax. Moreover, the *abandon* and the clear tracing
of the handwriting plainly indicate straightforwardness.
Nor is he a selfish man ; the only sign which might lead
us to think the contrary (the *e* of the word *time* curving
back to the left hand) is of no importance. We see, on
the contrary, a widely-formed handwriting with both
words and letters spaciously traced : generosity, and a
nature readily approached and easy of access, could
hardly be better shown than by these signs. He is
kind (rounded handwriting) and amiable (the *n* and *m*
shaped like the letter *u*) with an optimistic nature. His
liveliness is very apparent, and comes out turn by turn
as joviality, high spirits, and ready wit. This is shown
not only by isolated signs, but also by combinations of
signs. Thus :—

Graceful handwriting	.	.	*Gracefulness*	
Animated handwriting	.	.	*Imagination*	*Merriment*
Spontaneous handwriting	.	.	*Quick wit*	

The briskness of the lines of the specimen and the vivacity of some of the pen-strokes indicate eagerness, ardour. And joining ardour with merriment, we obtain a fresh psychological condition, high spirits.

Merriment . . . } *High spirits.*
Ardour . . . .

The first line of the specimen, which ascends so strikingly, expresses spontaneity ; it is an expansive, open-hearted movement, almost one of mirth. The line following, which becomes horizontal, is a sign of moderation. It is somewhat undulating, and indicates a struggle between two moods of its writer. The hand tries to ascend, being urged on by the temperament of the writer, but it is kept in check by his mind—a sign of moderation which has been acquired.

Natural liveliness. . } *Gaiety held in check.*
A mental restraint .

But such exuberance of spirits necessitates a re-action ; their plenitude comes near running over. This handwriting does not maintain its original ascend-ant movement. Several of the lines ascend at their commencement and descend at their end ; the restraint is painful, it leads to sadness, to melancholy. This con-trast, of which we know more than one example, is not altogether surprising in the present instance, owing to the sensitiveness and impressionability of Mr. Clemens' nature. But this reaction is not of much note ; the character is too strong in the other direction, and the termination of the letter is an instance of the upward rebound. The final stroke of " *very* " is pluckily thrown off with the wavy " *y*," a sign of gaiety. The following word (" *truly* "), although not very legible, has a power-

ful graphologic expression of great activity and liveliness.   The final of the letters " *S L*," which immediately
follow, is a good example of the sign of joviality.   And
the way the signature is underlined is a further indication of similar qualities.   There is an intense life in
these four words, and something like a hearty laugh.
And the laugh, moreover, is delicate, like the handwriting, honest like the character, and wounding no-
body.

We obtain another resultant from so much active and
intelligent gaiety :—

Intelligence	.	.	.	
Delicacy		.	.	
Activity	.	.	.	} *A keen and fine wit.*
Joviality		.	.	
Gaiety	.	.	.	

Will-power is not lacking, but Mr. Clemens has more
spirit and life than actual force of character.   He is
firm enough without being obstinate : we can scarcely
look for massiveness in so delicate and keen a mind.

SOME REMARKS UPON THE NUMERICAL EVALUATION OF CHARACTER.

PRACTICE is essential to the graphologist for the development of his judgment, and it is necessary to analyse many handwritings if we wish to gain facility in grasping the characteristic meaning of the written signs. For the use of those students who may be alarmed at the amount of work thereby entailed, but only for such as have passed beyond preliminary study, we give here a method that, with a minimum of work, will materially facilitate their progress.

Each of the three main divisions of character—intellect, morality, will-power—has been sub-divided into three classes of superiority, and three of inferiority. See the chapter upon *Resultant Characteristics*, which contains also a definition of each class.

As regards *intellect*, we have :—

Personal inferiority, viz. :

    I.   Mind of a low order.
    II. Insignificance.
    III. Mediocrity.

Personal superiority, viz. :

    I.   Intelligence.
    II. Talent.
    III. Genius.

Concerning *morality* and *will*, the grades are :—

Personal inferiority, viz. :

    I.   *Nil*, or nearly so.
    II. Feeble.
    III. Mediocre.

Personal superiority, viz. :

    I.   Sufficiently pronounced.
    II. Superior.
    III. Very superior.

The table which follows shows the value at which we estimate numerically our six grades of intellect, morality, and will, which have already been defined by us in words. Thus the section 0 to 9 represents the lowest degree of these three qualities ; 50 to 59 the highest. A feeble insufficiency is denoted by 10 to 19 ; mediocrity, or a relative insufficiency, by 20 to 29 ; a satisfactory development of the three qualities by 30 to 39 ; while the section marked 40 to 49 refers to a superior degree of intellect, morality, or power of will.

Numerical value.	Degrees of Intellect.	Degrees of Morality.	Degrees of Will.
0 to 9	Mind of a low order	*Nil*, or nearly so	*Nil*, or nearly so.
10 „ 19	Insignificance	Feeble	Feeble.
20 „ 29	Mediocrity	Mediocrity	Mediocrity.
30 „ 39	Intelligence	Sufficiently pronounced	Sufficiently pronounced.
40 „ 49	Talent	Superior	Superior.
50 „ 59	Genius	Very superior	Very superior.

(*For definition of the various degrees, see* " *Resultant Character-istics.*")

The more advanced student of the preceding chapters of this book can now sum up the general value of a specimen by combining the three numerical values. But we must remember that the totalization is not always comparable between specimen and specimen of handwriting. To illustrate this let us use two or three specific examples.

Thus a character made up of—

Intellect   45 degrees
Morality   15   „
Will   20   „
          ——
  Total   80   „

is, in our opinion, inferior to the more moral character composed of—

Intellect   15 degrees
Morality   45   „
Will   20   „
          ——
  Total   80   „

while we should class both of the preceding specimens below a handwriting which indicated to us the more harmonious personality comprising—

Intellect   30 degrees ‥
Morality   30   „
Will   20   „
          ——
  Total   80   „

Now, these three illustrations all give a total of eighty degrees, but, be it noted, the total number of degrees in each case is not equally distributed among the same *genres* of personality. Hence our distinctions just made. We may not come across such wide differences every day, but they certainly exist, and thus it is well for us to fully recognize that comparison of the *total* figures only may lead us to a faulty conclusion in our general practice.

In particular cases, we should be justified in according a pre-eminent ability, latent or exercised, for certain avocations, according to special circumstances. Thus a specimen which showed us: intellect, 45; morality, 10; will, 45; total, 100: might not unreasonably denote the capacity required by (say) a talented and unscrupulous financial schemer, or by a *fin de siècle* " Jim the Penman " ; while we could scarcely think that a man would be successful as a practising surgeon whose handwriting showed us 10 degrees of intellect, 50 degrees of morality, and 40 degrees of will-power—total, 100.[1]

We will now use an actual specimen of handwriting as a further illustration of the preceding table : The handwriting of " Mark Twain " (*see fig.* 1, p. 37) is clear and simple, very active, but nevertheless it is well controlled : we mark it at 50 degrees of intellect, and we readily ascribe to it the same grade of morality, this figure showing a superior rectitude of character, which can, however, like the intellect, be still further advanced by the aid of a little more precision and vigour. As to the grade of will-power, which quality is less prominently shown than intellectuality and morality, we may fairly pronounce it to be practically sufficient, if not superior, and we write down the will-power at the figure 40 ; $50 + 50 + 40 = 140$, which is thus the total value of this fine organization.

This numerical evaluation of character may be carried out with a considerable degree of precision. The process is, in any case, an interesting exercise for the capable student, and it is less fatiguing than that of making a graphologic portrait, or even a sketch. We

[1] Practically, we shall not meet with these identical figures, which are given here as a simple theoretical illustration. An elevated intelligence may be associated with very feeble morality, but a truly superior morality is necessarily accompanied by a sufficiently pronounced intelligence. Very superior will-power is equally associated with a certain intellectual capacity, for without this, the will-power would be merely the energy of brute force. Combinations that may be set out on paper are not all practically realizable to the same degree.

often experiment in this way with good graphologists : each one examines silently a given specimen of hand-writing, and jots down his figures upon a separate paper. Not infrequently the same number is found written upon several papers, while the others are not widely divergent. The satisfaction which is then evinced, is followed by a lively interchange of ideas and impressions, while we are all ready enough to repeat the experiment. In this way the more advanced students can obtain instructive recreation from the interesting study of personal gesture which is termed graphology.

ART IN HANDWRITING.

ACCORDING to the psychological division usually adopted, we possess three main faculties ; thought, feeling, and will. May we not regard the æsthetic sense as a fourth ? This is certainly a faculty not distinct from the other three, for it can exist only in conjunction with them, but, on the other hand, no one of these can produce it. In art there is feeling ; there is also a science and a harmony which depend upon intellect, and the activity which gives character to art, and aids its expression, connects it also with the will.

Dictionaries do not give a good definition of art, which is, perhaps, due to the diversity of its elements. Thus it will be well for us to define a term which we shall frequently use.

Art is a form of expression produced by the harmony of a whole with its parts. The manner in which a man is sensible of or appreciates this harmony constitutes the artistic side of his nature.

In psychology, why should we not assign a special place to art, since it is, or should be, the final and supreme resultant of things which are beautiful and good ?

The importance of art is very considerable ; it

colours, it charms, it is a moral teacher, and it assumes a thousand forms to produce its results. The tender-hearted look for emotional effect, the imaginative desire to be wafted to the ideal, the headstrong ask to be excited or subdued—we wish for manifestations of command, of action, of grace, of skill, of enthusiasm, in a word, of all that we conceive, of all that we experience —and art must respond to our demands. It needs but momentary reflection upon the inexhaustible variety of the forms of art to perceive the shortcomings of the graphologic data which relate to it. This is at present one of the most incomplete sections of graphology.

There is certainly no absolute sign of art contained in handwriting, for art is not an entity. Artistic productions viewed as responsive to the desires of the people, give us a fairly definite idea of the taste prevailing at the epoch of their production. But the most admired of these works cannot be viewed as the only, or as the highest expression of the beautiful. For instance, a play may be a very great success without being of the best art; it may show us the public feeling, but in many cases it is only a very poor exponent of the beautiful in art. Not only does æsthetic taste vary from epoch to epoch in the same country, but there is often such a divergence in this respect, between nation and nation, that what is beautiful under the brilliant sunshine of Southern Europe may be considered the reverse in the colder North. Now art, being a *resultant* of individual, as of national traits, the handwriting which yields these manifestations of character, ought also to contain the elements of such artistic sense. And we proceed to investigate these.

The relativity of artistic sense extends beyond the varying tastes of epochs or of countries, such relativity exists also for different degrees of intelligence. A child has a certain art, and we will look for its elementary factors in the actions of a child.

A little boy sits down to produce a letter to his father. He chooses a sheet of paper as clean as possible, and the better the paper, and the more ornamented, the more studied is his writing. If the paper chance to have a kind of lace-work border, as is sometimes seen, he will probably draw a margin round the edges, and make fanciful capital letters. Neatness, arrangement, and ornamentation show themselves as the principal elements of art from this child's point of view. His embellishments may sometimes be disfigurements, his studied neatness may be far from harmonious, but there is still a manifestation of artistic feeling and intention, however feeble it may be. Later on, should the child become a writing-master, and consider his capital letters and the headings of his writing-models of prime importance, there will be a development of this same art formed of the same elementary factors: *neatness, ornamentation, arrangement.*

These three signs viewed separately, are specially applicable to a condition of general inferiority, and constitute artistic inferiority.

> General inferiority .   . } *Artistic sense little*
> Arrangement or neatness } *developed.*
> or ornamentation .   .)

Arrangement and ornamentation accompanying a vulgar mind, can indicate, at the utmost, only a sense of symmetry.

Vulgarity . . . . ⎫
Arrangement . . . ⎬ *Symmetry.*
Ornamentation . . . ⎭

The handwriting of superior men containing these same signs, causes other meanings to be deduced.

A superior man's sense of neatness is less easily satisfied; it is improved upon and elevated. Not only does he begin again a letter which is soiled, but he chooses good paper to write upon, and he avoids the use of a pen which makes a little blot at each long up or down stroke. His taste for arranging his materials becomes order.

Superiority . . . ⎫
Arrangement . . . ⎬ *Order.*

Arrangement and neatness produce clearness.

Superiority . . . ⎫
Arrangement . . . ⎬ *Clearness.*
Neatness . . . . ⎭

Ornamentation is either replaced by simplicity, or else it develops into gracefulness.

Superiority . . . ⎫
Ornamentation . . . ⎬ *Gracefulness.*

Now if ornamentation combine with imagination we obtain fantasy.

Ornamentation . . . ⎫
Imagination . . . ⎬ *Fantasy.*

We must investigate the general condition of the writer as regards his superiority of character, to know if the manifestations of such fantasy be of a high or of a vulgar kind.

Arrangement is a fundamental quality of handwriting, ornamentation an accessory. We possess a letter from the Marquis de Beauharnais, a general in the French army, which might serve as a model of arrangement. The handwriting is very legible, and is moderately spaced-out. Between the date, the word *monsieur*, and the commencement of the letter, the spaces are carefully arranged, being neither too large nor too small. The

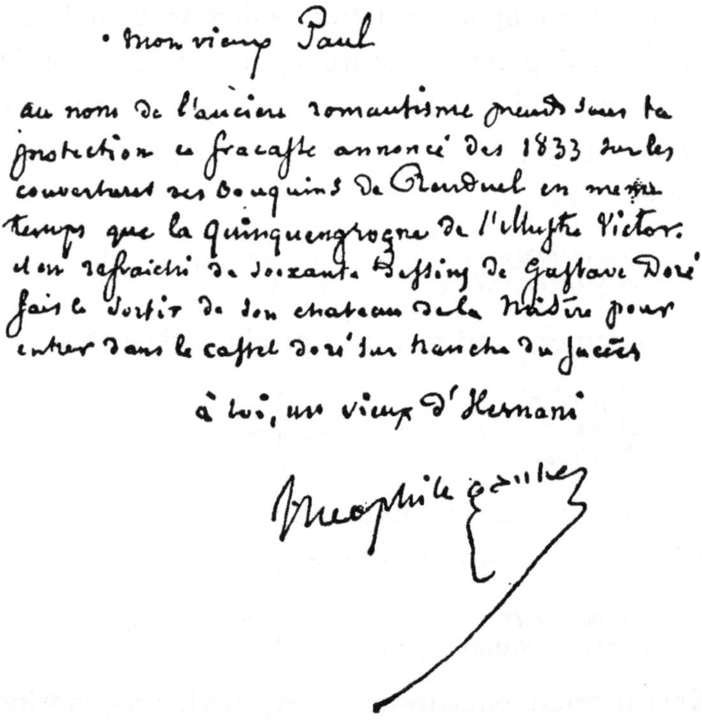
· Mon vieux Paul

au nom de l'ancien romantisme prends sous ta protection ce fracasse annoncé dès 1833 sur les couvertures des bouquins de Renduel en même temps que la quinquengrogne de l'illustre Victor. il s'est rafraichi de soixante dessins de Gustave Doré fais le sortir de son chateau de la Misère pour entrer dans le castel doré sur tranche du succès

à toi, un vieux d'Hernani

Théophile Gautier

Fig. 109.—(Théophile Gautier.)

margins at right and left hand, and at the bottom of the page, make a white framework for the text of the letter, which shows up the writing. Arrangement of this kind causes a certain pleasure, at least, to the eye of a graphologist, greater than the satisfaction produced by the sight of well-arranged letterpress, because there is a life and individuality about written signs that are wanting in printed matter. What pleases the eye is not the larger or smaller amount of white margin left on each side of

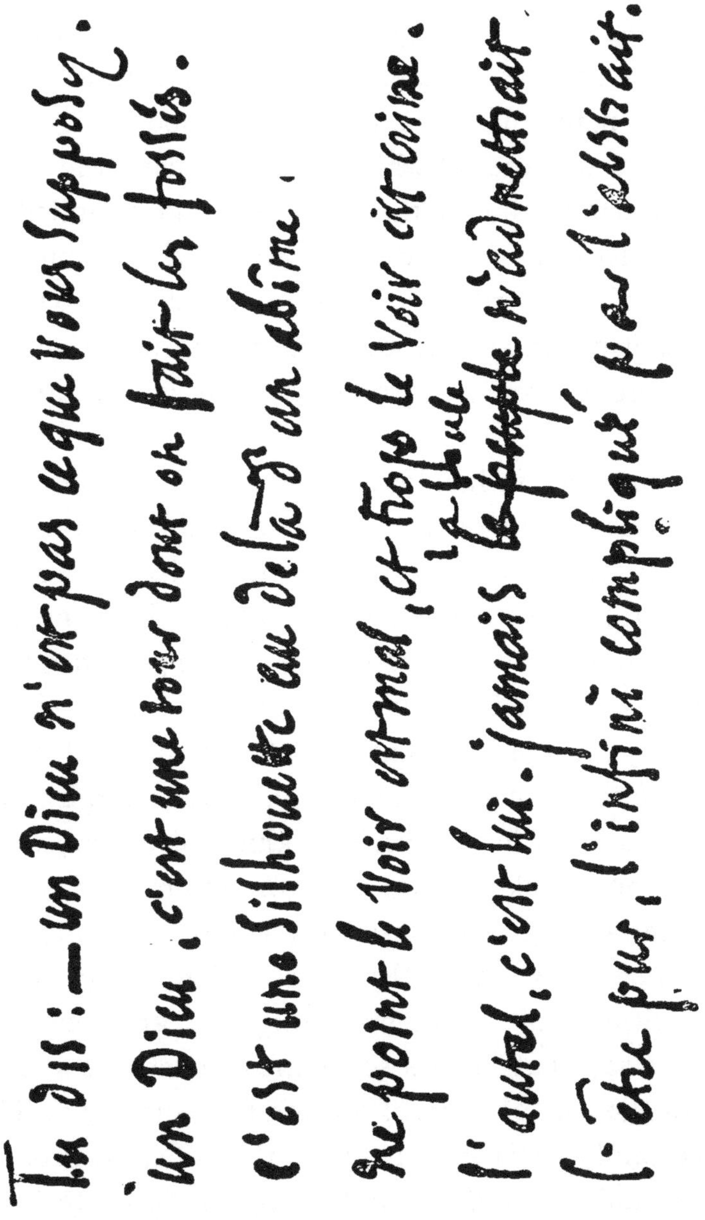
Tu dis : — un Dieu n'est pas ce que vous supposez.
Un Dieu, c'est une tour dont on fait les fossés.
C'est une silhouette au delà d'un abîme.
Ne point le voir est mal, et trop le voir est crime.
L'autel, c'est lui. Jamais n'admettrait
L'être pur, l'infini compliqué par l'abstrait.

Fig. 110.

the writing, but the harmony that exists between all the parts ; for large margins, especially on the right hand,

and disproportionate space between the date and the commencement of the letter, are as inharmonious to the eye as the opposite defects.

We have here (*fig.* 109) a letter written by Théophile Gautier, who was certainly a very accomplished and *distingué* man. He has turned to good account the little scrap of paper of which he made use; the spaces are well arranged, and the clearness and simplicity of the handwriting are well shown. Now, must we not say of the writers of specimens 96 and 97, that their writing shows an obscure mind, and that they are unable to properly appreciate what is beautiful and delicate.

The presence in handwriting of letters of typographical form is a sign of art. They contain several of the elements which we have mentioned: clearness, simplicity, regularity, symmetry (fig. 110). Thus no more explanation is needed to justify the importance which we have attributed to this description of written signs.

This typographical form is met with in small as well as in capital letters. We have compared a large number of the handwritings of various kinds of artists, and we have been struck by the rarity of letters so formed in the handwritings of musicians, composers, singers or instrumentalists, and by their frequency in the handwritings of architects, designers, and engravers. May we say that letters so shaped constitute a special sign of the love of form, of outline, for example? There are certainly variations between the different groups of artists, and this one just noted appears to us to be one of them. Yet a general rule has its exceptions. We come across the handwritings of very able designers which are without these letters of typographical form. With such men, their love of form is shown by other signs, and in this, as in other cases, we must use our general principles of graphologic analysis. There may even be shown graphologic signs *contrary* to the love

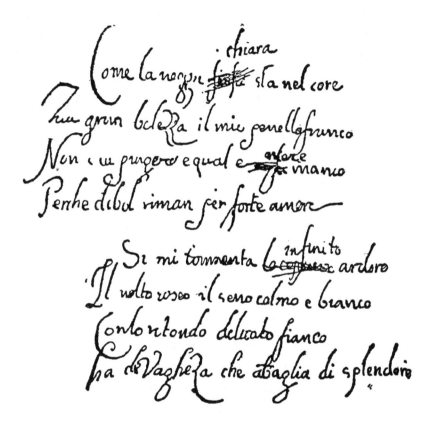

Fig. 111.—Raphaël.

of form : but the absence of any special sign does not authorize the assumption of the opposite quality, because we may still find the specified trait by the already explained method of resultants.

If we go to the Louvre and look at the signatures at the bottom of the pictures we shall see that they nearly all contain several letters of typographical form, in some cases the entire signature is so written.

Notice these lines written by Raphaël (fig. 111) in which the typographical form of letter is almost exclusively used.

There are some authors who have the taste for form well developed, and who, without being designers, frequently employ this form of letter. Théophile Gautier is one such (fig. 109) ; Töpffer and Arséne Houssaye, who are both graceful writers and skilful

Fig. 112.—Chardin.

draughtsmen, modify by their curved strokes of the pen, the typographical letters which they freely use.

The curve is a *compound* æsthetic sign of the highest order. Its graphologic characteristics are : gentleness and imagination, elements of grace. The association of the curve with the straight line much augments the value of the latter. Angular handwriting is never very graceful[1] (fig. 112) ; neither is handwrit-

---

[1] We give as an example the signature of Chardin, the celebrated traveller of the last century. He would certainly not be denied the trait of severity which is shown by very angular handwriting. He it was who wrote to his brother : "Again, my dear brother and friend, do I send my son into your charge ; do not hesitate to make him suffer and to put him to do menial and painful things if it be necessary to thus get rid of his idleness. I would sooner see my children dead than mean-spirited and lacking virtue."

ing graceful which is exclusively composed of curves (fig. 113) ; but notice a specimen where the curve and the straight line are in about equal proportion (fig. 87) (*a*). What harmony this combination gives to the handwriting ! Without noting the special signs that this specimen contains, we feel that it is not the handwriting of a fool nor of an evil person ; it allows us to see a pleasant nature.

The capital letters E, F, and L lend themselves specially to the formation of graceful and artistic curves.

Besides the primary and the compound indications of which we have just now written, there are signs which have a very close connection with art, so much so that they are concomitant with artistic feeling. *Imagination, sensibility,* and *intellectual capacity,* are most surely factors of art. It is imagination (large movements of the pen) which excites the creative genius of poets, painters, and composers ; it is their sensibility (sloping handwriting) which urges them to produce works which provoke emotion ; it is intellectual capacity (letters separated

Fig. 113.—G. Doré.

and placed side by side) which is their guide in seeking
the required effect. Therefore we frequently find
these graphologic signs in the handwriting of men who
follow art.

We notice inclined handwriting more often among
great dramatic artists than among painters, and the
latter show more imagination than poets. Painters
have to be constantly forming a mental picture of lines
and colours in order to revive their impressions, whilst
the poet ought rather to stimulate his intuition, and to

Fig. 114.

exercise intellectual capacity in composing his verse
and in considering its mental effect.

Activity is also one of the conditions of art, and is
therefore one of the signs which is revealed by the
handwriting. We give as an example a specimen by
Sir Frederick Leighton, P.R.A. (fig. 114).

Any work to which its author has not imparted a
certain life, will not hold the attention and will fail to
charm. A picture, a statue, or an opera, ought to be
definitely expressive of something, it ought to show a
certain activity. Thus a laboured and slow handwriting

even with indications of art is not that of a true artist. At the most it may belong to a savant who takes up art as a hobby, or to a designer of steam engines.

We perceive from the foregoing re-marks that the signs of art are very different, and that to ascertain its pre-sence in handwrit-ing is not so easy as some graphologic writers have sup-posed. In the hand-writing of Gounod (fig. 115) there are many indications of art; but the author [1] of *Pré-aux-Cleres* and of *Zampa* also possessed genius, but his handwriting (fig. 116) is far from resembling that of Gounod. We may even go farther, and say that by viewing this speci-men (fig. 116) no graphologist would deduce any artistic talent whatever.

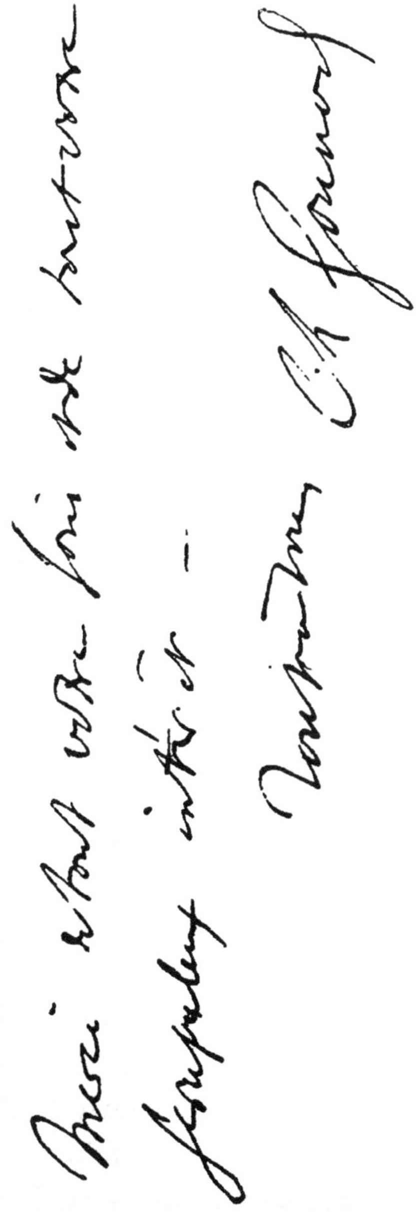

Fig. 115.—Gounod.

[1] Hérold.

The great Rubens had a splendid handwriting (fig. 117) ; all the signs of art are there prominent, as is also the case in that of Raphaël (fig. 111). But ·look at this letter by Léopold Robert (fig. 118), a Swiss painter of real talent. We see there much activity, ardour, and a quick sensibility ; but we do not see the graceful curves of typographical form that are characteristic of artistic ability.

Graphology, viewed as affording indications of art faculty, seems to us to show rather the general aptitude of a writer than the particular genus of his talent, and this limitation appears proper if we consider that the expression of art may run into many and various channels. We shall see this better by comparing the handwritings of very different artists. As an instance, Paul Baudry, who is a great painter (fig. 119), writes similarly to Alfred de Musset, the eminent author (fig. 120).

Fig. 116.—Herold.

Graphology as a study is sufficiently stable to allow of criticism and of the limits of its power being defined. In this chapter we have been thus occupied :

the art faculty is a resultant characteristic which is now and then very difficult to see in a handwriting, *if sensibility be the chief factor of that resultant.* Viewing the handwriting of Rachel (fig. 121), we can detail the traits of her character, state

[Fig. 117.—Rubens.

Fig. 118.—Léopold Robert.

that she was intelligent and very sensitive, with but little m ental culture ; but what is there in this specimen to tell us that Rachel was the greatest tragedienne of our age ? Her sensitive and impressionable nature coupled with the *timbre* of her voice, were probably the chief causes of her power. Now handwriting does not give us information about the voice, and the inclination or slope of this

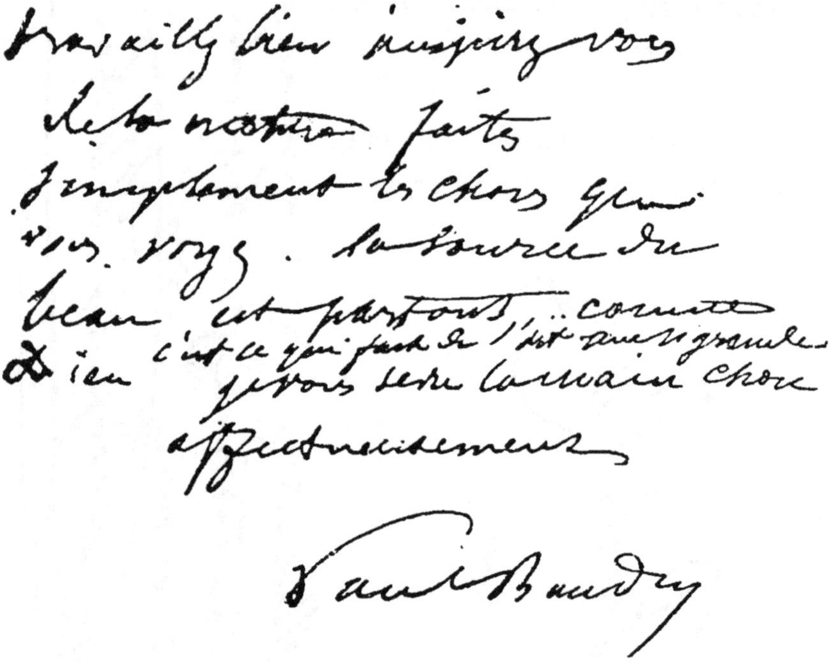
travaillez bien toujours voyez
de la nature faites
simplement les choses que
vous voyez. la source du
beau est partout... comme
Dieu c'est ce qui fait de l'art une si grande
je vous serre la main chose
affectueusement
Paul Baudry

Fig. 119.—Paul Baudry.

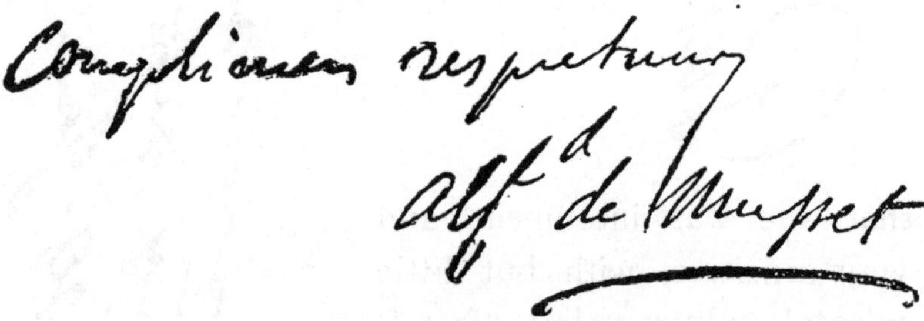
Compliments respectueux
alf de Musset

Fig. 120.—Alfred de Musset.

handwriting (fig. 121), tells us of only one of the sources of Rachel's talent, and we are here necessarily left in the dark as to the nature of the talent itself.

In ending this chapter we may say that certain difficulties which now lie in our way may possibly be removed in the future. We mean as regards the graphologic analysis of specific arts. What is wanted perhaps is the determination of the psychological conditions causing the evolution of the various orders of artistic talent. The brain of the sculptor works differ-

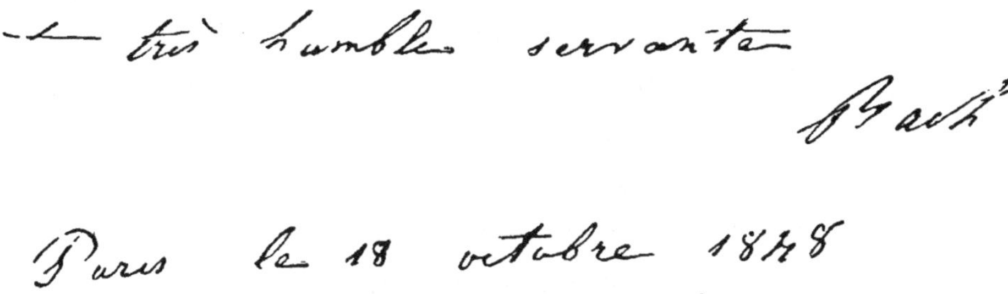
— très humble servante
Rachel
Paris le 18 octobre 1848

Fig. 121.—Rachel.

ently from that of the painter; the art of the singer is not made up of the same factors as that of the comedian. Delicate and difficult study of their respective psychological conditions might reveal the causes, and possibly the outward manifestation by means of written gesture, of these very different forms of artistic talent.

THE HANDWRITING OF THE SICK.

PERSONAL experience has probably caused most of our readers to notice that handwriting is influenced by various external phenomena which affect us. "*Please excuse this wretched scrawl, but my hands are so cold I can scarcely write*"—is a sufficiently familiar case in point. It needs but small powers of observation even for those unaware of the existence of graphologic study, to notice the agitation which is imparted to the handwriting when it is produced in a state of strong excitement or emotion, such as joy, grief, indignation or anger. Now illness also modifies our organism, profoundly in some cases, and it would indeed be surprising if it did not also affect or change our handwriting.

Very often the mere appearance of a sick person will put the medical diagnoser upon the right track even if there be no very obvious symptoms shown ; there are various unmistakable pathologic manifestations. We think that by examining the handwriting it is quite possible to see there also, some of these outward expressions of pathologic condition ; therefore we proceed to study this new order of facts with the hope that such research may lead to the discovery of useful signs for diagnostic purposes, or for throwing fresh light upon the condition of sick persons.

Here again it is the study of gesture which will serve as our guide.

Sportsmen know well that weariness is soon felt when no game is about; but after fair sport, a man who may just before have been lagging behind, becomes light of foot and carries his gun easily. The case is somewhat analogous when we have good news to announce. A joyful man does not feel the weight of a burden, and the pleasure which stimulates his organism as a whole, also raises the lines of his writing—gives them an ascendant direction.

Sadness, trouble, weariness, and all conditions which lower the vital forces, also render effort difficult and action laboured, even that of the pen, and under such circumstances the lines of writing will scarcely maintain a horizontal position across the page. Given a greater degree of lowered vitality, the lines will descend, and this handwriting is typical of discouraged and wearied men and of those lacking energy and power.

These phenomena, which have meaning in them for the graphologist, may be accidental or temporary, as in some of the cases just alluded to, but they may also reflect the habitual state of the writer.

At our University the professors announce the resumption of their classes by small written placards: their handwriting is then ascendant. They think while writing these notices of again meeting their students; they perhaps call to mind the applause which usually awaits them; they picture the activity of the days following the formal re-opening. But, one month later two little documents are added to the preceding notices; the handwriting of both of these is descendent. Two professors who are ill announce that they will not lecture until further notice.

The majority of diseases have a depressing effect upon our organism, and with a few rare exceptions, even those affections which are characterized by exaggerated nervous activity, show in the written tracing not the ascendant sign of power and ardour, but rather the disorder of an abnormal excitement.

Here are some words written upon a visiting card (*fig.* 122).

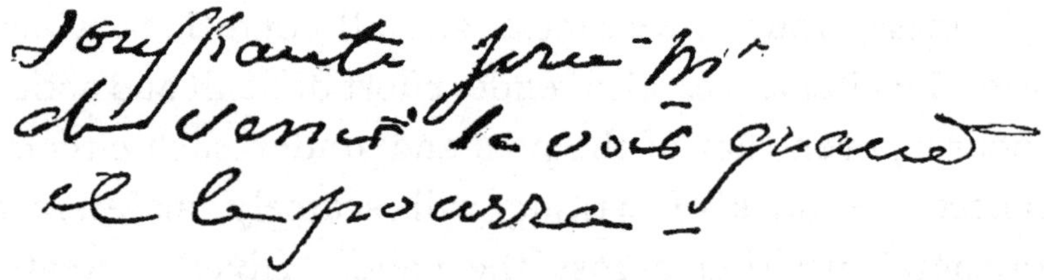

Fig. 122.—*souffrante prie Mr.*
de venir la voir quand
il le pourra.

This is a message such as physicians receive every day.   A slight examination of this writing shows some amount of excitement.   The dots are represented by little dashes placed considerably in advance of the small *i;* the upper part of the *d* in "*quand*" ends with a hasty stroke of the pen ; the letters of the second word ("*prie*") diminish in height ; the last word ("*pourra*") on the contrary grows larger towards its end.   The lines of the handwriting descend slightly.   Mme. X's doctor at once went to see her.   He found her restless and agitated, but not in any serious condition.   On the morning of the following day a second written message was brought to him (*fig.* 123): "*Mme. X. soùffre beaucoup plus, elle a eu la fièvre cette nuit et prie le Dr. de venir la revoir."*

The agitation of the sick person is here very noticeable. The words *"fièvre," " nuit," "prie,"* are illegible; the lines of the writing are serpentine, wavy in direction. The handwriting is much altered; but, although it was written during an attack of fever, it nevertheless descends.

The dreadful toothache which over-excites the nervous system also produces similar results. A sick-headache on the other hand is a particularly depressing illness, and shows us analogous signs to those we shall

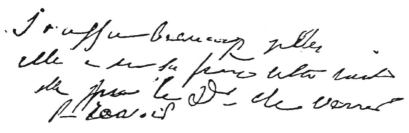

Fig. 123.

point out in cerebral congestion, or in the second period of general paralysis. These points being ascertained, let us see if handwriting can show us more than the expression of inordinate excitement, or of more or less marked depression, let us see whether it can furnish any indications of the nature of the illness or of its progress.

To begin with, we will state that we are not warranted in our observation of the handwriting of sick persons, in seeking by analogy some particular sign special to each malady. The graphologic sign of gastralgia no more exists than that of rheumatism. Pathologic

condition shows itself by graphic modifications, which
are all borrowed from those which relate to the
personality. If these modifications be characteristic,
and if they present themselves regularly in relation to a
given pathologic condition, it will at least be clear to us
that the ordinary signs in the handwriting of sick
persons ought to be considered, when we are engaged
upon a psychological study of a handwriting in respect
of which we possess no extraneous information.

The comparison of a page written prior to the illness
with one produced when the writer is suffering from
the malady, allows us to judge in most cases of the
direction in which the organism is thrown out of gear.
It is unnecessary to enlarge upon the importance of
such a comparison ; it is indispensable in order to see
the modifications caused by the illness in physical and
mental force, and to ascertain how far the nervous
system has been affected.

The confused condition characterized by a certain
disturbance of the faculties, or by a lack of bodily and
mental energy, which is termed apoplectic, whether it
be caused by troubles of the circulation, intoxication by
alcohol or tobacco, is one of those conditions which are
the most clearly shown to us by the handwriting. The
lines in this state are descendent, but not in the way we
have noted in our study of the handwriting of men
without ardour, without power or merely discouraged,
the lines have a drop so marked that we see it comes no
longer from merely a lack of energy, but from a certain
affection of the whole body which is unable to support
itself. We can observe this sign in the handwriting of
aged, drowsy, very sedentary persons, whose feet drag

as they walk.   This is also the handwriting of alcoholic subjects (*fig.* 124).

Liver complaints have afforded data for the following observation : time after time the handwriting was descendent and presented characteristics notified as belonging to bilious temperaments, viz., handwriting which is concentrated (non-expansive), turning back upon itself, sparing and without flourishes, and rarely much inclined to the right hand.   These signs constitute a conjectural resultant, because the influences of the temperament can be extracted from them ; but in a case of illness they might be usefully employed to aid diagnosis—although all bilious persons in whom the disease is not definite may not be suffering from liver complaint.

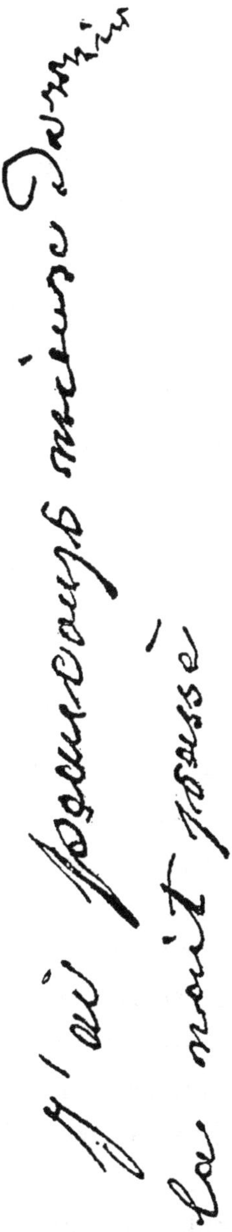

Out of forty-eight handwritings of sufferers from tuberculosis, forty-one were descendent, the others being horizontal across the page. We do not see our way to report any other fact.   And we have been similarly restricted in a rather important number of specimens relating to diseases of the stomach, to rheumatics and to diabetic patients; descending handwriting is the only

Fig. 124.—The handwriting of an alcoholic subject.

steady expression which we are able to connect with the condition of the writers.

The specimens of handwriting which served as our data were three-fourths of them letters addressed to medical men. In writing them the sick person was aware of illness, and we ought to take note of this fact, so as not to lay too much stress upon the descendent handwriting, for uneasiness is sufficient to produce this trait.

Examination of seventeen specimens of heart disease showed us fourteen cases of descending handwriting, two when it was horizontal, and one where it ascended upon the paper. This last belonged to a very intelligent

Fig. 125.—Fractured letters: anxiety.

man, gifted with much good taste. We have noticed several cases where a keen intellect acts as a preventive of descending handwriting.

Heart complaints are very numerous in their forms, lesions, and symptons; they certainly do not reveal themselves by any generic sign, but by a sign corresponding to a special reaction of the disease upon the organism. Twelve cases out of seventeen showed us an indication to which M. Hermite has given the meaning of trouble, of non-material sorrow. This sign is a break, a slight interruption in the up and down strokes, especially in the loops of the letters (*fig.* 125).

M. Hermite says, " These long, thin broken strokes of

the pen have always appeared to me analogous to the
slender bonds, but bonds so powerful over the heart,
threads so dear to poets and to eastern writers. They
break, as I think, when the bonds of affection are broken."[1]
This is indeed a mysterious idea of the analogy of forms.
The determination of the proper meaning of this sign in
the handwriting of persons suffering from heart disease,
should rather lead us to study the physiology of these
diseases in order to find a rational interpretation, instead
of indulging in the poetical imaginings of M. Hermite.
This fracture constitutes a point of suspension in the
tracing of the strokes by the pen ; it is in fact a momentary stoppage in the nervous functions, a sort of
very slight *absence* of the writer.   It is possible that the
condition of the person suffering from heart disease, by
necessitating the suppression of violent movement, and
by causing the writer to adopt an easy and precau-
tionary mode of outward expression, may be the cause
of this fracture in the pen-strokes ; for when we write
without putting much stress upon the pen, it is often
the case that at the outline of the curve of up and down
loops of letters, the pen leaves the paper for an instant.
This fracture of the letters may be then a sign of anxious
gesture, sufficiently characteristic of some diseases of
the heart.   It is noticed most frequently in cases of
palpitation, which malady causes a sort of pang, and a
disturbance in the irrigation of the brain and in the
action of the muscles.

Several of the handwritings that we have examined in
connection with affections of the heart were whimsically
punctuated.   In one the dots over the *i* were placed

[1] *journal, La Graphologie,* 15th September, 1883.

very low down and at (about) $\frac{1}{12}$th of an inch at the side
of the letter ; in two others, the commas were replaced
by mere dots ; and in another there were little super-
fluous points placed beween various words.

We owe the explanation of this singular trait
in handwriting to the sagacity of Dr. Paul Helot.
Having observed this sign in the letters of patients
with pulmonary disease, or with obesity, he wrote
to us : " Notice a short-breathed man upon a stair-

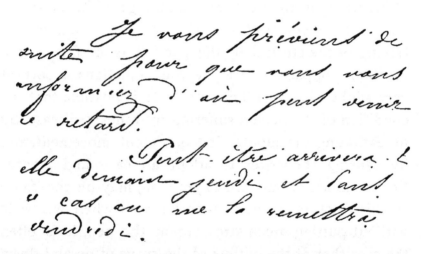

Fig. 126.—Little dots or points placed where they are not needed:
respiratory trouble.

case; he goes up a few steps, stops and supports
himself upon something, the handrail for example. He
starts off again only to rest afresh, and his power does
not match his courage, his foot tries to go ahead and
very likely stumbles close to the place where properly
it should alight safely. In the act of writing, such a man
instinctively rests himself by resting his pen upon the
paper, as he would also do with a stick when walking.
This is, I think, why you have come across these abnor-

mal points or dots instead of the comma.   The presence
of this sign in the handwriting of cardiacs is probably
also due to shortness of breath.   In fact, these dots and
little dashes scattered about the writing, and in the
neighbourhood of the bars of the *t*, or near the *d*, being
usually close to a pen-stroke that causes a certain effort,
tell us of *respiratory trouble* (*figs.* 126 and 127).   The
heavier dots appear to be caused by the affection of

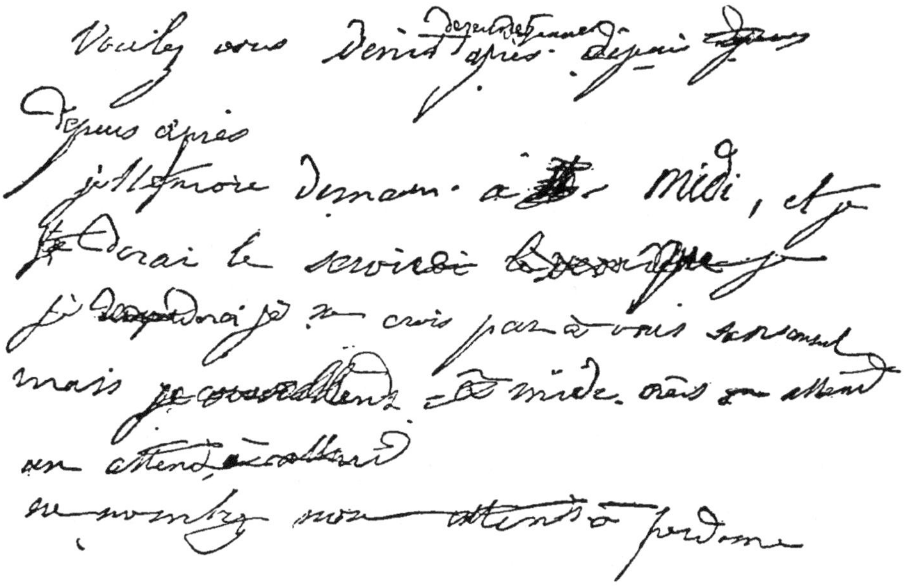

Fig. 127.—The handwriting of a woman suffering from aphasia.

obesity, and the little dashes and the very fine dots belong
to asthmatics."

" We have also noticed abnormal dots placed at the
commencement of phrases or words ; these do not
concern pathology, but denote hesitation, laboured
conception, reflection."

Aphasia, loss of power of accurate expression, is
characterized by a trouble of speech.   The intellect is

usually intact.   The person so affected may perhaps
speak, but he no longer says what he wishes to say.
Sometimes it is an unsuitable word which takes the place
of the right one, sometimes a word or a series of words,
always the same, is uttered, whatever may be the thought
that the patient may wish to express.   The handwriting
is modified similarly to the speech; indeed it often reveals
aphasia before we have been able to observe this affection
in the spoken language.   In other cases there are disturbances in the handwriting analogous to those caused
by aphasia, which are independent of disturbance in the
speech.   Marcé observed this as far back as 1856.[1]

More recently, cases of aphasia in the handwriting
have been reported, when there was no loss of power of
expression as regards speech ; and Ogle [2] in 1867 created
the word *agraphia* to specially denote the loss of power
of expression by means of writing.

The signs of agraphia are well known to doctors.
They occur with a very varied intensity.   Sometimes
the patient can trace only the letters, sometimes there
are incoherent words.   We have seen a woman who
said *armchair* for *table, bookcase* instead of *book*.   In her
handwriting there were no errors of this kind, but there
were frequent and unnecessary repetitions of words.

As illustrating a farther advanced stage, we can cite
the case of a young man who repeated at the commencement of each line the word which ended the one
preceding.

[1] Marcé. Biological Society, 1856. Memoir on some observations of pathological physiology, tending to prove the existence of
a co-ordinate principle of handwriting and its analogies with the
co-ordinate principle of speech.

[2] W. Ogle. *Aphasia and Agraphia.* St. George's Hospital
ports, 1867, vol. ii.

Bastian[1] speaks of a man partly insane and who wrote much. His letters were intelligible at first, then in place of some of the concluding letters of each word he would write *ffg*. Later on, the entire word was changed, and a reduplication of many of the consonants, added to the almost invariable termination by the letters *ndendd*, or at the least *endd*, became the most remarkable features of his manuscripts, which, while still voluminous, were absolutely unintelligible.

The same author mentions a still more curious case observed by Dr. Jackson. It was in connection with a woman who often made errors in speech, owing to loss of power of expression, and who called her children by names other than their own. But this was not very noticeable and might have passed unobserved if her friends had not been solicitous about her. When asked to write her name, she would write *Suunil Siclaa Satreni*, which had no resemblance to her own name either in sound or in mode of spelling. Her address she indicated by *suner nut ts mer tinn-lain*. And in all her autographs there was an assemblage of letters quite destitute of any meaning, remarkable only for the frequent repetition of small groups of letters. At this stage of the disease, agraphia evidently concerns the physician rather than the graphologist.

In our example (*fig.* 127) the sick person suffers from a heart affection which modifies the irrigation of the brain to such a degree, that at times she has attacks of aphasia and loses all or most of her power of expression.

---

[1] *The Brain as an Organ of Mind* (p. 255), by H. Charlton Bastian, M.D. International Scientific Series. Kegan Paul, Trench, Trübner & Co.

The lines reproduced here were written during one of these crises. We see there, not only repetitions of certain words and incoherent words, but also the signs of shortness of breath (dots and little dashes scattered about), and a trembling movement of the pen.

We have frequently noticed temporary agraphia following an excess of work, and also after an abuse of pleasures. Concurrently with a slight perplexity or derangement in the speech, forgetfulness of words or

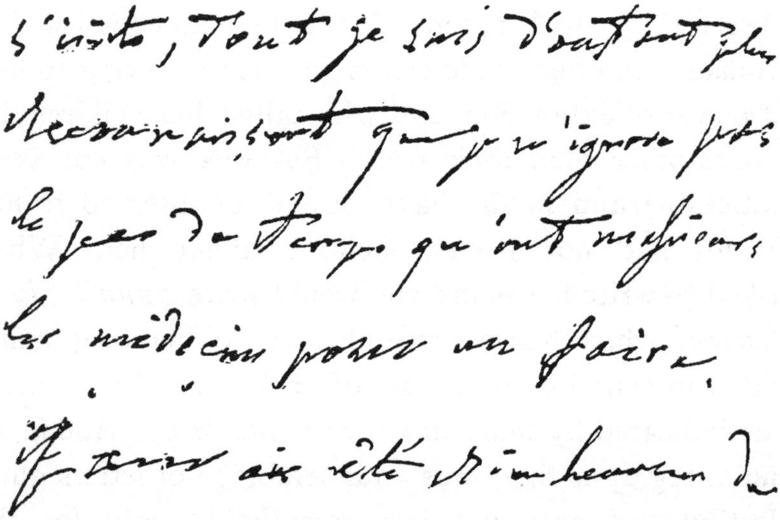

Fig. 128.—The handwriting of a man suffering from writer's cramp.

stammering, the cleanness of the pen-strokes, and the precision of their tracing are disturbed by corrections or erasures ; words are either needlessly reiterated or at least repeated at every opportunity—the writer's command of language having been decreased owing to a partial loss of memory. These phenomena cease to exist as soon as the writer recovers from his state of exhaustion.

Nervous diseases affect the handwriting considerably,

and the attention of physicians has often been directed to this matter, but apart from a little book by Dr. Erlenmayer,[1] there is no connected work upon this subject. Moreover, Dr. Erlenmayer treats the question from a point of view entirely different from our own.

Writer's cramp appears to show itself in handwriting by descendent lines and by letters traced with a trembling movement (*fig.* 128). When this malady is pronounced, the handwriting cannot be confused with that of persons whom age has rendered infirm; in the latter case the handwriting is tremulous, but it is regular in form, direction, etc., while in the former case it is particularly irregular. A legible word will be followed by one almost undecipherable, most of the letters forming it being represented by a shapeless horizontal stroke of the pen. Writer's cramp is not, properly speaking, an illness, although we deal with it in this chapter. It is an inaptitude of one or more muscles of the hand to work accurately in the production of handwriting.

Dr. Hammond has described writer's cramp particularly well.[2] He says that the first symptom usually noticed is a sensation of fatigue in the muscles which have worked together during the necessary movements. "The patient endeavours to get rid of his sensations of fatigue by grasping more firmly the pen or the graver, or by making a strong mental effort to regulate the muscular contractions which are concerned in the performance of these actions, that is to say, he trys to control the movements of the hand which holds the pen.

[1] *Physiologie und Pathologie. Handschrift durch* Dr. Erlenmeyer.

[2] *A treatise upon the maladies of the nervous system.* By W. Hammond.

But he only increases his difficulties, for fatigue and worry being augmented, the muscles become weak, and moreover, irregular contractions supervening, his handwriting is rendered more or less illegible, his execution more or less defective and imperfect. If he should persevere in his attempts, he will soon arrive at a phase of the malady where it will be impossible for him to direct the pen according to his intentions, and where automatic actions, which are of great importance in handwriting, will also be manifestly diminished."

" For a certain time he will write better when his mind does not pay attention to the formation of each letter, thus, so to say, allowing his muscles to look after themselves. He will, however, constantly feel the necessity for mental effort, and this effort invariably augments the trouble to such a degree that at last, when he trys to write, the pen, driven by the muscles of the fingers, executes such incoherent movements that they have no connection with the words he endeavours to trace on the paper. A paroxysm results, which lasts as long as the invalid persists in his attempts to write. When he puts down the pen, the spasm ceases, and he can perform any other action with his fingers without bringing it on afresh." [1]

It has been necessary to point out the modifications caused in handwriting by writer's cramp, because they might lead to error in the analysis of character unless the indications of this affection be known.

Paralysis agitans is a nervous disease characterized mainly by tremors of the limbs; in connection with this

---

[1] The two preceding paragraphs are not a literal transcript: they are translated from the French text.

malady we find the descendent lines of the handwriting of paralytics, and a tremulousness which varies with the intensity of the disease (*fig.* 129). We have no doubt that a profound study of this question would show the characteristic differences of the various kinds of tremulousness due to other causes, such for example as the forms of intoxication, etc.

Chorea, or St. Vitus's Dance, which has been termed "insanity of the muscles," is a disease which handwriting discloses in a remarkable manner. We do not see here the trembling that marks paralysis agitans, but on the contrary, the pen-strokes are vigorous, and are

Fig. 129.—Modifications produced in handwriting by paralysis agitans.

violently projected in a direction which is frequently different from that necessitated by a normal formation of the letters (*fig.* 130). The badly-managed pen chafes or tears the paper, and splutters the ink on every side. At a more advanced stage the patient will use a pencil instead of a pen, while, when this malady is confirmed, the sufferer will entirely cease to write.

We have studied numerous handwritings of hysterical persons. Several graphologists have searched for the written characteristic of hysteria, and, as might be expected, have lost their way. Under this term are included so many and such complex conditions that no sign can be held to specially relate to it.

P

Hysteria is convulsive or non-convulsive. Those who suffer from more or less pronounced crises of the disease do not write during the convulsive state; all that

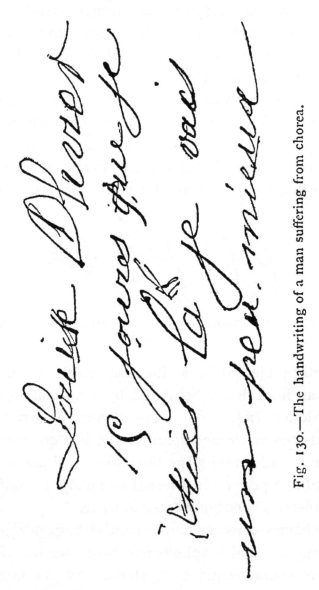

Fig. 130.—The handwriting of a man suffering from chorea.

could be noticed in their handwriting at other times would be various general tendencies, a certain tension, a sort of nervous excitement, showing the possibility of an attack ; and, the crisis being over, a relaxation would be perceptible, indicating that calm had returned.

In non-convulsive hysteria are found various paralyses, contractions, disturbances of sensation. The circulation, the digestive functions, may undergo injury. At other times the intellectual or moral faculties may be perverted.

It is these latter features of the disease which handwriting shows more clearly by aid of our ordinary graphologic signs.

M. Barbier de Montault has pointed out nineteen signs which relate to hysteria ; but it appears easy, we think, to increase this number without arriving at more precision of results, and we are unable to agree with this writer, that it suffices to encounter some ten or twelve of these signs in a handwriting in order to diagnose hysteria. Physicians do not proceed thus in their diagnosis; it is not the number of symptoms that decides their opinion, but rather the special character that these symptoms assume. A hysterical person will sometimes present the appearance of being unduly sensitive, a liar, or extravagant in speech. His impressions as well as his expressions have a particular *cachet* of which the graphologic sign is wanting. It is probably to be found in one or in several combinations of signs, in which the nature of the elementary traits is of more importance than their number.

The examination of forty-five handwritings of hysterical persons revealed hysteria in twenty-four instances by the marked agitation and the abnormally large movements of the pen ; nine times by the same signs and by the presence of single letters of exaggerated size ; three times by abnormally large pen-movement coupled with the confusion of the writing ; five times by very sloping handwriting and by hasty pen-strokes ; and four times by a very sloping hand-writing and hastiness, which latter trait was evi-dently moderated or held in check.

This experience recalls to our memory some re-marks made to us at the prison of St. Lazare by a man who was well informed of Parisian events. Refer-ring to the prisoners, he said : " These poor wretches, many of whom suffer from disease in some form, show for the most part the signs of a very ill-regulated imagination and will : this is all that I have been able to see in their handwritings." We now give some autographs of hysterical persons. The first (*fig.* 131) is a good example of serpentine or undulating handwriting which is also agitated. The small *s* is higher than the other small letters (notice the *s* in the words *vous, expression, sympathie, recon-*

Fig. 131.—The handwriting of a female hysterical patient.

naissance). This is a sign of exaltation, or morbid excitation, which we again see in *fig.* 132. Here the abnormal imagination of the writer shows itself especially in the word *Monsieur.* The *bizarre* shape of the *M*, the marked upward prolongation of the *s*, and the disorderly and uncontrolled final stroke, put the exaltation of the writer beyond all doubt. " *Je ne vais guère mieux* " (*I am hardly any better*), writes the invalid. The *v* of the word *vais* and the *m* of *mieux* terminate by strokes which are raised much above the normal level. In writing that she has had *une forte crise* (*a bad attack*), her hysterical nature is again revealed ; these two words are formed of larger letters than the rest. It is a kind of unconscious underlining; if the invalid had wished to underline

Fig. 132.—The handwriting of a female hysterical patient.

her words, she would have done so with the exaggeration that is habitual with her. The handwriting of a hysterical male is given in *fig.* 133. The loops of the letters *g*, *z*, *l*, and *d*, at once tell us of the vivid imagination of the writer. The large movements of the pen, the confusion resulting therefrom, and the elevation of the *s* in the words *assurance* and *reconnaissance* are also signs of imagination and exaltation. The union of all these signs gives us a resultant of intensity, which enables us to say, at the least, that the writer is very far from a condition of mental equilibrium.

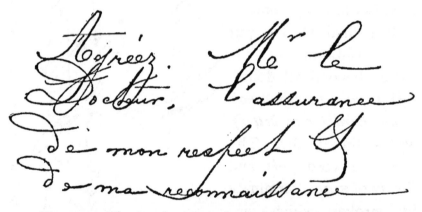

Fig. 133.—The handwriting of a male hysterical patient.

There are some lunatics whose appearance is so characteristic of their condition that no one would hesitate to class them as such. We also see autographs which are so extravagant, that each one appears to cry out that its writer is mad. In other cases it is more difficult to recognize mental derangement, and the most skilful specialists will have much hesitation in giving an opinion. And similarly there are some lunatics whose handwriting reveals no trace of their disorder.

The handwriting of *fig.* 134 is that of a person suffer-

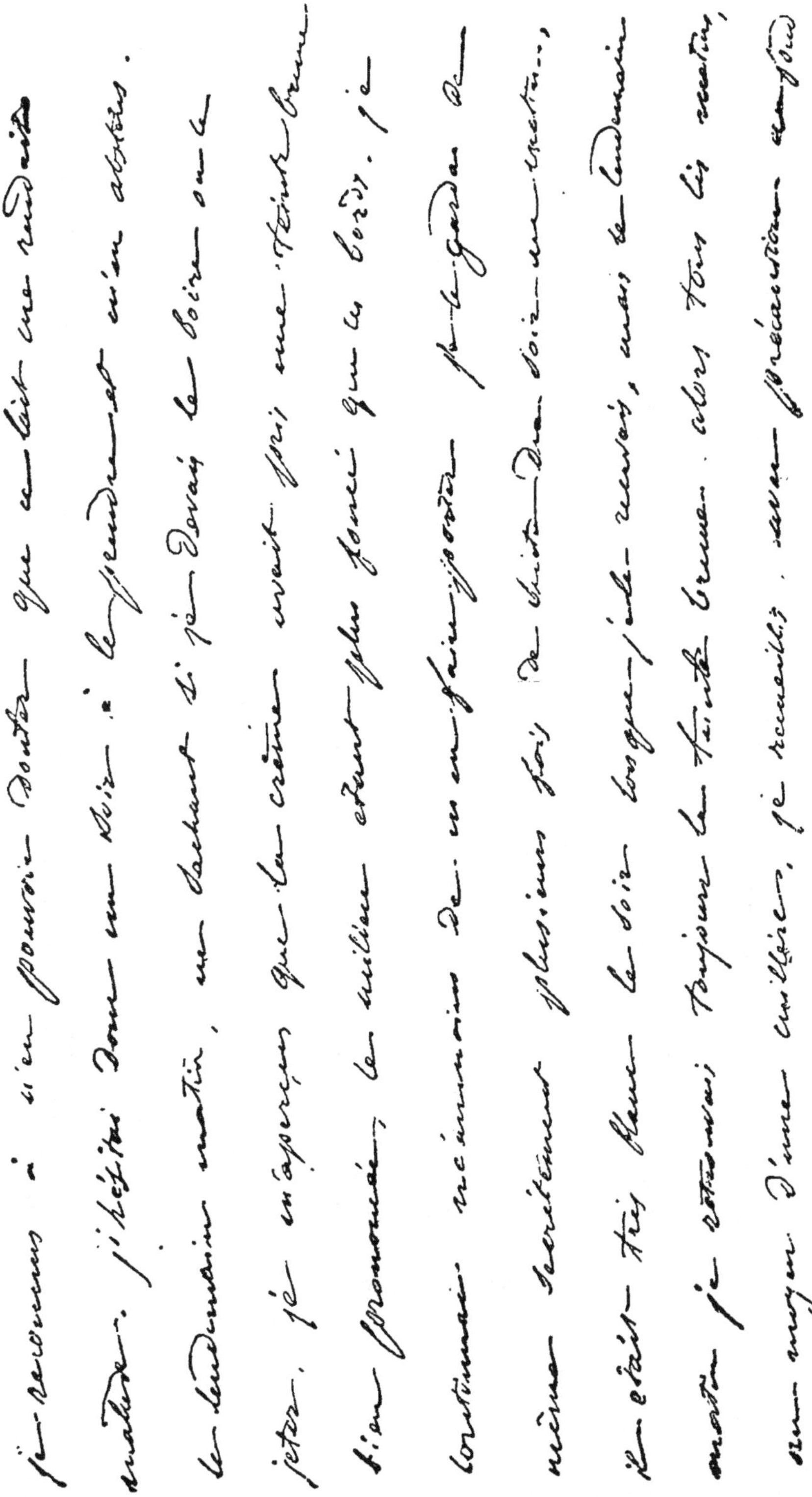

Fig. 134.—*See p.* 214.

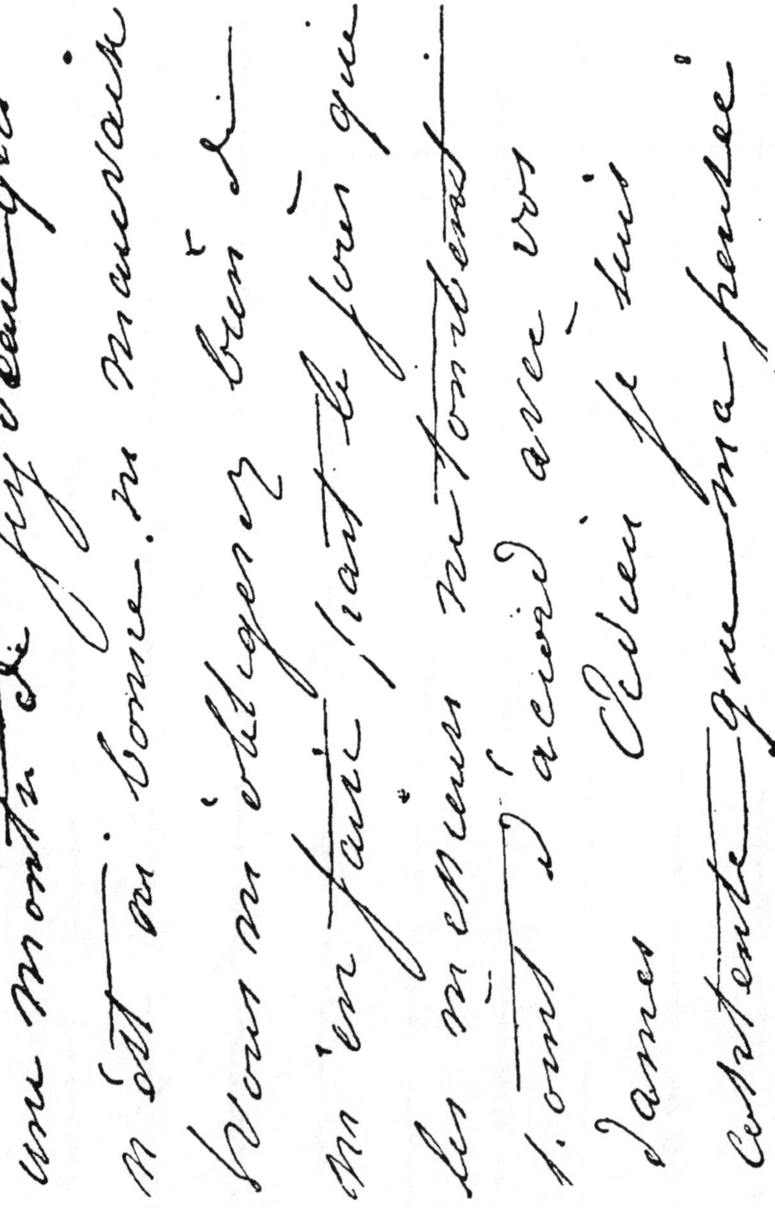

Fig. 135.—*See p.* 217.

ing from lypemania, with the delusion of persecution, and a suspicion of being poisoned.[1] It contains no sign of madness.

Here is part of a letter (*fig.* 135) written by a lady aged fifty-one:[2] the style of the whole letter clearly shows madness ; but we do not think that any graphologist would ascertain this fact by merely confining himself to observation of the handwriting itself.

We have another lunatic's handwriting in *fig.* 136. Gautrin is a lypemanic, and has hallucinations and believes he is persecuted.

He sometimes signs himself *B. Gautrin, a political victim.* A chief *employé* in a large house of business, a most intelligent man moreover, but very fanatical, he resigned his position in order to engage in politics. He undertook to disclose the mysteries of the secret police, the corruption of the Government, and especially that of the President of the Republic ; and he produced a series of violent pamphlets, of which he made written copies, distributing them himself among the shops of the quarter in which he lived.[3] Ultimately he was arrested on account of these writings, and from that time his fanaticism increased. His fear of being poisoned was as pronounced as his joy at being arrested, the joy being due to the fact that at last he could give expression to his opinions before the judges of his country. After medical examination he was placed in a lunatic asylum. Now Gautrin's con-

---

[1] Ambrose Tardieu. *Medico-legal studies of madness.* Facsimile VI.

[2] Idem. Facsimile IV.

[3] Idem. Case XVIII.

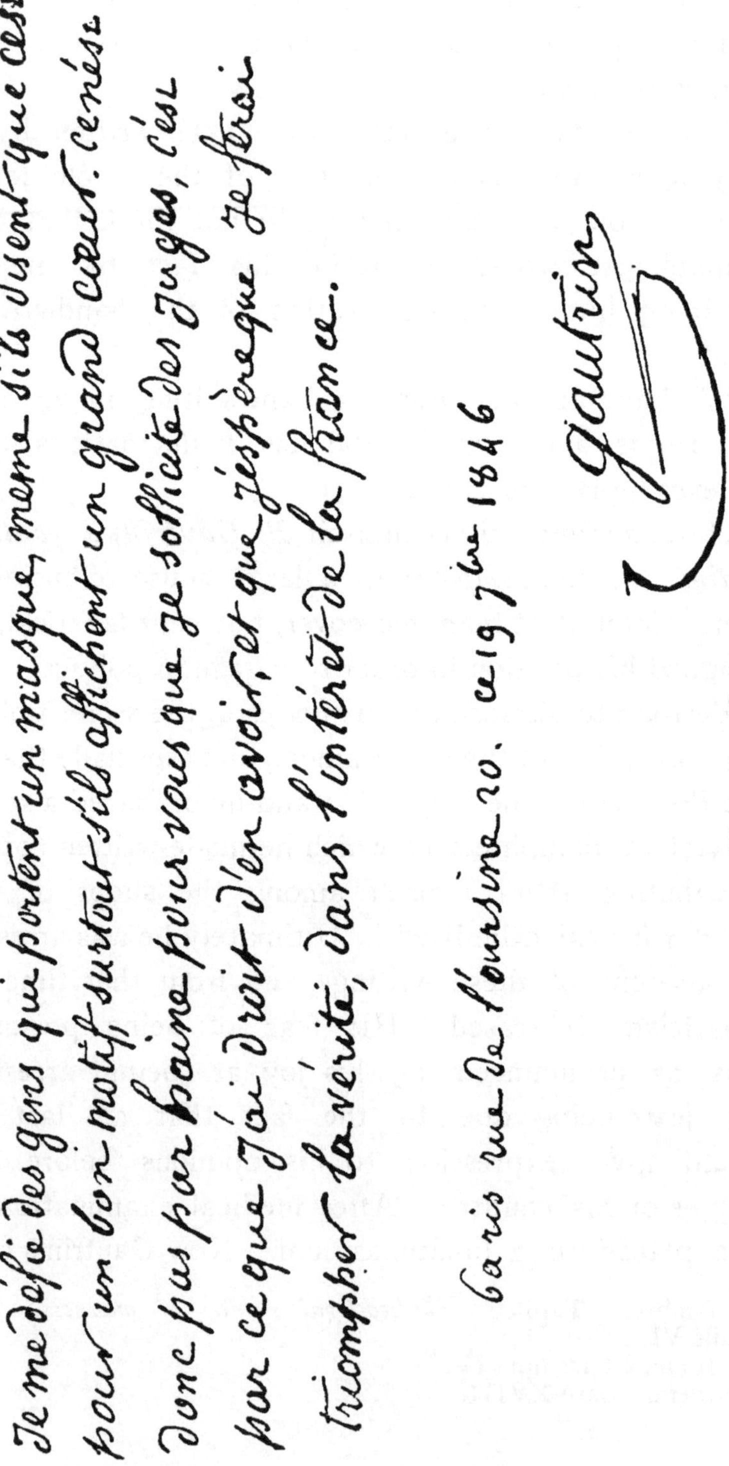

Je me défie des gens qui portent un masque, même s'ils disent que c'est pour un bon motif surtout s'ils affichent un grand cœur. Cenèse. Donc pas par haine pour vous que je sollicite des Juges, c'est par ce que j'ai droit d'en avoir, et que j'espère que je ferai triompher la vérité, dans l'intérêt de la France.

Paris rue de l'oursine 20. le 19 7bre 1846

Gautier

Fig. 136.—See p. 217.

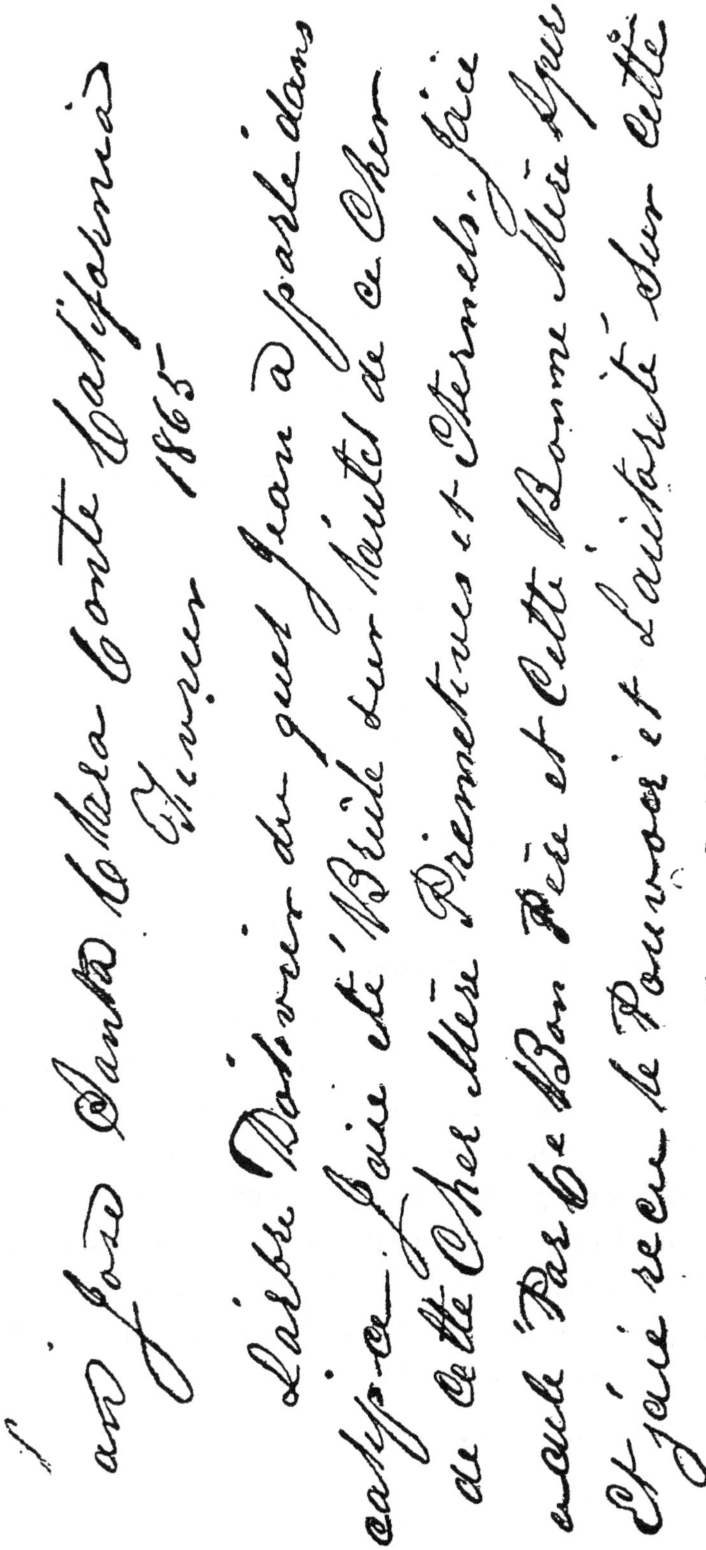

Fig. 137.—See p. 220.

dition is not apparent in his handwriting (*fig.* 136), which is very clear and shows the superior intelligence that we have mentioned.

In *fig.* 137, on the other hand, we easily recognize the handwriting of a lunatic.[1] The capital *S* of *San*, the numerous capital letters which are used instead of small letters, and the general agitation of the writing, entirely confirm the madness which characterizes the style of the letter and the condition of its writer.

We encounter the same signs in *fig.* 138. According to Dr. Tardieu,[2] the writer of this specimen is eccentric, insane. Many of the small letters are replaced by capitals ; we notice the words *triste ressource* which are characteristic of exaltation. The handwriting is thick, crowded together, very agitated ; there are frequent touchings-up, and omissions of letters that cannot be attributed to faulty spelling : thus in the letter of which this specimen forms part, we find written *renter* for *rentrer, trait* for *traître, tin* for *tient, troube* instead of *trouble.* This is quite characteristic of the handwriting of the insane ; but the preceding facts relating to *figs.* 134, 135, and 136 show that gesture, while keeping within normal limits of expression, may in some cases relate to ideas and conceptions which are insane ; they lead to the deduction that the absence of graphologic signs which may be connected with madness, is not in itself a sure proof of the existence of reason.

Dr. Tardieu says that the psychological indication of madness does not exist. " It would certainly be desirable to be able to define surely the character of mental alienation, and to fix a limit between madness

[1] Tardieu. Facsimile XIV.   [2] Tardieu. Case VII.

Fig. 138.—See p. 220.

and reason.   Several have tried to do this, but without
success ; and I think it useless for me to enter into a
purely technical discussion concerning the various kinds
of criteria proposed for this purpose, by sundry philo-
sophical and medical writers upon the subject.   The
psychological indication of madness is wanting ; it is
trouble thrown away to seek for it, and no useful purpose will be gained by these sterile efforts to discover
it."[1]

The same writer mentions later on some signs in the
handwriting indicative of madness, and Dr. Tardieu's
remarks confirm our own opinion : that all signs of
marked disorder in the handwriting, whether due to
exaggerated action of the pen, to omissions of letters
or words in the text, or to abnormal adjunctions to the
handwriting, are possible graphologic signs of a disordered mind.   Before we became acquainted with
Dr. Tardieu's investigations, we wrote in our *Traité
pratique de graphologie*[2] that the search for specific indications of madness is utopian.   " Graphology does not at
present allow of a precise definition of the signs characteristic of madness, and in our opinion it never will. . . .
We do not know where reason ends and madness
begins : nor is the starting-point of the latter the same
for all ; this is a matter of constitutional vigour as well as
of mental equilibrium. . . . All that graphology can do
as regards madness, is to ascertain the presence in handwriting of tendencies in that direction, and thus act as a
possible deterrent."

We can perceive a tendency to mental derangement

[1] Ambrose Tardieu.   *Medico-legal studies of madness*, p. 59.
[2] Page 176.

when there is a too-pronounced spontaneous excitement (the bars of the *t* rapid and very long), excessive

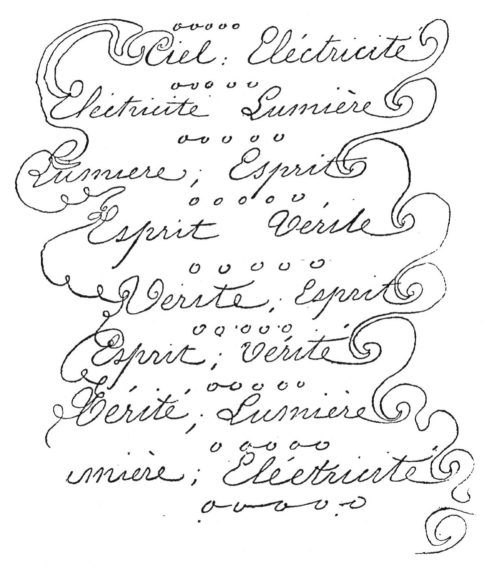

Fig. 139.—Extravagant and bizarre ornamentation : madness.

imagination (large pen movements, very tall capital
letters), or undue sensibility (very sloping handwriting),
because these traits of character are opposed to a state

of sound reason in thought and act, and madness comes from the entire or partial absence of reason. But there are four other signs which appear to be characteristic of madness and of exaltation : the small *s* or *r* being taller than the other small letters; the final strokes, especially that of the small *d*, ascending in a rounded coil; the use of capitals in place of small letters, and frequent underlining.

Moreover, superadded marks, bizarre ornamentation (*fig.* 139), are indicative of madness.

One of our illustrations (*fig.* 140) deserves some little attention.

Maillard, the writer of *fig.* 140, is a monomaniac with religious delusions. He is not God Himself, but he is God's prophet. He has been able during this state of frenzy to preach his religion in all parts of the world. At the present time he issues his benedictions from a lunatic asylum and promulgates his dogmas therein.

His personality, blending as it does with the excessive exaltation characteristic of his mental state, causes him to project to an abnormal height the first up-stroke of the *M* of his signature (*fig.* 140), which stretches upward through some eight lines of his own writing, while the second stroke of the *M* is normal in height. If we needed a demonstration of the sign indicating pride of comparing one's self with others (see p. 78), we could see it here without a doubt.

Looking more closely at this specimen, we find other signs of considerable weight, that confirm the opinion which the extravagance of the *M* causes in the mind of the graphologist.

The *R* of *Religion*, with its bizarre ornamentation,

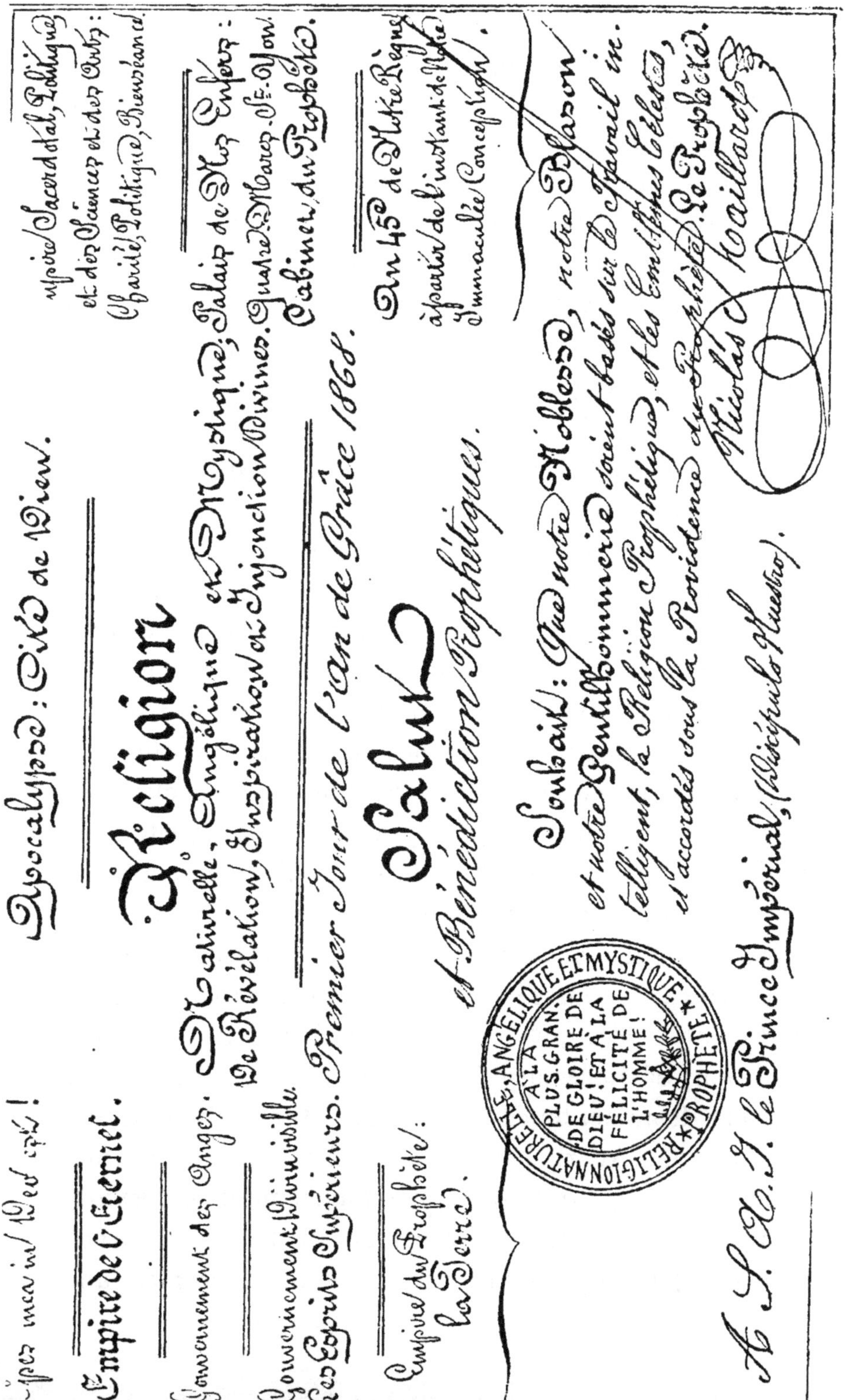

Fig. 140.—The handwriting of a monomaniac with religious delusions. See p. 224.

the multiplicity of capital letters, the diversity of the written characters employed, which might tax the technical skill of a writing-master, are all salient features leading to the diagnostic of madness ; and the delicate ascendant finals of many of the words show us the mystical tendency of the writer's mania.

The progress of general paralysis of the insane is fully set out in the handwriting of those who are thus afflicted. At first, during the period of excitation, the future victim of general paralysis, who is already in a diseased state, if not a partial paralytic, reveals the disturbance of his organism by the exaggeration in various downstrokes of the letters of his handwriting. Sometimes capital letters assume an abnormal importance, they are used instead of small letters, and then it is that the writer will talk about his imaginary good fortune, its power, and the pleasure of it ; then it is that he will relate personal exploits which exist only in his diseased mind. At this period the lines of the handwriting are sometimes ascendant. This trait, however, lacks constancy, as does his temporary vigour, and lassitude is indicated by failure in the control of the words and of the lines of his writing. When the period of excitation lapses and the disease sets in, the lines of writing assume a downward course; and there soon arrive physical and mental decay, characterized in handwriting by the omission of necessary letters from words, by words missing from sentences which may themselves be left unfinished. At the same time the lines of writing descend more, and their commencement is usually straighter than their end, which is apt to take a curved direction ; the letters are very imperfectly formed and look broken up into pieces; in some cases they are indecipherable, unduly large, or so tiny that a magnifying glass is needed to recognize them.

The mind being now more disordered, we find quite

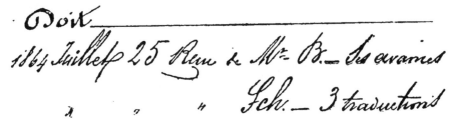

Fig. 141.—The six specimens, 141 to 146, show the gradual alteration in the handwriting of a man attacked by locomotor ataxy. Fig. 141 gives the normal handwriting of the patient in 1864. (*See p.* 230.)

inappropriate words written in place of those intended. A person afflicted with general paralysis wrote thus on his card to a friend who had just lost a parent, "*congratulations sympatitique*" (sympathetic congratula-

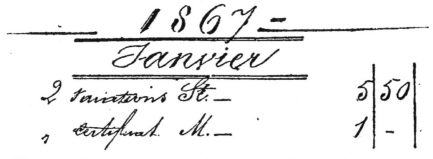

Fig. 142.—Commencement of the alteration in 1867. See Fig. 141.

tions), two words only, but one of which (*congratulations* was, of course, just the opposite to his intention, while the other had a syllable repeated (*ti*) and also contained an orthographical mistake (*sympatitique* should have been written *sympathiques*). We have since had the opportunity of seeing the handwriting of this person when a remission of his disease permitted a partial recuperation. It was remarked that he wrote *better* than before his illness. As a matter of fact, his handwriting is now more legible than it was formerly. But

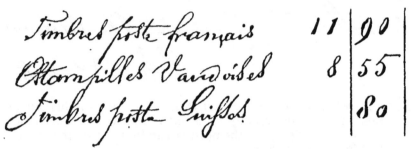

Fig. 143.—The modification became more pronounced in 1871. See Fig. 141.

this man, who is naturally quick and intelligent, used then to write too quickly for the pen to follow his thoughts, whilst now his hand has no difficulty in forming his words, which, like his thoughts, come to him only in a slow and laboured fashion.

The disturbances we have mentioned in the hand-

I ig. 144.—Profound change in 1876. See Fig. 141.

writing of general paralytics, are not the only ones that may be observed before decrepitude causes the entire cessation of writing. By comparing various autographs, we are able to follow the different phases of decay that the intellect, the will, and the sensibility of the invalid undergo, without having recourse to special signs.

Dr. C. Lauzit, who in his book[1] has dealt with the handwriting of lunatics, lays stress upon the importance of erasures in the handwriting of these persons, and adds that the long up and down strokes, and any prolonged pen-strokes, are characterized by tremulousness.

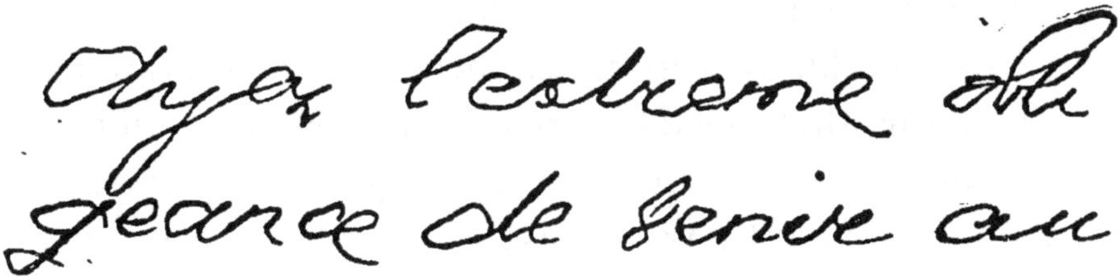

Fig. 145.—(*See p.* 230.) See Fig. 141.

Locomotor ataxy is characterized by an unsteadiness in the performance of voluntary movements, while the muscular energy may be retained, although there is a loss of power to control the action of the muscles. In

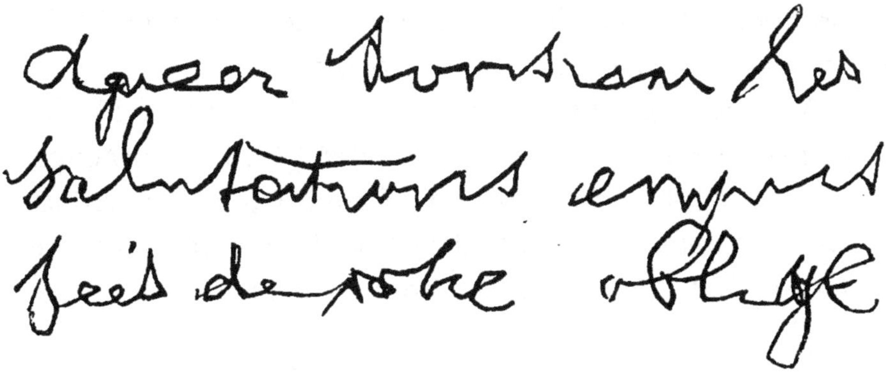

Fig. 146.—The handwriting in 1884. (Patient died the 15th February, 1885.) See Fig. 141.

this condition the invalid ceases to be master of his movements; he overshoots his mark or fails to attain it. The power, the extent, and the direction of his

[1] *Aperçu général sur les écrits des malades.* By Dr. C. Lauzit. Paris, 1888. Ollier-Henry.

movements are no longer regulated with precision by his will.

Handwriting will often show signs of this malady before the writer is aware of his condition.

Some interesting observations made by Dr. Prévost, of Geneva, furnish us with an illustration.[1]

"In 1868 M. W. first experienced trouble in walking. He told us that one day when he was with his wife on the promenade, he himself pushing a baby-carriage containing his little two-year-old daughter, the passers-by made fun at his expense, accusing him of being intoxicated, although he was, as usual, quite sober ; and a dispute ensued upon this occasion. This was the first time that it was apparent his walk was not normal. Since then the illness gradually advanced in severity. The disturbance in the lower extremities became more pronounced, and then spread to the upper limbs, in which ataxy was later on very marked."

We see in *fig.* 141 the normal handwriting of M. W. in the year 1864. Three years later (*fig.* 142), although he (M. W.) had no suspicion of anything being wrong, we can detect a slight alteration in the form of the letters, but this is much more evident in 1871 (*fig.* 143).

In 1876 (*fig.* 144) the handwriting is very much altered, while in 1883 (*fig.* 145) the invalid wrote but rarely, usually to his doctor when he felt very ill. In 1884 (*fig.* 146) he could use only a pencil, and that even less often than formerly. Finally, death released him from his suffering early in 1885.

---

[1] *Néorites périphériques dans le tabes dorsalis.* By J. L. Prévost.

Graphologic observation applied to the handwriting of the sick is certainly inadequate, but we think we have shown that it is by no means useless. We may compare the importance of deductions from graphologic signs in the handwriting of sick persons, to those drawn from examinations of the tongue, of the temperature, and of the pulse. However valuable these latter may be in establishing a diagnostic, it is but seldom that they suffice to enlighten the physician in a sure degree as to the specific illness, and he who would accept such tests as an absolute guide, might reasonably be taxed with imprudence.

STATISTICS have been compiled upon such a host of different subjects that it may seem impossible almost to discover another that has escaped notice. However, statistics relating to mental phenomena touch comparatively new ground. M. de Candolle, of Geneva, and Mr. Francis Galton, of London, have made inquiries in this sense from the standpoint of heredity; they have not endeavoured to investigate under what conditions of intelligence and of morality we live. In fact, the means were wanting of judging these conditions. But to-day, to some extent, such facility exists, for the study of handwritings allows of the investigation of certain qualities in the units composing a mass of human data. Graphologic study is superior to physiognomy as a means of psychological inquiry; it is more convenient as regards the observation of facts, for there is no need, as in physiognomical analysis, to have a human face before us in order to note its attitude and expression. The results are reliable and relatively complete, and the data are more trustworthy than information furnished by interested persons. For example, Mr. Galton addressed himself to the literary public by means of the press. He asked for confidential information as to height, as to family resemblances, as to good or bad character. The printed questions certainly facilitated the task of correspondents ; but we cannot generalize from such materials, for the reason that only the literary public replied to the questions, or perhaps for the contrary reason, that the literary public did not reply. Out of 100 individuals, Mr. Galton found that 48 were known for their good character, but that does not tell us much. Such indication of good character has about the same degree of significance as the term "*good fellow*," which is frequently and rather indiscriminately used. A question of this kind is too general, and may be a fruitful source of error ; but in spite of its broad generality, it did not appear easy to obtain a sufficient number of replies. What, then, could we expect should we ask if those interested be intelligent, selfish, amiable, etc.? All would be intelligent, no one would be selfish, and the psychological inquirer would merely have to make his bow to each of the excellent characters brought before him, and report upon the general excellence of humanity. We fear that this statistical research cannot aid such investigation.

But in estimating character from the *handwritings* of the very same persons we have to do with facts of a different class. If the specimens be written under normal conditions they afford a kind of psychological photograph of the writers ; the habitual expressions are all registered therein, and the great objective difficulty of the former data being removed, any that remains is subjective, and rests with the graphologist in his analysis of the characteristic traits.

We know for each country the proportion of its in-
habitants who can read or write, but this is only a very
scanty indication of the intellectual level of a people.
In Geneva, where education has been compulsory for
a long while, the statistics of the school of recruits give
the figure of three per 1000 for men who can neither
read nor write.   A lower figure could hardly be expected
taking into account a fair proportion of idiots, etc., but
nevertheless we must admit that the intellectual level of
Geneva is still capable of being raised.   It has appeared
interesting to us to search for some average of the
mental value of a man under certain conditions.   An
exceptional circumstance placed at our disposal a large
quantity of different handwritings, which we classified
into groups, marking the distinction between males and
females.   These specimens, 3000 in all, were supplied to
us by a French manufacturer, 2000 being males, and
1000 females.   This mass contained the handwritings
of an entire community ; the head of the firm, his family,
his friends, his advisers were there, all well represented
alongside of his contractors, workmen, and workwomen.
The data at hand for graphologic analysis appear to us,
under such conditions, to be comparable to those which
might be obtained by observation of an industrial centre
of equal importance, such, for instance, as the small towns
of the Jura, of the Ain, or of the Rhone.

We have separated the characters into three broad
categories : superior persons, mediocrities, and inferiors,
without reference to the social rank of the writers.

By a state of superiority, we mean the possession of at
least sufficient intellectual culture to allow of a writer
taking up mental work with ease, and consequently the

faculties of assimilation of facts, and their correct appreciation, are also inferred.

By the term mediocrity we denote a decidedly incomplete development of the intellect. A mediocrity is not without intelligence, but he gives no proof of superiority, and his mind applies itself to more or less commonplace or even vulgar affairs.

Inferior men are those whose minds are essentially of a low type or who are practically wanting in intellect. In this class we include insignificant persons of no individuality and force, although when the latter are young, their minds might often be strengthened and they themselves removed from a colourless state of personality.

Out of 2000 men we have found only 74 whose handwriting bore the signs of superiority, viz. clearness, simplicity, and sobriety of handwriting; 1132 were mediocrities, and 794 inferior or insignificant men. As concerns the 1000 females, only 22 came under the head of superiority; there were 460 mediocrities and 518 inferiorities. This large proportion of female inferiorities, nearly 52 per cent., is explained by the presence of 431 insignificants among the 518 specimens just referred to.

It may be thought, perhaps, that we have been unduly severe upon such of the intelligent class as have been included with the mediocrities, when the handwriting of the former contained no sign of culture, but we shall now see—and this renders our classification just—that we have not confounded mental culture with good sense, judgment.

CLASSIFICATION OF THE 3000 SPECIMENS AS REGARDS
GENERAL SUPERIORITY, MEDIOCRITY, INFERIORITY.

Sex.	No. of speci-mens.	Superiority.		Mediocrity		Inferiority.		All classes.	
		No.	Ratio per cent.	No.	Ratio per cent.	No.	Ratio per cent.	No	Ratio per cent.
Men	2000	74	3.7	1132	56.6	794	39.7	2000	100.0
Women	1000	22	2.2	460	46.0	518	51.8	1000	100.0

CLASSIFICATION OF THE ABOVE 6 SECTIONS (3 MALE
AND 3 FEMALE CLASSES) AS REGARDS THE
FACULTY OF JUDGMENT.

Sex and class.	No. of speci-mens.	Correct judgment.		Mediocre judgment.		Judgment nil, or almost nil.		All classes.	
		No	Ratio per cent.	No.	Ratio per cent.	No.	Ratio per cent.	No.	Ratio per cent.
Superior men	74	61	82.4	13	17.6	..	..	74	100.0
Superior women .	22	15	68.2	7	31.8	..	..	22	100.0
Mediocre men	1132	226	20.0	872	77.0	34	3.0	1132	100.0
Mediocre women .	460	45	9.8	322	70.0	93	20.2	460	100.0
Inferior men	794	41	5.1	634	79.9	119	15.0	794	100 0
Inferior women	518	12	2.3	325	62.8	181	34.9	518	100.0
Total	3000	400	13.3	2173	72.5	427	14.2	3000	100.0

After making the classification at the head of this
little table, we again examined the data and obtained
the results shown in its lower part.

We have awarded a correct judgment where we have
found mental clearness, a certain reserve or moderation
of character, and no passion; but we do not pretend
that of the 74 *superior* men whose handwritings we have
studied, 61—to quote from our table—are gifted with a
superior judgment; we merely say that in these 61
instances we have found the conditions of a *generally
correct* judgment.

A mediocre judgment has been indicated to us by one or more traits incompatible with a correct judgment: sensitiveness, a too pronounced imagination, touchiness, passion, exaggerated *amour-propre*, etc. No one of these signs shows radically bad judgment, because we do not always have to form an opinion concerning those things which quickly excite our sensitiveness, our imagination, our self-love, etc.

We have classed under the head of "*judgment nil, or almost nil*," those specimens showing a confused mind, an excess of susceptibility, and those where several of the signs indicative of a mediocre judgment were united in one handwriting.

Thus we have found that out of 74 superior men, 61 had a generally correct judgment; 13 were not so well off in this respect, but none were wanting in judgment. Fifteen women out of 22 of a superior type, come under "correct judgment," and 7 are ranked as mediocre; female imagination, and especially their pronounced sensitiveness, being the causes of the female ratios in the fourth column of the table comparing unfavourably with those of the males.

As regards male mediocrities, we have 226 out of the 1132, under our heading "correct judgment"; 872 being in the middle class, and 34 practically without judgment.

Female mediocrities show here a marked inferiority to the males; only 45 out of 460 judge as a rule well; 322 have a mediocre judgment, and the remaining 93 specimens are of no account as regards this faculty.

Thirdly, we have ascertained that of the 794 inferior

men, 41 have what we may term a rough and ready
good sense ; 634 are greatly confused as to what decision to make, and frequently make a wrong one, while
119 are obtuse.   In the same category, of our lowest
class of female in the table, 12 know how to get fairly
near the mark in their opinions ; 325 want another's
advice, and 181 have, instead of any power of judgment,
a faculty of mere imitation of precedents.

Finally out of 3000 persons we have found good
sense more or less prominent among 400, or a ratio of
13·3 per cent. ; a middling power of judgment in 2173
cases, 72·5 per cent., and judgment wanting in the remaining 427 persons, a ratio of 14·2 per cent.

We have also made comparative investigations between the male and the female character as regards
another feature.   Three thousand female handwritings
considered from the point of view of sensitiveness have
enabled us to state the following résults : with 60, reason
and good sense dominated their sensitiveness ; 537 had
a moderate amount of sensitiveness ; 2208 were very
sensitive, and capable of letting passion run away with
reason, while 195 were morbidly sensitive to impressions.

Three thousand male handwritings gave very
different results.   Reason dominated in 242 cases ;
moderate sensitiveness was present in 1980 ; 724 were
passionate natures, and 54 were morbidly and un-
healthily sensitive.[1]

---

[1] These results have been obtained by the aid of Schwiedland's
graphometer, which is described in M. Crépieux-Jamin's work,
" Traité pratique de Graphologie."

Sex.	No: of speci- mens.	Sensitiveness weak.		A moderate amount of sensitive- ness.		Sensitiveness strong. Passion.		An unhealthy and morbid suscepti- bility.		All classes.	
		No.	Ratio per cent.	No.	Ratio per cent.	No.	Ratio per cent.	No.	Ratio per cent.	No.	Ratio per cent
Women ..	3000	60	2.0	537	17.9	2208	73 6	195	6.5	3000	100.0
Men ..	3000	242	8 0	1980	66.0	724	24.2	54	1.8	3000	100.0

We have submitted to several other psychologists a portion of the handwritings which served as our data in these investigations. The differences between their results and our own were not considerable.

We must here make special reference to Dr. Paul Helot, who has very kindly checked our own results. One hundred handwritings were separated into six groups by Dr. Helot, who was guided in his classification by personal knowledge of the writers; these specimens were sent to us without any information whatever as to the respective characters. Our opinion arrived at by graphologic analysis, agreed with that of Dr. Helot in seventy-three cases, and as regards the other twenty-seven, we differed so slightly from his opinion, that we may say there was in no case any important variation in the results.

Dr. Helot wrote to us : " In three instances I altered a first number to a second, and in each case the first classification I made agrees with your own. As regards four other specimens, I am content to accept your opinion in preference to my own."

Dr. Helot was desirous of conducting a similar experiment, so our positions being reversed, 100 specimens classified by us were submitted to him. The results were pretty nearly alike. In sixty-four cases the two groupings agreed, and in all the others our respective opinions were very closely allied.

If Dr. Helot and ourselves had confined the classification to the three broad groups of superior men, mediocrities, and inferiorities, as in the first portion of the statistical table in this chapter, our differences might have been nil. This first experience, satisfactory as it was, has been repeated, producing results that left us fully satisfied.

REFERENCE-TABLE TO THE ILLUSTRA-
TIONS.

THE arrangement of the illustrations in the French original was
not quite satisfactory, for if the reader wished to refer to any particular specimen, indicated by its number in the paragraph he was
reading, he did not know what page to turn to, and as in many
instances there were numerous consecutive pages of text containing
no illustrations, some inconvenience resulted before the desired
specimen could be found.

It will be observed that in *Handwriting and Expression* the 154
numbered specimens (those in the *Introduction* and *Appendix* are
not numbered) do not all follow in consecutive numerical order.
The reason for this is, that, as the references in the text to the illustrations are very numerous, a single specimen being sometimes
noticed many times, it would have been necessary to almost
entirely upset the connection between the reference in the French
text, and the respective numbers of the illustrations indicated
therein, if it had been decided to let all the present illustrations
run in strict numerical order.

This upsetting of so many references was undesirable, if only
for the increased probability of error caused thereby; and the
method now adopted places the various specimens as close as
possible to the *most important* text-reference to each; the original
numbering of the illustrations has been kept intact where possible,
both as concerns the specimens transferred from the French book
and those newly placed as substitutes in the English version;
while any objection to the non-numerical order just mentioned has

been obviated, and the original inconvenience has been avoided, by preparing the following table, which shows at a glance upon what page any desired illustration is printed.

Number of Illust.	Page.	Number of Illust.	Page.	Number of Illust.	Page.	Number of Illust.	Page.
1	37	38	86	77	88	110	183
2	38	39	86	77(a)	88	111	185
3	39	40	86	78	88	112	186
4	40	41	86	79	70	113	187
5	41	42	86	80	70	114	188
6	42	43	86	81	70	115	189
7	43	44	86	82	71	116	190
8	44	45	86	82(a)	71	117	191
9	45	46	86	83	71	118	191
10	46	47	87	84	71	119	192
11	47	48	87	85	71	120	192
12	48	49	87	86	71	121	193
13	66	50	87	87	100	122	196
14	57	51	87	87(a)	101	123	197
15	58	52	87	88	102	124	199
16	59	53	87	89	103	125	200
17	60	54	87	90	103	126	202
18	61	55	87	91	104	127	203
19	62	56	87	92	104	128	206
20	63	57	87	93	105	129	209
21	63	58	87	94	105	130	210
22	64	59	87	95	105	131	212
23	66	60	87	96	106	132	213
24	67	61	87	97	107	133	214
25	67	62	87	98	108	134	215
26	68	63	87	99	108	135	216
27	68	64	87	100	108	136	218
28	68	65	87	101	109	137	219
29	69	66	87	102	109	138	221
30	69	67	88	103	109	139	225
30(a)	69	68	88	103(a)	146	140	227
31	85	69	88	104	147	141	227
32	85	70	88	105	149	142	227
33	85	71	88	106	151	143	228
33(a)	70	72	88	107	155	144	228
34	85	73	88	107(a)	157	145	229
35	86	74	88	108	161	146	229
36	86	75	88	108(a)	168	Total—154 Illustrations.	
37	86	76	88	109	182		

284 out of next pay
unblotted & caps
diversity letters use
late = leaving out letters
leaving nr words lines
writing slopes down

SD - #0022 - 100823 - C0 - 229/152/14 - PB - 9780282841621 - Gloss Lamination